Henry VIII
and the Reformation
Parliament

"Reacting to the Past" Series

Henry VIII
and the Reformation
Parliament

J. Patrick Coby

Smith College

PEARSON
Longman

New York Boston San Francisco
London Toronto Sydney Tokyo Singapore Madrid
Mexico City Munich Paris Cape Town Hong Kong Montreal

Senior Acquisitions Editor: Janet Lanphier

Editorial Assistant: Stephanie Ricotta

Executive Marketing Manager: Sue Westmoreland

Production Coordinator: Virginia Riker

Cover Designer/Manager: Nancy Danahy

Cover Illustration/Photo: #97 Henry VIII (1491-1547) by Joos van Cleve, (c. 1485-1541)

Burghley House Collection, Lincolnshire, UK, Netherlandish/Bridgeman Art Library

Senior Manufacturing Buyer: Al Dorsey

Printer and Binder: Command Web Offset Company

Cover Printer: Coral Graphic Services

Library of Congress Cataloging-in-Publication Data

Coby, Patrick,
  Henry VIII and the Reformation Parliament / J. Patrick Coby.
    p. cm. -- ("Reacting to the past" series)
  Includes bibliographical references.
  ISBN 0-321-41878-6
  1. Great Britain--Politics and government--1509-1547. 2. Henry VIII, King of England,
1491-1547--Relations with legislators.   3. Great Britain. Parliament--History--16th
century. 4. Reformation--England. I. Title. II. Series.
DA338.C63 2005
942.05'2--dc22   2005023790

Please visit us at www.ablongman.com

ISBN 0-321-41878-6

1 2 3 4 5 6 7 8 9 10—BJP—09 08 07 06

Table of Contents

Acknowledgments

I wish to thank my colleague William Oram, of the Smith College English department, for sharing with me his extensive knowledge of Renaissance England and for his assistance with compiling the supplementary texts; and my colleague Howard Nenner, of the Smith History department, for his critical review of the manuscript. Also, special thanks are due to Kelsey Livingston, who provided the genealogy, drew maps, transcribed texts, edited statutes, and worked tirelessly at bringing the various parts together; and to Mallory SoRelle, Jaci Eisenberg, and Cate Hirschbiel, who assisted with research, maps, and preliminary role descriptions. The Fund for the Improvement of Post-Secondary Education helped underwrite the project. Smith College has been similarly generous and the administration unflaggingly supportive. Finally, and most of all, Mark Carnes, Ann Whitney Olin Professor of History at Barnard College, is owed congratulations for conceiving of this role-playing pedagogy and for inspiring me and numerous others to aid in its development and dissemination.

Introduction: Historical Fiction

COMING TO LONDON

Up ahead you see the torches illuminating the towers of the Great Stone Gateway. The Gateway guards the southern entrance to the London bridge; and the flaming torches announce that the bridge is closed for the evening. The news is most disconcerting, since your accommodations lie on the other side of the Thames. You left your coastal home days ago, in plenty of time, you thought, for the opening ceremonies of the newly summoned parliament, of which you are an elected member. But the overland coach suffered numerous breakdowns on England's rutted roads and has arrived too late for passage over the bridge. You could hire a ferryman to carry you to the north bank, but the people milling around warn against a nighttime crossing. It seems you're stuck in the London's Southwark suburb; and you're due at Blackfriars tomorrow noon.

Lodging, you are told, can be found upriver a short distance. You thank these strangers for their kind assistance; they snicker as you depart. For upriver are the brothels, called stew houses, and the prostitutes are called geese. As it happens, you are a little surprised to encounter so many women out and about. Still, it is flattering that they notice you and comforting that they invite you in. When you ask for a room and inquire as to the cost, the declared price astounds you, until the matron at the desk specifies the services provided. You are embarrassed by your naïveté and concerned for your reputation, for what, you wonder, would the world think if a parliamentarian were ever caught in an establishment such as this? But you reason that it is too late to be wandering farther up Bankside, especially since more of the same is all that awaits you. So you take the room, but with assurances to yourself that the balance of the evening hours will be spent elsewhere, in more respectable surroundings.

You spy an arena nearby, in fact, two of them. They are theaters, you suppose, for London is the country's largest and most cosmopolitan city. (But, no, they won't be theaters for some decades yet, when they become the sites of the Rose, the Swan, the Globe, and the Hope theaters. The recreational tastes of this generation of Londoners run a notch or two lower—bear-baiting and bull-baiting are the entertainments within.) You enter and observe in the center of the ring, not an actor, as you imagined, but a huge black bear, chained at the leg, surrounded by a pack of snarling, yelping dogs. The spectators, in full-throated holler themselves, root on the dogs, root on the bear, depending on which of the animals they have placed their bets. A similar contest is underway in the adjacent arena, but with an untethered bull struggling to gore the swarming dogs before they succeed in tearing at its legs and bringing it down. You quickly are caught up in the excitement, notwithstanding the vulgarity of it all, and so fail to notice that a melee has broken out in the seats above. Soon the fighting in the stands exceeds that in the ring, and soon after a constable arrives supported by a squad of police. No attempt is made to separate the guilty from the innocent; all are driven outside, wrapped in an encircling rope, and as one large crowd escorted down Bankside to Winchester house.

Your fellow detainees explain that the bishop of Winchester, with his London residence near London bridge, has jurisdiction over the south bank of the Thames and that within his palace is a jail called the Clink. It is to the Clink that you are sent, placed in a cell with four other men, though none of them are the rowdies from the bear-baiting fracas. On the contrary, they are sober, somber, and severe, engaged in earnest talk about scripture and the church. Huddled around a candle, they thumb the pages of a Bible or recite biblical passages from memory. One declaims: "It is evident that no man is justified before God by law." And another answers: "For by grace you have been saved through faith, not because of works." They are not disputing; they are supporting and confirming what each believes. On they go, quoting the Bible and fortifying their courage. You later learn that they are sectarians accused of heresy and facing interrogation before an ecclesiastical tribunal in the coming days. They pay you no mind, but eventually the jailer does, who communicates to his superior your asserted status as a parliamentarian and your indignant protestation over false arrest. Satisfied on both counts, the warden tenders his apology and releases you from incarceration just as the sun is rising. It is November, which means that morning is well under way; but there is yet time to collect your belongings, left at the stew house, to attend morning services, and to partake of breakfast at a tavern before crossing into London and traveling up Thames Street to Blackfriars monastery.

The mass you attend is at the chapel on London bridge, which amazingly is not only a bridge but a street lined with shops, offices, inns—and a chapel. The service is punctuated by a sermon, delivered by a skillful and erudite prelate, who denounces what he calls the Bohemian infection of the one true faith and who defends church teachings, church practices, and church personnel. You make the required donation upon departing and ponder the fate of your jailhouse companions, whom you now suspect are the very Bohemians the prelate was denouncing.

Breakfast is taken at a tavern farther down the bridge. The breakfast fare is merely fair, but the conversation at the nearby table is quite exceptional indeed. The patrons there are lamenting the humiliation of the queen and deriding the king for his lust, his arrogance, and his heresy—words of rebuke not ordinarily heard—and are speculating that the emperor might just invade England to deliver his aunt from harm. The cause of their displeasure is no mystery, for all of England is aware that the king now regards his marriage of 20 years as invalid and his daughter by that marriage as illegitimate; also that the king, in his quest for an annulment, gives friendly hearing to innovative and unorthodox ideas. The diners' conversation reminds you that your one previous visit to the city, as a child, coincided with the arrival of a Spanish princess sent to England to marry royalty and reign as queen. That was not 20, but 28 years ago, and the fact that the princess came early and married twice is the source of all of the controversy. The queen is still at court but made to endure the presence of a mistress treated as a wife.

When finally over the bridge and in London proper, you observe an ecclesiastical establishment beyond all reckoning: the great St. Paul's cathedral, religious houses of every drab coloration—Greyfriars, Whitefriars, Blackfriars—gilded crosses at every street corner, and over 100 parish churches within the city walls alone. You conclude that more piety must reside in London than in any city on the planet, more even than in Rome. But as you pass by one of these parish churches, a quarrel erupts inside. Some parishioners are in high dudgeon over the fee charged for the burial of a child. The curate responds to their complaints by explaining how this and other fees go to the purchase of holy relics. But the parishioners are unappeased, and as they push toward the front door, the curate, ahead of them, is shoved down the church stairs. He argues no more, but picks himself up and runs toward the protection of a friary, with the angry laymen in hot pursuit. Perhaps Londoners are not as pious as you first supposed—and the paper at your feet provides immediate confirmation. It is a broadsheet titled *A Supplication for the Beggars*. Looking ahead, you see that it litters the street and is nailed to posts and walls along the way. One quick glance at the opening paragraphs tells you that anticlerical passions run deep and that the church stands accused of multiple and longstanding offenses.

Indeed, much else is not well in this glistening city on the Thames. Off the main thoroughfares lives a population of beggars, crowded into hovels along streets stinking from sewage and from mud. The sight of you, a stranger, draws them forth, whereupon many tell tales about how they were sturdy plowmen once until the conversion of tilled fields to pasture for sheep removed them from their homes and reduced them to beggary. You pity their plight and hope that parliament can attend to their needs; but coming yourself from a port city in the south, you know well the importance of wool to the country's economy. Fixing this problem may require some careful lawmaking.

Beyond St. Paul's on the right and Baynard's castle on the left lies Blackfriars monastery, your destination. The hour is late; you have barely time to dispose of your luggage before taking your place in the receiving line of commoners. When you do, there is tittering, pointing, and guffawing all up and down the line. And when those antics change to the honking sound of geese, you realize what has happened: news of your evening at the stew house and in the Clink reached Blackfriars before you. You are mortified. But no defense can you offer, since at that very moment the procession of lords and royalty begins. First come the lords spiritual, led by the archbishop; then come the ceremonial officials, the Lord Chancellor among them; the king himself, attended by courtiers, comes next; after whom, and finishing the procession, come the lords temporal, led by the dukes. These bejeweled noblemen march over the covered footbridge connecting Blackfriars with Brideswell, a royal palace situated just across the Fleet rivulet trickling into the Thames. As the king approaches, a courtier whispers in his ear; and as the king passes, he winks at you. Your mortification deepens.

The king and lords retire to the monastery's church, where a solemn high mass is sung by the royal choristers. After the mass—to which the commoners are not admitted—the combined party assembles in the great chamber for the opening session of parliament (but with all subsequent sessions to take place at Westminster, a mile or so upriver.). At one end of the chamber sits the king, on his throne. Down the chamber, on his right, sit the bishops and abbots, and on his left the dukes, marquesses, earls, viscounts, and barons. Opposite the king, behind a rail, you and your fellow commoners stand. The king rises, and with him all the lords. When the room is perfectly still, the king, scepter in hand, begins to speak: "Our liege subjects, we have summoned you here, in parliament assembled . . ."

And so it begins. But where, you wonder, will it end? Will revolution come to England, as it has come to the continent? Will war come, too? Will England remain loyal to the Catholic faith and obedient to the pope? Will the ecclesiastical establishment retain its power and wealth, or will the monarchy assert its supremacy and confiscate church lands? Will the king divorce his wife and disinherit his child? And will a new wife produce an heir to continue the Tudor line? Despite the pomp and circumstance, despite the thrill of participating in a momentous historical event, your mood is anxious and distressed, for you know that the times are troubled and that the future is uncertain.

Plus you now have a reputation to live down.

A FAREWELL LETTER

Daughter:

Believe always that adversity is God's blessing in disguise. God does test us, but not without purpose and not without our well-being assured.

I am ill, daughter, sorely ill. I must write you now before strength of body and clarity of mind desert me. My great regret is that these past years you and I have been kept apart. I was not present to see you grow; to advise and comfort you; to laugh and cry with you as mother and daughter should. Do not despise me. And do not hate your father. He loves you, even if now he persecutes you. He is headstrong, and you and I thwart his will. Cares of state weigh heavy upon his heart. Passion too possesses him—of that I say no more—and wicked advisers have made him cruel. But he is a good man, I believe, generous, godly, and grandly ambitioned. In time he will come back to you, though sadly not to me. My time is nearing its end, and the king still denies our marriage.

Our lives, daughter, have been hard of late. Am I to blame? Should I have yielded my position as wife and queen and retreated to a nunnery? The pope's emissary urged such a course on me, to save England for the church. Perhaps he was right, considering what since has transpired: Rome's supremacy has been denied; the king is titled head of the church in his realm; heresy is rife; monasteries are looted; clerics are abused; good men die on the gallows. All because I would not yield. Can such harm brought to this land by me be God's work? Have I sinned? Everyone says that I have.

But how can untruth be holy? It is untruth to affirm that my marriage to the king's brother was consummated. Should I have sworn before God that it was? The position I hold is unassailable, I believe: that since the marriage lacked consummation, no proper marriage occurred; and with no marriage, no impediment preventing marriage to his majesty the king; with no impediment, no need for a papal dispensation to remove the impediment; and with no dispensation, no dispute over its legality. Just think on all of the useless labor of scholars and divines debating endlessly the worth of a dispensation to annul a marriage that never existed! Was I to be party to such mendacious madness?

I have been asked to declare my life a lie and a sin, to avow that I have lived as concubine, not as wife, of a king. I have been asked to bastardize my child, to deny you your birthright as princess and heir to the throne. Can it be God's will that I attest to such lies? I confess that the consequences of my truthfulness have so far been unwelcome; but surely God wants us to remain true, having faith that somehow calamity He will turn into triumph. God's ways are inscrutable. Our souls' destinies are ours to win or lose. Be ever true, and trust ever in God.

Thankfully his Holiness did finally rule—after five years of delay—that the marriage betwixt me and the king is and always has been valid before God. Had his Holiness acted more promptly, I am confidant that the king would never have ventured down so disastrous a path. But now his parliament calls him supreme, and so the pontiff's ruling comes too late to keep England Catholic.

I rejoice and thank God that your health has been restored. I feared for you and beseeched the king to have you sent here so that I could nurse you and protect you. But that was not to be. Reports of your person and whereabouts come to me irregularly and late. What last I heard is that you have been returned to Hatfield Hall, that you serve in the household staff of your half-sister, and that you have been placed under the close supervision of a lady instructed to offend your dignity in all ways possible. I lament these humiliations visited upon you. They have only one cause—the king's determination to take from you your title of Princess of Wales and to confer it upon another. Be firm, my child, no matter the insults; do not yield. Agents of the king have frequently harried me too, demanding that I trade my title of queen for that of dowager princess. Servants refusing this style of address have been threatened with arrest. Most have in fact refused, and most are gone; my household is not what it once was. Only a few loyal maids, my confessor, physician, and apothecary are still with me, their defiance of the royal decree notwithstanding. All others are spies.

There is strength in resistance. We are beloved of the people, whose support grows deeper the more hardship we are made to endure. The king is constrained by our resolve. This I know from past experience. Two years back a deputation arrived led by a duke of great eminence. As usual the purpose of the visit was to compel the surrender of my title and the rescission of my appeal to Rome, to bully the servants, and this time to carry me off to some dank and dreary fortress. I barricaded myself inside my bed chamber, the duke and his party kept at bay by a locked oaken door. For five days the duke pounded and hollered, for five days he stormed about the corridor; but his fulminations and curses availed him nothing. He commanded local magistrates to deliver me to him; they paid him no heed. He wrote the Council asking for instruction; the Council never responded. The people of the neighborhood assembled without, sporting make-shift weapons and countenances full of menace. The duke paused, thinking better of forcing my removal; and after pillaging the palace and snatching up a few servants for show, he went meekly away, never to bother me again.

They dare not attack us directly, daughter; the people of England will not allow it. Still our lives are greatly imperiled. Take utmost care about what you eat and drink—test every morsel and sip. I worry that the "Italian disease" has infected our land; perhaps I myself have been stricken by it. Look after your health as best you can, for a "natural" death of England's princess would be to the liking of many persons well positioned and ill-willed. You have enemies; be on guard. I shudder, and I rail, that such advice I must give you. But trust in God; all will be well. Also, daughter, be careful of the company you keep. Your enemies may try through temptation to besmirch your reputation, to ruin thereby your marriage prospects, your use to the realm, and your standing with the people. Be ever chaste and trouble not about your future until this time of trial has passed.

The emperor's ambassador was recently here. Word of my illness reached the court, and he petitioned the king for leave to visit me at Kimbolton castle. A dear and loyal friend is the ambassador. Keep him close to you, daughter; he will not disappoint. We spoke of pleasanter times, of journeys once taken and of pilgrimages to come—for ever the sanguinist is he. We delighted in the memory of his previous visit, a year and a half past. Then I was housed at Buckden palace. Though lacking royal permission to visit, he departed London with a grand and decorous cortege of cavaliers and minstrels; and though cautioned not to proceed farther, and so staying back himself, he sent ahead his merry band of revelers to storm the palace with song and dance and acrobatics. A fool, more clown than acrobat, somersaulted himself clean into the moat. So amazed were the guards, so entertained by the spectacle, that they relented and lowered the drawbridge, opened the gates, and admitted the troop. The feast that night was heaven-sent and wanted only the ambassador's presence to count as divine deliverance.

Countess Willoughby, my dearest friend, is by my bed. Unlike the ambassador, just departed, she had no warrant for entering the castle. So outside the walls she feigned a fall from her horse; and muddied and limping she prevailed upon the constable to grant her admittance, though strictly instructed was she not to approach me. Once in, and with the constable's attention diverted, she hastened up the stairs—her injured leg miraculously healed—and locked herself inside my chamber. Here she has been ever since.

We have our small victories. Even in darkness there is light; even in grief there is joy.

My possessions have all been removed, except for a few furs, meager and worn, and a gold chain and cross I brought with me from Spain. These modest endearments I bequeath to you.

Be strong, my daughter. Live long and well in the years ahead. Pray for me. And remember me, your loving mother—

Catherine, the Queen
6 January 1536

Background: Political and Intellectual History

THE "GREAT MATTER"

A fateful decision it was when the newly proclaimed boy-monarch, **Henry VIII**, chose to marry his deceased elder brother's widow, Catherine. Catherine, or **Catherine of Aragon**, was the daughter of Ferdinand and Isabella of Spain, the king and queen famous for having sent Columbus in 1492 on his voyage of discovery. In 1501 they sent their daughter Catherine to marry Arthur, Henry VII's first-born son and Prince of Wales. Arthur was 15, and Catherine was 16. The marriage, though, was short-lived, as the sickly Arthur died of consumption five months later. Seven years later, in 1509, Catherine (who had remained in England) was married to the seventeen-year old Henry, Henry VII's second-born son. Henry married Catherine, six years his senior, upon his father's death, just days before his coronation as king and just days before his eighteenth birthday. It was a magnanimous gesture, but one of dubious religious legality, for it is written in the Book of Leviticus (20:21): "If a man takes his brother's wife, it is impurity; he has uncovered his brother's nakedness, they shall be childless." Henry VII, who first arranged the marriage, later decided against it, fearing that it would put in jeopardy the line of succession and unsettle an already shaky Tudor dynasty. But young Henry, now his own man, was determined to act magnanimously, and the pope in Rome (Julius II) had previously granted him a dispensation.

The marriage was not quite childless. Catherine did give birth to a daughter, **Mary** (1516–1558), who would go on to become Queen of England (1553–1558). But a male issue was what was required, and Catherine, though pregnant many times, never managed to produce a male heir who survived. By the mid-1520s, Catherine's child-bearing years had passed, as had her middling good looks. Indeed, she had become quite frumpy, while her husband—tall, strong, handsome, and athletic—was still the picture-perfect Renaissance prince. Henry had always been a beautiful specimen, and as king his opportunities for amorous dalliance were ample, if not limitless. One paramour of significance was Elizabeth Blount, a lady-in-waiting who bore Henry a son, Henry Fitzroy (Fitzroy being the standard name for a king's bastard—*fils du roi*). So desperate was Henry for a male heir that he considered legitimizing Fitzroy, and to that end had him named Duke of Richmond. But the paramour of real consequence was **Anne Boleyn** (whose sister, Mary, Henry had already come to appreciate—a fact that would later prove damaging to Anne). Henry first noticed Anne in 1525. In 1527 he announced that he no longer considered Catherine his lawful wife. For the next six years he turned his kingdom upside down trying to secure a divorce from Catherine and a marriage to Anne, and trying through Anne, once married, to have his a much-desired male heir. Anne bore him **Elizabeth** (1533; queen 1558–1603)—too bad for Anne!

This protracted divorce effort, called the king's **Great Matter**, was inspired by something more than Henry's lust and paternal pride. As mentioned, the marriage to Catherine was sufficiently irregular as to call for and receive a papal dispensation. Henry professed himself worried that this union was in violation of divine law; and Catherine's many miscarriages and stillbirths may have convinced him of God's disfavor, it being a commonly held belief of the time that divine intervention determined the health and sex of the child. Also, the Tudor house was of suspect legitimacy, as had been the York and Lancaster houses that preceded it. Without an heir widely accepted and able to defend the throne, Henry could not presume that the Tudor line would survive. The past burdened and distracted him—in particular, the War of the Roses, England's fifteenth-century civil war.

THE WAR OF THE ROSES

A quick telling of events will allow for a better understanding of Henry's situation. The roots of the war lay in the reign of Edward III (r. 1327–1377). Edward fathered five sons: Edward, Prince of Wales; Lionel, Duke of Clarence; John of Gaunt, Duke of Lancaster; Edmund, Duke of York; and Thomas, Duke of Gloucester. Edward, the firstborn and nicknamed the Black Prince for his ferocity in the Hundred Years War (1337–1453), died fighting the French before ever becoming king (1376). On the death of his father the following year, the throne passed to his son, Richard (1377). Richard II performed poorly as monarch. He so offended and imperiled the English nobility that one of their number, Henry Bolingbroke, son of Lancaster, led a revolt that deposed Richard and made Henry king (1399). Henry—Henry IV—was thus a usurper, strictly speaking. Even so, he handed the crown on successfully to his son, Henry V. This was the Henry, immortalized by Shakespeare, who with a small band of English volunteers defeated the flower of the French nobility at Agincourt (1415). English control over French territory reached its apex during Henry V's reign, plus Henry married the daughter of the French king and arranged by treaty that the son of their union would one day rule as king of England and of France. (English kings into the nineteenth century continued to call themselves king of France.) That day came sooner than anyone expected as Henry V died young and suddenly, leaving both thrones to his infant son, Henry VI (1422). A protectorate was thus needed until Henry came of age, and even then Henry proved singularly unsuited for royal power—shy, feeble, and for 15 months stark raving mad.

The situation was made worse by the end of the Hundred Years War (1453) and the return of angry veterans convinced that folly and corruption in high places had brought about England's slow but steady defeat (the tide turned in France's favor with the appearance of Joan of Arc (1429–1431]). These soldiers quickly formed private armies in the pay of rival nobles. The king's law meant little to the nobles and their retainers, whose violence reduced once proud and cultured England to a state of near anarchy. The best man of the realm at the time, able to restore order when in positions of authority but suspected and ill-treated by the crown, was Richard, Duke of York. Disaffected parties of all stripes looked to Richard for deliverance, whose claim to the throne was arguably as good or better than Henry's (Richard descended on the male side from the fourth son of Edward III, but on the female side from the second son; Henry descended only on the male side from the third of Edward's sons). Richard, though, was loyal, also patient, awaiting the day when childless Henry, the last of the Lancastrian line, would yield the crown to the house of York. But then childless Henry fathered a son, and the War of the Roses was on (red rose for Lancaster, white rose for York).

The fortunes of this thirty-year civil war oscillated wildly. Twice the king was captured; twice he was released. Richard died early, as did most of his generation (wholesale executions of captured nobles followed every battle). His son Edward led the forces of York to victory at Towton and himself to the throne as Edward IV (1461). But the forces of Lancaster, under the command of Henry's wife, Margaret of Anjou, conspired from afar. A division inside the Yorkish ranks reignited the conflict when the Earl of Warwick, the "kingmaker," turned on Edward for marrying beneath his station (thereby creating a parvenu nobility) and adopting a foreign policy friendly to Burgundy and hostile to France. Warwick briefly held the upper hand, and briefly he restored Henry VI to the throne as a puppet king. But Edward regrouped and in due course prevailed, defeating Warwick at Barnet and Margaret (and her teenage son) at Tewkesbury (1471) and ordering the death of king Henry, whom Warwick had returned to the Tower for safekeeping.

All was quiet for a while until the premature death of Edward at age 40 put his young children in the care of their uncle, Richard, who imprisoned (then murdered) the boys and seized the throne (1483). Richard III ruled for two years, and notwithstanding his intermittent efforts at good administration, he was never able to shake off the stink of usurpation and tyranny. Factions formed at home and abroad. A rebellion was put down led by a once-trusted ally. When his son died in 1484, Richard turned a suspicious and anxious eye toward Henry Tudor, Earl of Richmond and one of the last of the nobles descended from Edward III. In thick with the rebels, Henry fled to Brittany, where he busied himself gathering an army with which to challenge Richard. The following year he landed in Wales, his home country, rallied new forces to his cause, and marched toward Richard at Nottingham. Their armies met at Bosworth Field where Richard was defeated and killed (1485). Afterward Henry, of a cadet branch of the Lancaster line, married Elizabeth of York, daughter of Edward IV. With this victory and this marriage, the War of the Roses came to an end.

The Tudor dynasty, resting thus on the right of conquest, required a strong hand at the helm, and even with that hand, as during the reign of Henry VII, numerous conspiracies and rebellions occurred. The situation improved somewhat during Henry VIII's reign, as the feudal nobility, exhausted by war, had begun to adjust to the new order. Henry could afford to relax a little, but he dared not excite the ambitions of pretenders by leaving the throne to a vulnerable heir (one pretender, the Duke of Buckingham, he had executed in 1521). All in all, Henry needed a son (and all in all, he wanted, really wanted, Anne).

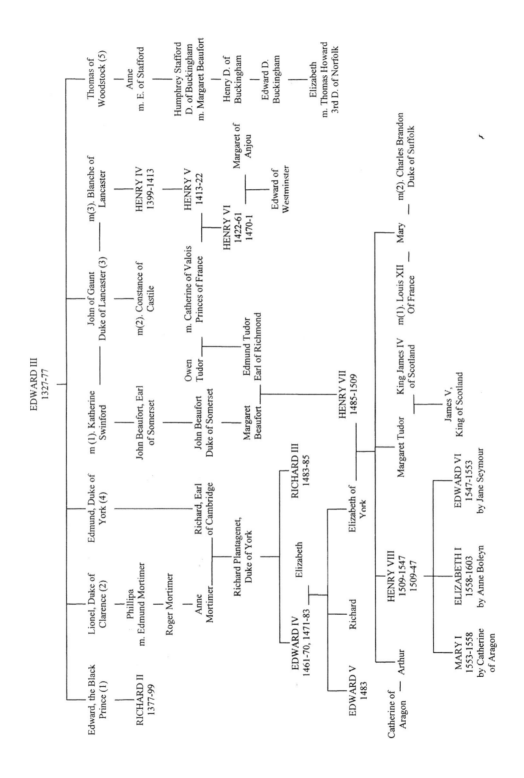

HENRICIAN DIPLOMACY PRIOR TO THE KING'S "GREAT MATTER"

Henry VIII reigned from 1509 to 1547. When he assumed the throne, expectations ran high that the Renaissance, an Italian enterprise of the fifteenth century, would now come to England. Henry was just the person to inspire a renaissance of art and learning, because Henry was, in the estimation of many, the proverbial Renaissance man. He knew four languages, composed music (much of which survives), wrote poetry, studied astronomy and cartography, tinkered with inventions, and was an immense builder and acquirer of palaces, mansions, castles, and the like. He hunted (on his many game parks), played tennis (quite expertly for the time), and jousted (well into his 40s). Henry was a large man (his body armor measured 6'2''), energetic and gifted; but because he was the second-born son, he received an education meant to ready him for the clergy. He took religion seriously and understood it well enough to engage in published controversy with **Martin Luther**. At an early age he made the acquaintance of **Desiderius Erasmus**, Europe's leading intellectual, and **Thomas More**, soon-to-be author of *Utopia*. But while Henry was a sometimes student and patron of the **Humanists** (scholars who made human nature rather than divine nature their principal concern), he did not share their cosmopolitan outlook or their passion for peace. Too English and too spirited was Henry to be satisfied with a world united and domesticated under the banner of international Christianity. Henry longed for glory, to be won at sea (Henry gave England its first great navy) or won on the battlefields of France.

The two continental powers of the time were Spain and France, countries ahead of England in transforming themselves into nation-states. Spain under **Charles V** enjoyed the immense advantage of possessing southern Italy through conquest and central Europe—i.e., the **Holy Roman Empire**—through marriage with the Habsburgs. Charles was the grandson of Ferdinand and Isabella and the grandson of Maximillian (of Germany). When Ferdinand died in 1516, Charles became king of Spain; and when Maximillian died, in 1519, Charles became Holy Roman Emperor. Spain then was the colossus. France's situation was somewhat less favorable. It had prospered since the end of the Hundred Years War, and it had a new and resourceful king in **Francis I** (1515-1547). But its invasion of Italy, begun by Charles VIII in 1494, then renewed by Louis XII in 1499 and by Francis in 1515, had not gone well. Spain entered the fray, and by the late 1520s Spain was the dominant power on the peninsula. Indeed, at Pavia in 1525, Francis himself was captured and forced to pay ransom for his release and to accept ignominious terms of surrender.

Because England under Henry still smarted from the loss of (most of) its French possessions half a century earlier, England saw France as its foe and by default saw Spain as its friend. To cement the alliance Catherine was married to Arthur—and the fact that Henry married her, too, helped to keep England inside the Spanish fold. Henry's first martial adventure was in 1513 as an auxiliary to Ferdinand, where at the head of an army of 30,000 Henry defeated the French at the battle of the Spurs (so named because of the enemy's hasty retreat) and captured the French town of Tournai (which he garrisoned and held for six years). The French retaliated by stirring up the Scots (standard practice), who under their king, James IV (husband of Henry's sister, Margaret Tudor) crossed the northern border and captured several towns. But at Flodden Field (while Henry was still in France) the English army inflicted a terrible defeat upon the Scots, who lost their king in the fighting. For a vigorous young monarch like Henry, this seizing of cities and killing of kings was wonderful sport, but not much of the same was to follow, as diplomacy subordinated warfare throughout the balance of Henry's reign.

Henry's chief diplomat was **Thomas Cardinal Wolsey**. Of humble beginnings (a butcher's son), Wolsey rose quickly in the ranks of courtiers (most of whom were prelates), first as chaplain to Henry VII, then as King's Almoner to Henry VIII, as Keeper of the Great Seal, and as Lord Chancellor. His intelligence and indefatigable energy were the qualities that catapulted him past all others. Wolsey happily performed the work of government (always cognizant of and compliant with Henry's wishes), while Henry entertained himself with tournaments, progresses (movings of the court from palace to palace), and love affairs. On the diplomatic front Wolsey established his preeminence in the aftermath of the combat of 1513. Ferdinand and Maximillian had each made a separate peace with France, leaving England to confront its implacable foe alone. But Henry, through Wolsey, did them one better by marrying his other sister, Mary Tudor, to the French king, Louis XII (1514). Mary was young and beautiful; Louis was old and infirm—and dead within two months of the wedding. Louis's heir, Francis (a cousin and son-in-law), was, like Henry, proud, ambitious, and hungry for glory. He invaded Italy and won a signal victory at Marignano against Swiss mercenaries in the pay of pope Leo X (1515). Desperate for allies, the pope offered concessions to the English, including a cardinal's hat for Wolsey (known to be the power behind the throne) and later the title of papal legate (lifting Wolsey's religious authority above that of the archbishop of Canterbury). England reciprocated with financial support, but in time the anti-French coalition failed again when Maximillian and then Charles (king of Spain since 1516) made peace with France. Leo, too, shifted his focus, since with a new Turkish sultan on the throne (Soleiman the Magnificent), the threat to Italy came mainly from the east. The belligerents then assembled in London, and under Wolsey's direction they agreed to a European peace whereby captured properties were restored, indemnities paid, and a crusade against the Turks declared. This was the treaty of London, signed in 1518; it marked the high point of Wolsey's diplomatic career.

One other moment followed, though it was more theatrical than substantive. The **Field of Cloth of Gold** (June 1520) was a meeting of heads of state which for its grandiosity and expense rivaled a Hollywood movie set and a modern-day Olympics. Henry and Francis, each accompanied by thousands of nobles, courtiers, prelates, and servants, met on a field in between Guisnes (English territory) and Ardes (French territory). For two weeks the French and English parties housed themselves under 2800 tents and in a temporary palace constructed for the occasion. There was feasting, jousting, athletic competitions (including a wrestling match between the kings), and entertainments of various descriptions. And there was politicking—e.g., Henry's daughter, princess Mary, was formally engaged to Francis's son, the dauphin. Fearing that the politicking would do him harm, the uninvited guest to the party, emperor Charles V, insisted upon meeting Henry in England before and after the festivities. England was riding high, and Wolsey higher still, for he was the majordomo and impresario of this ostentatious event.

Remember the European peace and the war against the Turks? Instead, there was war between Spain and France and a forgetting of the Turks, notwithstanding the fact that Soleiman was laying siege to Belgrade. England tried negotiating a truce while all along hatching plots with the emperor toward the goal of conquering France and installing Henry as king. The betrothal of Mary to the dauphin now became the betrothal of Mary to the emperor (she was five, he was 21). As a reward for Wolsey, again the dark genius behind events, the emperor promised to have his supporters on the College of Cardinals vote for Wolsey as pope (Leo X would die in late 1521). England declared war against France in 1522 (citing violations of the treaty of London) and together with imperial forces advanced 50 miles inside of French territory before withdrawing to winter quarters.

A war had begun that would last for 40 years. But it was not England's war primarily. England had little at stake beyond royal ambition and a strategy of balance of power. Nor was England's contribution significant, continuous, or even consistent. England could not find the cash to support an army, though Henry summoned parliament for the purpose and had it pass a war tax (1523), which supplemented a series of forced loans, the last one called euphemistically the Amicable Grant. Lacking the resources and sometimes the will, England failed to provide Spain with useful and steady assistance. And when Spain was successful on its own, at Pavia especially (1525), England was not counted an equal with rights to the spoils. Accordingly, Charles broke off his engagement to Mary, having twice previously reneged on his promise to make Wolsey pope (Leo was succeeded by Adrian VI, who two years later was succeeded by **Clement VII**—of the Medici family and cousin to Leo). England responded by withdrawing from the imperial alliance and signing a treaty (treaty of the More) with France, which renewed hostilities, once Francis, its king, was released from captivity. Rather than fight on the French side, England reverted to a position of neutrality, attempting to broker a continental peace. But in 1527 imperial forces overran and sacked the city of Rome. Spain now was triumphant, and the policy of England, which tracked closely the policy of the papacy—i.e., weaken France without strengthening Spain—was in tatters. The defeat of French forces at Landriano in 1529 was the final nail in the coffin.

CONTENDING IDEAS AT THE TIME OF THE REFORMATION

The treaty of London envisioned a united, Christian Europe standing shoulder to shoulder against the invading Muslim Turk. But something of moment happened the previous year, in 1517, which set in motion the fracturing of Europe along religious lines. Martin Luther nailed his *Ninety-five Theses* to the Wittenberg church door and ushered in the **Protestant Reformation**. Peace and unity were never serious possibilities.

Lutheranism began as an attack upon church abuses. But what was the church, abuses aside, that structured the beliefs and influenced the politics of Europeans on the eve of the Reformation?

Medieval Catholicism

Learned reasoning during the Middle Ages went by the name of **Scholasticism** (from schoolmen). It applied logic to the questions of theology, philosophy, politics, and ethics. St. Thomas Aquinas (1225–1274) was its supreme practitioner. Aquinas undertook to reconcile classical philosophy (newly recovered) with the revealed word of scripture. His assumption was that all truth is of a piece since all truth is from God—hence revelation ought to make sense to natural reason. Aquinas's method (and that of scholastics generally) was to pose a question, state objections thereto (the conventional wisdom of the day), quote scripture and/or church fathers on the subject, then proceed to answer rationally all objections in a way consistent with the teachings of the church. The *Summa Theologica* was his crowning achievement.

After Aquinas, scholasticism lost its confidence in the unity of truth (Duns Scotus, William of Occam); and its penchant for abstraction (the notorious angels-on-the-head-of-a-pin debate) and its use of a terminology ever more obscure and barbarous did further damage to its good name. It seemed not to connect with people's religious experience (mysticism represented the extreme alternative), to say nothing of original Christianity and the life of Jesus, the carpenter. It fell into disrepute, ridiculed by critics as diverse as Luther (*Three Treatises*, pp. 92–94, 147–48) and More (*Utopia*, p. 49), though at the time of the Reformation it still constituted the orthodox curriculum taught at the universities. (Apparently not much changed with the Reformation, for similarly critical assessments of university education can be found among Enlightenment authors. See, for example, Adam Smith, *Wealth of Nations*, V.i.f.19-32 (vol. II, pp. 765–72 of Liberty Fund edition).

Two other features of medieval Catholicism deserve notice: sacramentalism and the cult of the saints. Salvation, it was taught, came through receipt of the sacraments, performed by church clergy for the benefit of church members. Seven such sacraments in all were—are—there: baptism, confirmation (a supplement to infant baptism), communion, penance, marriage, holy orders, and extreme unction (a blessing at the hour of death). Additionally, the celebration of the mass, a restaging of the Last Supper and the sacrifice of Christ, provides the liturgical occasion for the distribution of communion. The eucharist was understood as the body and blood of Christ, miraculously transformed from the bread and wine present on the altar (more particularly—and drawing on the scholastic distinction between substance and accident [Fourth Lateran Council of 1215]—the substance, or inner essence, changes, while the accident, or outward form, remains the same; thus bread and wine continue to look and taste like bread and wine [accidents] even though their transformed nature [substance] is now the body and blood of Christ). **Transubstantiation** is the name of this miracle.

As for the cult of the saints, it might be regarded as Christianity's concession to paganism. Saints are not gods. In life they were men and women of exceptional holiness—and to whom miracles are attributed—who in death serve as intermediaries between God and man. The God of the Middle Ages was distant and judgmental, the laws of nature unknown; saints were prayed to so that they might intercede with God to grant the suppliant's worldly and otherworldly wishes. In time, this "people's" Christianity became tantamount to saint worship, complete with relics, shrines, and pilgrimages.

There is, of course, more, much more. The Roman Catholic church—with its popes, cardinals, bishops, and abbots, its priests, deacons, monks, and nuns—had been the religious power in Europe ever since the fall of Rome; but it also was a secular power of considerable import. It ruled over central Italy (the Papal States), and it claimed the right of anointing the Holy Roman Emperor. (Charlemagne was the first; Napoleon was the last of these super-kings, who at various times aspired to the governance of a pan-European state with Christianity as its religion.) Emperors had special obligations to and rights over the church and were at once the church's protectors and oppressors. They mostly were German princes (chosen by seven German princes, both secular and religious) who, because they tried to establish their authority in Italy (every new emperor would go to Rome to be crowned, and not infrequently the going required an invasion), failed to unite the provinces at home and ended up generally weaker than the kings of France, Spain, and England (see Luther, *Three Treatises*, pp. 100–05.) Other ecclesiastical powers, such as excommunication and interdiction (denial of the sacraments), extended the church's control over all of the princes of Europe. Also, church personnel were landowners comparable to the nobility as well as ministers of state. England's Lord Chancellor was typically the Archbishop of Canterbury. In many ways, therefore, European monarchs found themselves governed by Rome—and paying for the privilege. Taxes were collected for use by the church, and with the appointment of new bishops and abbots to offices called **benefices**, huge sums of money called **annates** or **first-fruits** were transferred to Rome.

What, though, accounted for this intricate interlacing of church-state relations so foreign to us today? The answer is as simple as the meaning of life. Life's purpose is not mere existence. Nor is it agreeable existence as provided by wealth, power, love, tranquillity, esteem. To think so is to prize the body and its momentary desires ahead of the soul and its eternal destiny. The soul's salvation is what matters most, and those best trained to chart the soul's progress to heaven are the rightful rulers of society. Society is a hierarchy, and sitting atop this structure is the person or persons with the most comprehensive knowledge of the most important things. The principle at work here is actually classical, that knowledge rules over ignorance (natural right, as it is called). Plato says as much when he declares that philosophers, not statesmen, should be kings (*Republic, Gorgias*). (We say something similar when we affirm that pilots, not passengers, should fly planes and that doctors, not patients, should diagnose disease.) But with the advent of Christianity, the word of God becomes the most comprehensive knowledge (not philosophy), and openness to and dependence on God becomes the most important thing (not self-sufficiency). Hence society's supreme ruler is, or ought to be, the pope in Rome. Kings in their states are unqualified as leaders; but they are useful agents when they agree to submit to the authority of the church, in which case the law and order they provide are valuable aids in keeping people from violence and temptation. Royal authority has, then, a role to play, but as a subordinate to sacred authority. In medieval parlance, royal authority is the regnum; sacred authority is the sacerdotium.

This position of the medieval church was developed over centuries of controversy. And controversy aplenty there was, for, suffice it to say, kings and emperors had a different take on the matter. If a bishop was going to govern a district inside the emperor's realm, then, by God, the emperor was going to appoint the bishop—so said (Germany's) Henry IV to pope Gregory VII. Gregory's response was to excommunicate Henry, forcing him to walk "barefoot" over the Alps to seek the pope's forgiveness. (This dispute was the start of the **Investiture Conflict,** which was waged for fifty years—1075–1122.) If popes were going to excommunicate emperors, then the emperor was going to choose his own pope—so reasoned Frederick Barbarossa, who gave himself three rival popes (1159–1177). If Christendom divided over the question of who rightfully was pope, then some institution other than the papacy would be needed to decide among the contenders—hence arose the **Conciliar Movement** of the fifteenth century (though it produced more rivals than it eliminated). And so it went. (For a clear and concise introduction, see Roland Bainton, *The Reformation of the Sixteenth Century* [Boston: Beacon Press, 1952], pp. 6–21 [on reserve].)

Both sides to the controversy accepted the premise that church and state were inextricably bound; they haggled over which of the parties should be in charge. One disputant on the secular side was **Marsilius of Padua**, author of *Defender of the Peace*. This fourteenth-century philosopher was well schooled in classical thought; thus, he understood the argument from natural right that those who know should govern those who do not know. But Marsilius distinguished between governing (judging) as an exercise of coercive power and governing as an apprehension of proper ends. The priest may be expert in matters of true faith, but the priest does not for that reason punish the heretic, anymore than does the goldsmith, expert in metallurgy, punish the counterfeiter or does the physician, expert in medicine, punish the quack. Punishment is left to civil authority. Experts give advice to civil authority, but civil authority decides whether to make that advice law. Otherwise, as many governments would exist as there exist experts or fields of expertise. But multiple governments are an evident danger to peace—and Marsilius is a "defender of the peace." Thus, for the sake of peace, all must submit to the one, civil government, religious experts included.

When Henry could not persuade the pope to grant him a divorce, some of Henry's ministers discovered Marsilius and put his ideas to good use.

Lutheranism

Marsilius orchestrated an attack on the structure of the church that to many in the sixteenth century seemed like a forerunner of the attack launched by Martin Luther.

Luther was an Augustinian monk and professor of theology at the newly founded University of Wittenberg. His reading of scripture led him to discover a primitive Christianity antedating the clerical establishment, and his reflections on scripture led him to conclude that salvation rested on faith alone. No doing of good works would make any difference given the radical unworthiness of fallen man. Only God's mercy, bestowed on some as the gift of faith, cleansed the soul and delivered it to heaven. This conviction put Luther at odds with established church doctrine, which taught that salvation was partly earned (through works) and partly given (through grace).

While the difference in teachings might seem small and negotiable, Luther's rejection of works actually made the Catholic church quite superfluous, as did Luther's treatment of the Bible as the sole source of truth and authority. Priests were unnecessary as intermediaries between God and man, because God, through scripture, spoke directly to the individual. Sacraments were discounted (other than those specifically authorized by scripture—baptism, communion, and [sometimes] penance), since sacraments were ritualistic acts designed to win the favor and forgiveness of God; they thus fell into the category of works. Similarly, the liturgy of the mass was a work and so was replaced by learned preaching of the word. The veneration of saints was condemned, since veneration supposed that saints by their holiness had the power to intercede with God on the suppliant's behalf. Images, relics, and pilgrimages were also of no use, as were cloistered monks and nuns devoting their lives to prayer. And for its practical consequence, of greatest importance was the doctrine of **purgatory**, defined as a time and place of punishment where souls of the deceased expiate their sins. Expiation was but another form of work, implying that humans could achieve, or contribute to, salvation. It also meant that others could assist through their prayers and could lessen their own time of suffering through the granting of **indulgences**. Private masses privately paid for were the preferred form of prayers for the dead; and church-approved behaviors (e.g., visitation of shrines), plus donations to the church, were how indulgences were earned and/or purchased. Indeed, it was the sale of indulgences for the financing of St. Peter's basilica that provoked Luther in the first place.

Indulgences were not a new church practice, nor were they without theological rationale: Christ and the saints, so the argument went, had amassed a surplus of merit available to ordinary sinners through distribution by the church. Penance absolved sins but did not remit all punishments due. Good works were needed to balance the books, or reduce the time required in purgatory, and those whose lives were insufficiently good could draw upon the good works of Christ and the saints. But purgatory and indulgences were doctrines that lent themselves to abuse and misunderstanding. The church treated passage to the afterlife as a cash-cow for funding the activities of the present life; the laity believed that they were buying salvation and resented what sometimes seemed like extortionist prices set by the church. This entire apparatus of salvation Luther called into question when he announced his doctrine of **justification by faith alone**.

What follows is a list of essential Lutheran beliefs:

> **Predestination.** Life is not meaningless; there is a divine plan. Salvation is this plan, and it details have all been worked out in advance. Accordingly, salvation is not earned; man is too unworthy, and his will is not free. Rather, salvation depends upon election determined by God from the beginning of time. The elect are identified by their yearning for God's presence, their determination to do God's will, and their repentance of their sins.

> **Justification by faith alone.** Belief in Christ the savior is Christianity's core principle and is what justifies, or saves, Christian souls. Faith is a gift of God, not an achievement of man. Good works, understood as charitable acts (as in "love thy neighbor") or as observance of ceremonial rules (so important to the Pharisees), contribute nothing to justification; they are instead caused by justification, since without faith sinful men cannot keep the commandments of God (*Three Treatises*, pp. 280–85). **Justification by works** is a throwback to the Pelagian heresy of St. Augustine's day.

> **Christian freedom.** The promises of God, communicated by his word, liberate believers from all worldly concerns and constraints. Believers are free of law, though they obey law in order not to give offense (*Three Treatises*, pp. 284, 305–06).

> **Scripture as the only source of truth.** Centuries of papal decrees, canon law, and scholastic theology carry no authority. Only scripture counts (*Three Treatises*, pp. 97–99), and scripture is to be interpreted by the individual—hence accurate translations are a must, as is their dissemination to the laity (made possible by the recent invention of the printing press).

> **Preaching the word as true liturgy.** Communion (the desideratum of the mass) is but a symbolic act (though Luther was less insistent than his followers in denying the transubstantiation of the bread and wine into the body and blood of Christ). The other sacraments of holy orders, confirmation, extreme unction, and marriage are human-made and not true sacraments.

> **Pope as Antichrist.** The pope has no more status than any other bishop of the church; his claim to superiority is the work of the devil. What's

more, all clerical hierarchy is suspect, since the church is an egalitarian community of the faithful.

> **Priesthood of all believers.** While there still are ministers trained in biblical studies, the church as a separate society of celibate men and women is no more (*Three Treatises*, pp. 244–50).

After Luther posted his *Ninety-five Theses* attacking indulgences, the church decided to investigate, and the following year it summoned him to Augsburg to explain himself before the papal legate. There Luther made his case for the authority of scripture, while the legate made his case for the authority of the pope and of the church. Luther was hoping to reform the church, not rebel against it, but with the publication of his three most important treatises, *Address to the Christian Nobility of the German Nation concerning the Reformation of the Christian Estate*, *The Babylonian Captivity of the Church*, and *Concerning Christian Liberty*—all works attacking the papacy and the curia—it became clear that a split was inevitable.

In 1520 Luther was excommunicated by the pope, who additionally demanded that Luther be placed under imperial ban and declared an outlaw. Luther was summoned to the Diet of Worms, where he was interrogated but not punished, after which his protector, Frederick the Wise, elector of Saxony, removed him to the safety of Wartburg. (Because Germany was a collection of semi-autonomous states, and because the emperor, Charles, had recently made concessions in order to secure his election, imperial authority was reluctant to suppress Lutheranism in its origins.) A year later, in 1522, he returned to Wittenberg, married a former nun, and with her started a family (six children in all).

While Luther occupied himself with work and domesticity, his country occupied itself with the Peasants' Revolt (1524–1525), an uprising partly inspired by Luther's anti-authoritarianism and much denounced by him for that reason. The princes stepped in to give order to the Reformation, some declaring for and some against Luther. The emperor was able to impose his (Catholic) will only on the Low Countries; and when he tried for more, revoking the freedom of conscience decreed by the Diet of Speyer (1526), the princes "protested"—and were forever after known as **Protestants** (second Diet of Speyer, 1529). (The final settlement came in 1555 at a second Diet of Augsburg. Princes were granted the right to decide for themselves and their subjects which faith they collectively would profess. State churches were thus created, and dissenting subjects were required to emigrate.)

In the 1530s and 1540s Luther turned his attention to the task of churchbuilding. He completed a German translation of the Bible, while his colleague, Philip Melanchthon, authored the *Augsburg Confession*, the catechism of the Lutheran faith. Luther had many followers of note (Karlstadt, Zwingli, Oecolampadius), many of whom he denounced over doctrinal disputes; but his most important follower, who in Britain at least surpassed Luther in fame and influence, was John Calvin of Geneva (1509-1564). Luther died in 1546.

Renaissance Humanism

Catholic Christianity's first opponents were not the Lutherans. That distinction belongs to the humanists of the Northern Renaissance. The word "renaissance" means rebirth, and **the Renaissance** generally means a rebirth of classical civilization. Italian humanists rediscovered classical art and literature. Northern humanists applied the same reclamation techniques to the texts of ancient Christianity, in particular the New Testament. Erasmus produced a new translation from the original Greek (Septuagint), bypassing the Latin translation available during the Middle Ages (Vulgate). Whereas the Italian Renaissance was pagan (i.e., Greeks and Romans) and aesthetic (e.g., Leonardo, Michelangelo, Raphael), the Northern Renaissance was Christian and political. Humanists of the north were advisers to emperors, kings, popes, and bishops. Erasmus was in correspondence with nearly every secular and religious leader of Europe, and Thomas More was a member of Henry's cabinet before becoming Henry's Lord Chancellor. The advice they gave was for moderate reform designed to draw on and energize the piety of laypeople (among other recommendations, e.g., peace, poor relief). Humanists wished to revive the faith of the laity by what Erasmus called the "philosophy of Christ" (doctrinal simplicity, rational morality, inner commitment, the Holy Spirit as guide to true understanding, the common man as theologian and preacher). Humanists, therefore, were particularly annoyed by the elitist obscurantism of scholastics.

But humanists, too, were intellectual elitists, and they took delight in poking sophisticated fun at the foibles of courts and consistories. Gentle prodding, they hoped, would prick the consciences of powerful persons sufficiently to bring about needed reforms in belief and practice. Erasmus's most famous book, *The Praise of Folly*, marvels at the harmless failings of common humanity before satirizing with increasing severity the prideful selfishness of society's well-to-do—merchants, philosophers, courtiers, princes, cardinals, and popes. Thomas More's *Utopia* recounts a fictional conversation with a fictional world traveler whose exposure to unknown places, particularly the "nowhere" land of Utopia, casts the customs of English society in a harsh and unflattering light. More and Erasmus were good friends and close collaborators in this project of religious, social, and educational reform called the "new learning." Other English contributors were John Colet, dean of St. Paul's cathedral; Thomas Linacre, the king's physician; and William Grocyn, translator of Aristotle.

When Luther burst upon the scene, humanist reaction was mixed. More immediately threw himself into polemical mode, defending the faith against this heresy from abroad. Erasmus was less quick to judge, in part because he thought himself implicated in Luther's protest, saying—or having it said of him—that he laid the egg that Luther sat upon and hatched. Erasmus eventually declared against Luther, but other humanists did not. In England the reform of the church became entangled with the king's divorce. Those humanists who supported the divorce went one way, enjoying the king's patronage, while those who opposed the divorce went the other way, in some cases to their deaths.

Machiavellianism

There was in fact one humanist of the Italian Renaissance who interested himself in politics; this was **Niccolò Machiavelli**. At about the time Thomas More was publishing *Utopia* and Martin Luther was circulating his *Ninety-five Theses*, Machiavelli was writing a revised dedication to his notorious handbook of statecraft, *The Prince*.

Machiavelli (1469–1527) was an important government official of the Florentine republic, serving as secretary to the Second Chancery and to the Ten of War (equivalent to secretaries of State and Defense) from 1499 to 1512. On behalf of Florence he visited imperial, royal, and princely courts all over Europe and Italy. He was a player on the international scene (albeit for a tiny state) just in advance of Henry's entering the game. (Machiavelli never met Henry, though he wrote of him.) In 1512 a Spanish army defeated a Florentine garrison at Prato. The loss so frightened the Florentines that they agreed to a change of government, restoring the Medicis, who had ruled the city during its heyday in the fifteenth century, and removing officers of the republic, Machiavelli included. Shortly thereafter Machiavelli was implicated (falsely) in a conspiracy, arrested, imprisoned, tortured, and then released, along with others, upon the installation of Giovanni de' Medici as pope Leo X in March of 1513. Forbidden to live in Florence proper, he took up residence at the family farm a few miles away and set about writing his books: *The Prince, Discourses on Livy, The Art of War, Mandragola* (a play), *Florentine Histories*, and others.

Machiavelli is most famous as author of *The Prince*. It is a book meant mainly to instruct "new princes" (i.e., usurpers) in the arts of seizing, keeping, and expanding power. The instruction is scandalously indifferent to questions of legitimacy, common goods, natural law, and divine purpose. Princely character is discussed, but in ways altogether revolutionary. Rather than encourage a prince to practice the classical and Christian virtues of wisdom, justice, moderation, piety, charity, clemency, etc. (as would a "mirror of a prince" treatise so common during the Middle Ages), the book reduces virtue (*virtù*) to the qualities useful for acquisition—boldness and cleverness (the lion and the fox). All other qualities are like costumes, to be put on or taken off depending on the role the prince is playing. Sometimes it advantages a prince to rule by love, in which case he should appear generous, merciful, humane; other times it behooves a prince to rule by fear, in which case ferocity, cruelty, gravity are the appropriate qualities. Success in this world depends on flexibility, and a prince who feels himself bound to keep faith with his promises or who more generally strives always to be good will likely lose his state, since any one who would act up to a perfect standard of goodness in everything, must be ruined among so many who are not good. It is essential, therefore, for a prince who desires to maintain his position, to have learned how to be other than good, and to use or not to use his goodness as necessity requires (*Prince* 15).

The Prince was not published until 1532, five years after Machiavelli's death, but it circulated in manuscript form soon after its composition in 1513. One of those manuscripts, it is thought, made its way to England and into the hands of **Thomas Cromwell**, Henry's chief minister after the fall of Thomas More. (Cromwell was in Florence working for the Frescobaldi banking house during some of the time that Machiavelli was in office.) An account of Cromwell's Machiavellian affinities is provided by **Reginald Pole**, Henry's cousin and a cardinal of the church. Pole tells of a conversation he had with Cromwell (in the late 1520s) about the duties of a courtier. Whereas Pole offered the humanist opinion that courtiers should advise their prince honestly, Cromwell replied that a successful courtier is one who divines his prince's unspoken wishes and proceeds to satisfy them, whatever their nature, while talking always of virtue and seeming never to veer from its path. Cromwell went on to belittle the idealism of writers like Plato who outline societies and prescribe behaviors too good for this world and ruinous to those who take the advice seriously. But Cromwell made an exception for a recent author, unnamed, who combined learning with experience to produce a true account of politics; and he promised to lend the book to Pole. Now Machiavelli was likely the author referred to by Cromwell, since Machiavelli claims political knowledge based on "long experience with modern affairs and continual study of antiquity" (*Prince*, Dedication), and since Machiavelli announces the realistic purpose his writing is meant to serve:

But since it is my object to write what shall be useful to whosoever understands it, it seems to me better to follow the real truth of things than an imaginary view of them. For many republics and princedoms have been imagined that were never seen or known to exist in reality. And the manner in which we live, and that in which we ought to live, are things so wide asunder, that he who quits the one to betake himself to the other is more likely to destroy than to save himself (*Prince* 15).

Pole was the first to damn Machiavelli (many would do so after him), and he described Cromwell's reformation of the English church as the work of a Machiavellian prince.

Maps

KEY

.   Seat of Diocese

————   Diocese Border

—— · ——   National Border

DURHAM

CARLISLE

YORK

BANGOR

St ASAPH

COVENTRY & LICHFIELD

LINCOLN

NORWICH

ELY

HEREFORD

WORCESTER

St DAVIDS

LLANDAFF

LONDON

ROCHESTER

CANTERBURY

BATH & WELLS

SALISBURY

WINCHESTER

CHICHESTER

EXETER

Bedfordshire
Berkshire
Buckinghamshire
Cambridgeshire
Cheshire
Cornwall
Cumberland
Derbyshire
Devonshire
Dorset
Durham
Essex
Gloucestershire
Hampshire
Herefordshire
Hertforshire
Huntingdonshire
Kent
Lancashire
Leicestershire
Lincolnshire
London and Middlesex
Norfolk
Northamptonshire
Northumberland
Nottinghamshire
Oxfordshire
Rutland
Shropshire
Sommerset
Staffordshire
Suffolk
Surrey
Sussex
Warwickshire
Westmorland
Wiltshire
Worcestershire
Yorkshire

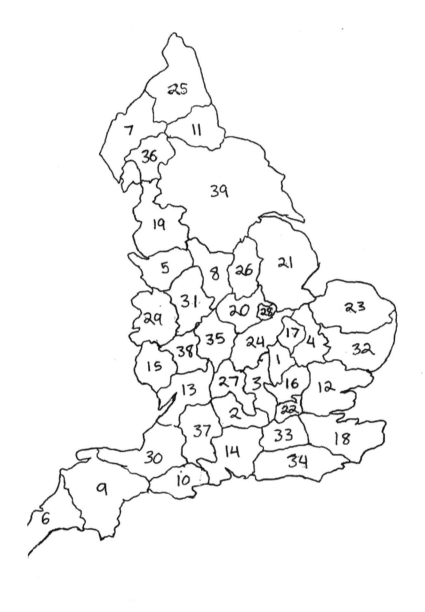

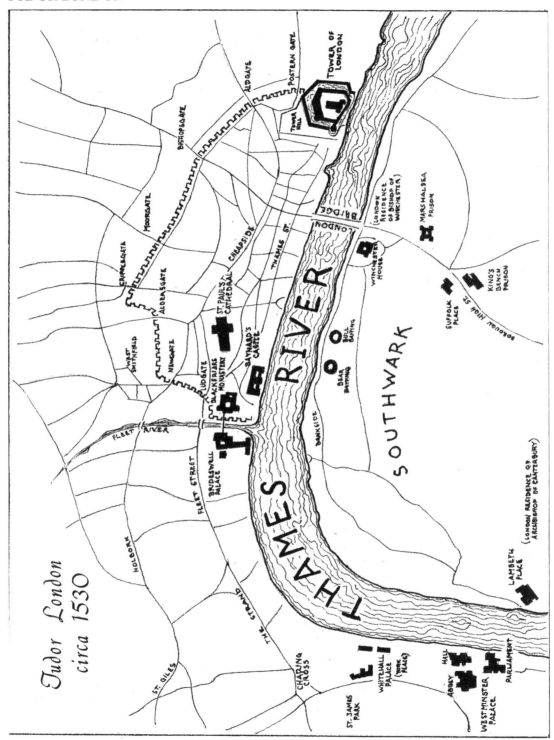

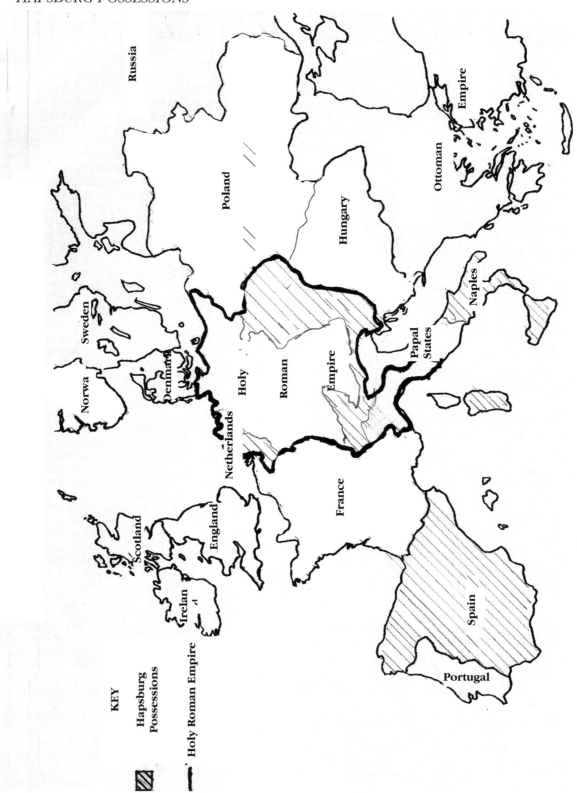

Russia

Empire

Poland

Ottoman

Hungary

Sweden

Naples

Norwa

Denmark

Holy

Roman

Empire

Papal
States

Netherlands

France

Scotland

England

Ireland

Spain

Portugal

KEY

Hapsburg
Possessions

Holy Roman Empire

Henry VIII and the Reformation Parliament

The Game

PARLIAMENT

The game covers the years 1529 to 1536. Wolsey has just fallen from office on a charge of **Praemunire** (allegiance to a foreign power—e.g., Wolsey's service as papal legate, a fourteenth-century law, rarely invoked, that sought to protect the rights of the king and his secular courts against invasions by the church), and Thomas More has succeeded him as Lord Chancellor. Wolsey had promised to deliver Henry his divorce, claiming that only he, Wolsey, as papal legate, could bring the pope around to the English position. But the pope at the time was a virtual prisoner of Emperor Charles, and Emperor Charles was the nephew of Henry's wife, Catherine. Charles would not countenance a divorce, and Clement, the pope, had little choice but to side with Charles.

Wolsey, then, was out because securing the divorce from Clement was out, and because other advisers had persuaded Henry that the church and parliament of England could accomplish Henry's objective. But at what price? A break with Rome? A schism within Christianity? Acceptance of Protestant heresy? The wrath of the emperor and of Catholic Europe?

The debates take place inside of parliament, which met seven times during the seven years and came to be known as the **Reformation Parliament**. But parliament was composed of two houses, Lords and Commons, and a fair portion of legislative work occurred outside of parliament in a religious assembly called **Convocation**, also divided into upper and lower houses. (The church was an independent legislative/judicial body with power over marriages, burials, wills, contracts, morals, heresy, etc. The Convocation of Canterbury, outside of London, governed the southern half of England, while the Convocation of York governed the northern half.) Unfortunately, as a counterfactual, this multi-layered legislative structure must be compressed into a single chamber. Its members, though, will still be drawn from all of the sectors of society actually represented: **temporal lords**, members of the peerage (dukes, marquesses, earls, viscounts, and barons); **spiritual lords**, high clergy (archbishops, bishops, abbots, and priors); **temporal commoners**, members of parliament from municipalities (burgesses) and members of parliament from counties (knights of the shire) (all of them called M.P.s for short); and **spiritual commoners**, low clergy (archdeacons, priests, and monks). (This last group had representation only in Convocation, and so their inclusion in parliament is another counterfactual.) The interests and opinions of these various groups differ widely.

For some issues the spiritual lords and spiritual commoners will convene separately as Convocation or as an ecclesiastical court (e.g., the prosecution of heretics). Other groups, such as temporal lords, are free to caucus together; in a couple of instances, only Commons, or M.Ps., vote.

Joint presidents, the Lord Chancellor and the Speaker of the House, will preside over sessions of parliament. (Thomas More is Lord Chancellor when the game begins; **Thomas Audley** is Speaker of the House.) Rules of procedure will be established by the presidents at the outset with amendments allowed as the game progresses. If the presidents are unable to agree, parliament will decide the matter, with each parliamentarian casting a single vote. Here are some rules known to have been in place at the time:

> The Speaker of the House petitions the king for freedom to speak (granted on condition that M.Ps. confine themselves to the issues at hand, say nothing of a treasonous or heretical nature, and are physically within the precinct of the parliament).

> Parliamentarians are granted freedom from arrest on private matters (e.g., debt) during sessions of parliament.

> Proceedings of parliament are secret.

> Attendance is mandatory for commoners; only with a license from the Speaker may a member be absent. Lords, though, may vote by proxy.

> Lords have their votes recorded; commoners (because of their greater number—though not an issue here) vote by acclamation. (See "Voting Procedures" below.)

> Bills are read three times before being presented to the king for his approval (perhaps the most important procedural development of the period, but one that, because of time constraints, cannot likely be observed here).

> The king convokes and adjourns (prorogues) each session of parliament. When adjourning, the king gives or denies his assent to legislation. (Henry, though, attended on other occasions.) In the king's presence, parliamentarians all stand.

> Legislative committees are sometimes utilized; joint committees of lords and commoners are called conferences.

For more on procedures, see Michael Graves, *The Tudor Parliaments: Crown, Lords and Commons, 1485–1603* (London: Longman, 1985); G. R. Elton, *The Tudor Constitution: Documents and Commentary*, 2nd ed. (Cambridge: Cambridge University Press, 1982), pp. 249–54; S. E. Lehmberg, "Early Tudor Parliamentary Procedure: Provisos in the Legislation of the Reformation Parliament," *English Historical Review*, 81 (1961) 225 ff. The Avalon Project provides an account of parliamentary procedures in the very early years of the English monarchy. See: *http://www.yale.edu/lawweb/avalon/medieval/manner.htm*.

One minor post is created for use in the game, namely parliament historian. The bishop of Lincoln serves in this capacity.

Also, the Lord Chancellor and the Speaker are responsible for keeping records of the laws passed by parliament (posted later on the class Web site), or they may wish to appoint someone to serve as parliament recorder.

The business of parliament, from the king's perspective, is to pronounce the marriage to Catherine unlawful and void. But from the perspective of lords and commoners, there is much else besides: church reform, relations with Rome, dissolution of monasteries, heresy, commerce, exploration, war, loan repayment, agriculture, poor relief, trials, etc.

Around these issues of the day, and around more permanent interests, numerous factions formed.

FACTIONS

Clergy

The male high clergy of the church consists of archbishops, bishops, abbots, and priors (a prior is the chief officer under an abbot or the head of a smaller, offshoot house). They rule over, respectively, archdioceses, dioceses, and monastic orders. (Archbishops and bishops belong to the "secular" clergy, since they and their priests live in the world; abbots and priors belong to the "religious" clergy, since they and their monks live in monasteries apart from the world.) The high clergy are members of the House of Lords, even though they are appointed by Catholic popes and not by English kings. Much property do they possess, and some are fabulously wealthy. Wolsey, archbishop of York, had pensions paid to him by princes from all over Europe; he was as rich as or richer than Henry.

The high clergy are resented by nearly all segments of English society. These princes of the church seem indifferent to their vows, neglectful of their ministries, and abusive of their authority. Ecclesiastical courts wield awesome powers, just as threatening to the lives, liberties, and properties of laymen as are the courts of the king. At the first session of the Reformation Parliament, a torrent of complaint comes pouring forth, targeting high and low clergy alike: that clergy charge to perform the sacraments; that they overcharge for burials and wills (mortuary and probate fees); that they compete with secular businesses; that they recognize too many holy days (suppressing work and wages); that they are uneducated; that they hold multiple benefices (**pluralism**) and thus are absent from their ministries (**non-residence**); that they respond to justified criticism with charges of heresy and then deny due process in their courts; that the ordinances of Convocation go sometimes unpublished; that the monasteries, countless in number but with ever-declining membership, own vast tracts of land constituting much of the nation's wealth; and that the monasteries are sinkholes of corruption. The low clergy share none of the riches, power, and perquisites of the high clergy; but the low clergy come in contact with the lay populace, and the scandal of the clergy's sexual morals brings added reproach upon the church. Citing these and other failings, a propagandist named **Simon Fish** has helped prepare the ground for parliament's anticlerical attack with his pamphlet, *A Supplication for the Beggars* (in Appendix A).

The high clergy, understandably, have an explanation for the good life they lead. The church, they say, ceased being a persecuted body existing on the margins of society long ago. It now is a governing body responsible for the stability and good order of the state. Because church officials must parlay with the powerful more than they minister to the poor, church officials must play—and dress—the part of rulers. By contrast, the low clergy still find appealing and relevant the simplicity of the primitive church and are open to calls for reform. Reform to the high clergy generally means the suppression of heresy.

Nobility

Led by the **Dukes of Norfolk and Suffolk** (Thomas Howard and Charles Brandon), the English peerage are resentful of the fact that their place at court is being undermined by a new class of low-born ministers—Wolsey, More, Cromwell, and others. These ministers are educated and enterprising professionals, but they have no family claims to power. England is emerging from the feudal Middle Ages, and the nobility is slow to comprehend, much less reconcile to, the new order. On the other hand, a devastating civil war (the War of the Roses) has left the nobility depleted, fatigued, and unambitious. No peer openly challenges Henry's claim to the throne. But then no peer needs to, since the throne may be vacant and up for grabs upon Henry's demise.

Apart from class interest, the peers compete for personal advancement, for titles, offices, pensions, and land; but these preferments depend entirely upon the favor of the king. As is true of all courts, proximity to the king is golden, and marriage constitutes the tightest of bonds. Providing the king with a wife (though a mistress will do) is an ambition of many of the families, none more so than the Boleyns.

Regarding the issues of the day, the peers share the general dissatisfaction with the church, but individually they wax more or less ardent. Some are rather conservative and would like to see reform confined to the divorce and the chastisement of Rome. Others betray Lutheran sympathies and conspire to bring about a total overhaul of doctrine, liturgy, and personnel. Others still are patrons of the humanists. All imagine themselves men of the world, but few have the intelligence or resolve to qualify as Machiavellians.

Commoners

Commoners divide between town and country. Municipalities, as a rule, send lawyers and merchants to represent them in parliament. The countryside sends knights of the shire, a sub-peerage, quasi-nobility (in former days, soldiers of the king), drawn from the landed gentry but with the non-hereditary title of "sir." There are 74 knights in parliament (from 37 counties) and 236 burgesses (from

117 towns). The total membership of Commons is 310 (two from each county and town, with an extra two from London).

The commoners are of a single mind when church reform is the issue—all want more freedom and less interference from papal Rome. Commons, more than Lords, is eager for religious reformation. But when economics is the issue, commoners have varying and sometimes contrary interests. Wool is the principal commodity of the day. English agriculture is converting to sheep grazing, and those in the sheep business want fields enclosed for pasturage. Those not in the sheep business, or those sympathizing with the farming poor, want laws passed proscribing **enclosure**. Merchants who traffic in wool (and other commodities) want price controls in some cases and in other cases want free(er) trade. Certainly they want peace with the Low Countries, imperial provinces, since Flemish mills are where some of the wool is manufactured into finished cloth. Lawyers have their own, sometimes conflicting, professional interests depending on whether they practice at the King's Bench and Common Pleas (common law courts committed to precedent) or at the courts of the Chancery and Star Chamber (equity courts relying on common-sense judgments of right and wrong). Wolsey reinvigorated the latter courts, and More utilizes them extensively. While members of Commons are individually well-to-do, they, more than Lords, are inclined to concern themselves with the relief needs of the poor.

Boleyn-Howard Faction

Like several ladies of the court, Anne Boleyn captured the heart of Henry VIII—for a time. But unlike the others, she resisted Henry's advances until just before their wedding in January 1533. During these many years of courtship, royal favors were bestowed upon her family (her father, Thomas, became **Earl of Wiltshire** in 1529) and upon supporters of her cause (e.g., the Howard family, whose head, Thomas, the Duke of Norfolk, is Anne's uncle). Her interests, and the interests of her faction, are opposite the interests of Catherine and the Aragon faction on three counts: Anne wants to replace Catherine as wife and queen; Anne wants her daughter, Elizabeth, to replace Catherine's daughter, Mary, as heir-presumptive; and Anne wants Lutheranism to replace Catholicism as the state religion. Household, dynastic, and religious issues are all at stake. Anne's chief asset is the love of the king. The king wants Anne, and courtiers looking for advancement want whatever the king wants. Anne's chief liability is her imperious personality (she is bossy, even of the king). But there are other problems: A match with the Boleyns provides no diplomatic payoff for the Tudors (Wolsey's complaint); Catherine is beloved by the people and has an incomparable paladin in the emperor, her nephew; Henry is tentative about what a divorce may imply—i.e., reform of the church; and the people, though anticlerical, are habituated to Catholic practices.

Cromwell Faction

Thomas Cromwell was first a minister to Cardinal Wolsey before (following Wolsey's demise) applying his considerable talents to the service of Henry. Cromwell never advanced to the office of Lord Chancellor (perhaps by his own choice), but he gradually elevated a mere ministership to the status of prime minister. By the start of 1532 (while More was still Lord Chancellor), Cromwell was effectively in charge of Henry's policy.

Cromwell has four ambitions: to satisfy the king; to modernize the government; to reform the church; and to protect anti-papal England from the combined might of Catholic France and Spain. The first of these ambitions requires securing Henry his divorce from Catherine, to be achieved not by appeal to the pope but by decision of Convocation ratified by legislation passed in parliament. The second requires professionalizing the membership of the king's cabinet, named the **Privy Council**; lessening the power of the **Privy Chamber**, a department of the court or royal household, itself a vestige of medieval governance; and laying the foundation for a unified nation-state governed by a constitutional monarchy (described, though, as a despotism by his critics). The third ambition requires dissolving the monasteries (work begun by Wolsey) and introducing as many Lutheran elements into English worship as Henry will allow. What Henry will allow is anyone's guess, and so Cromwell opts for a middle way (*via media*) that concentrates on the essentials of religion and dispenses with liturgical superfluities or with things indifferent (*adiaphora*). He has in his pay a large cadre of ministers, prelates, and intellectuals who serve as propagandists for the "middle way" faith, or what will in time become the **Anglican Church**. Foremost among these lieutenants are Thomas Starkey, idea-man for *via media* policies; William Marshall, translator of Marsilius; Richard Taverner, popularizer of Erasmus; and Richard Morison, first English scholar to obtain a working knowledge of Machiavelli. The fourth ambition requires establishing diplomatic ties with the Lutheran princes of northern Europe (the Protestant League of Schmalkalden) and brokering, eventually, a marriage alliance with the house of Cleves (Anne of Cleves was to be Henry's fourth wife).

Lutheran Faction

Lutheranism planted its first English seed in 1518, at Cambridge's White Horse tavern, known as "Little Germany." It bore a close resemblance to a suppressed heresy of the previous century, **Lollardy**, first propagated by John Wycliffe in the 1370s and 1380s. Lollardy (a middle-Dutch term for "mumbling"—as in the mumbling of prayers) prefigured all of the important points of Lutheranism, save the main one, justification by faith alone. But whereas Lollardy was a proletarian faith shunned by the social elite, Lutheranism appealed to the upper and literate classes; and it spread by means of contraband publications, in particular the English translation of the New Testament by **William Tyndale** with Lutheran prologues and anti-Catholic marginalia (1525). It spread also because of the anticlericalism rife in the land, because king Henry was at loggerheads with the pope, and because his second wife, Anne, was a devout, if secretive, Lutheran.

English Lutherans, at the time of the game, have very many friends in very high places. But they haven't quite a friend in the highest place of all—the monarchy—and they are as yet a proscribed and heretical sect. To be a publicly professed Lutheran is to be burned at the stake (six were burned during More's chancellorship). To be accused of Lutheran beliefs is to be hauled into an ecclesiastical court, forced to confess (whether truthfully or not), offered one chance to recant, failing which . . . to be burned at the stake. (Relapsed Lutherans re-recanting are automatically burned at the stake.) On the other hand, the tide is clearly with them, and with a little luck they might become persecutors themselves. Cromwell is friendly, though he is prudent and will advance their agenda only with the king's permission or when the king is not looking. He encourages translations of the Bible, for example, and he is responsible for the import of books of suspect orthodoxy from the continent.

Aragon Faction

Catherine of Aragon, who has spurned and who continues to spurn all appeals that she step aside as wife and queen, has her supporters in the clergy, the parliament, the court, and the Council. She also has the sympathy of Catholics abroad and much more than the sympathy of the emperor, her nephew. Wolsey was never her friend, but as long as Wolsey was in power, the king was tethered to the pope, the pope was tethered to the emperor, and the emperor was tethered to her. But with the removal of Wolsey, new avenues to a divorce have opened. Catherine's position is collapsing, therefore; but it is not entirely hopeless. More, who succeeded Wolsey as Chancellor, is against the divorce. The king is far from deciding that a break with Rome is what he desires. Not a decade ago Henry was named "Defender of the Faith" by Leo X in gratitude for Henry's book defending the sacraments against attack by Luther. Henry is still very much a Catholic, and as a sign of his continued devotion he allows (perhaps requires) his ministers and clergy to persecute the Lutherans. Thus if Henry stays bound to the church, a decision against Catherine here in England could be reversed on appeal by the pope in Rome. Time might just be Catherine's ally, since Henry's infatuation with Anne might pass over time, or over time diplomatic imperatives might make a divorce unthinkable. Would Henry chance a divorce if Catholic Spain and Catholic France threatened to wage war against him? Would Henry countenance an alliance with the lesser, Protestant powers of Germany? Ostensibly absolute, Henry is not entirely free in this matter.

Those elements of English society that support Catherine also support the dynastic claims of Mary, her daughter. In 1529 Mary is Henry's only legitimate child; in 1533 she has a rival in her half-sister Elizabeth. Three years later, after Catherine's death, disgruntled Englishmen, some with sympathies for Mary, stage a rebellion in the north, called the **Pilgrimage of Grace**. Implicated in the struggle is Reginald Pole (living in Europe), whose family is executed when the rebellion fails.

Foreign Powers

All of the European powers have ambassadors at the court of Henry VIII. (The most important of these—whose dispatches have survived—is **Eustace Chapuys**, ambassador for the emperor.) They also have some members of parliament friendly to their interests or simply in their pay. Representation of the Roman church is fuller still—and aboveboard—since the higher clergy are members of the House of Lords. **Lorenzo Campeggio**, the Italian papal legate (who with Wolsey heard Henry's divorce case) is the bishop of Salisbury (until 1535), and Catherine's Spanish confessor, George de Athequa, is the bishop of Llandaff.

DISTRIBUTION OF ROLES

Of the eight factions given above, three of them make up the **Henry Party**, the game's dominant voting bloc: Boleyn-Howard, Cromwell, and Lutheran. They are opposed by the **Aragon Party**, or the **Aragonese**. The three social orders of clergy, nobles, and commoners provide a second, albeit minor, division in the game. The foreign powers—consisting of Spain (emperor), France, the German states, and the papacy—exert influence, but for the most part they are not in the game, and for the most part they do not work together.

There are 21 characters in the game, if all roles are in use. Some characters leave early, and other characters take their place. The 21 who start the game are as follows:

	Temporal Lords	Spiritual Lords
House of Lords	Thomas More, Lord Chancellor Thomas Howard, Duke of Norfolk Charles Brandon, Duke of Suffolk Thomas Boleyn, Earl of Wiltshire and Ormonde Earl of Shrewsbury	William Warham, Archbishop of Canterbury John Fisher, Bishop of Rochester Stephen Gardiner, Bishop of Winchester Bishop of Worcester Bishop of Hereford Bishop of Lincoln
	Temporal Commoners	**Spiritual Commoners**
House of Commons	Thomas Audley, Speaker of the House and Knight of the Shire for Essex Knight of the Shire for Northamptonshire Knight of the Shire for Berkshire Nicolas Carew, Knight of the Shire for Surrey George Throckmorton, Knight of the Shire for Warwickshire Thomas Cromwell, Burgess for Taunton Burgess for Colchester Burgess for Maldon Burgess for Plymouth	Archdeacon of Barnstable and Proctor of the Clergy for Exeter

Loose Alliances

In most cases, the factions are not discrete and well defined groups. Members of the nobility may be Catholic, proto-Anglican, or crypto-Lutheran; supporters of Catherine or of Anne; agents of Spain, France, Protestant principalities, or Catholic Rome. Likewise, members of the clergy may align with any one of the denominations (or with any two, since opinions are changing) and have interests overlapping with various other factions. Commoners may espouse humanists ideas, or they may endorse Cromwell's Machiavellian tactics.

Extended Time Frame

A second unusual feature of the game is its extended time frame—1529–1536. The above accounts of backgrounds and factions reference events occurring within this seven year period: e.g., Henry's marriage to Anne, More's execution, the break with Rome. But once the game begins, students are historical actors free to do as they wish—more or less: more, because individuals matter, and because chance intervenes; less, because students are arrayed in counterbalancing formations, and because the rules of the game create a path of least resistance faithful to the historical record. Catherine might in fact hold on to her crown—and More on to his head—but the odds are decidedly against them both.

Planned Confusion

In order that students might experience the English Reformation as did the people of the day—with memories of the past, actions in the present, and expectations for the future—period information is provided, but in pieces and scattered across the 21 or so roles. Students are told where they come from, how they view the current situation (November 1529), and some of what happens to them during the Reformation years. But what happens to the state as a whole is a mystery until the various pieces of the puzzle are assembled through debates and votes taken in the parliament. There should, therefore, be confusion and surprise (true for all historical actors), since students glimpse the Reformation from the perspective of one person only. The game is on track, however, if students advance from wanting to be told what to do, to discovering what actually was done, to doing as their characters might have done and making a little history of their own.

Named Characters

There are more named figures in this game than is usual. Thomas More is in the game, as are Thomas Howard, Charles Brandon, Thomas Boleyn, Stephen Gardiner, and Thomas Cromwell—all members of the king's Privy Council. Some religious lords are also named, such as John Fisher, William Warham, and

Thomas Cranmer. Even some members of Commons are actual historical personages—Thomas Audley, for example, and George Throckmorton. (Of course, depending on class size, several of these characters might not be included.) Those who are not named have individualized role descriptions, and students who assume these roles are free to adopt the personae of actual M.Ps. whose biographies are compatible. See S. T. Bindoff, ed., *The House of Commons, 1509–1558* (1982); also Stephen Leslie and Sidney Lee, eds., *Dictionary of National Biography: From Earliest Times to 1900* (London: Oxford University Press, 1917); also online under *http://www.oxford.dnb.com*.

Indeterminates

No member of the game is entirely an indeterminate. Each player has victory objectives best achieved through alignment with the factions (though alignments may be fluid and occasional). Conversely, few members of the game are entirely determined—that is, always aligned with the same people for the accomplishment of group objectives. It is less important in the "Henry" game that there be a body of pure indeterminates acting as neutral judges, since the complexity of the roles prevents factional lock-up, and since the purpose of speechmaking is to impress one's patron or attract the attention of other patrons, as much as it is to persuade the parliament. Occasional secret balloting allows some characters the chance to express whatever indeterminacy may be contained in their roles (see "Embassies Abroad" below).

Henry VIII and His Queens

King Henry is not a role assigned to any student in the class (he is too powerful and would overwhelm any opposition). Nevertheless, Henry is in the game (sort of) in the person of the gamemaster, who appears as Henry at the start and finish of every parliamentary session (though is free to attend at other times), and who intervenes from afar with proclamations and decrees. Die roles are often used to determine the occurrence and outcome of these interventions, since Henry, unsure of his objectives (besides the divorce) and unpredictable in his actions, represents chance more than he represents omnipotence.

Henry cannot himself punish any member of parliament, but Henry can instruct his supporters to use parliament to move against an offending individual. Henry can make demands of parliament, say for taxes; but parliament can resist his demands (as parliament often did) without fear of reprisals, except those taken also by parliament (changing its mind), say against leaders of the resistance.

Henry's wives, Catherine and Anne, are not in the game, since they have no seat in parliament. Catherine, historically, was away from court (as of 1531), under house arrest, and incommunicado. She was powerless except as an inspiration for rebellion and invasion. Anne was at court, first as mistress, then as queen. She was quite powerful, and in the game she does exert influence; also, if a student preceptor is on scene, the preceptor can advise the Henry party adopting the persona of Anne.

Patronage and Patronage Chits

In most games students participate as equals. In the "Henry" game, however, students are not quite equals, even though they operate as members of a single legislative body. Rather, they are lords and commoners, subjects of a class society where birth and connections determine place and provide opportunity. Inequality, privilege, subordination, deference—these are the characteristics of aristocratic England, not liberty, equality, fraternity.

In order to capture the flavor of life in a rank-ordered society, patronage, or the patron-client relationship, is a dominant feature of this game. Those occupying the higher rungs of the social ladder have patronage to confer; those occupying the lower rungs seek and receive patronage in exchange for loyalty and services. For convenience sake, patronage power is divided into units called "chits."

Patronage chits are poker chips stamped with the patron's insignia. They are differentiated by color to reflect the social order to which the patron belongs (blue for royalty, red for nobility, white for clergy). On one side are letters designating the primary patron; on the other side, if the chit has been given to another, are smaller letters designating the secondary patron. (Some instructors might prefer Mardi Gras necklaces to poker chips.) The insignia are as follows:

Faction	Patrons	Insignia
ROYALS	Henry	"H"
	Anne	"A"
LORDS TEMPORAL	More	"LC" (Lord Chancellor)
	Howard	"DN" (Duke of Norfolk)
	Brandon	"DS" (Duke of Suffolk)
	Boleyn	"EWO" (Earl of Wiltshire and Ormonde)
	Shrewsbury	"ES" (Earl of Shrewsbury)
	Darcy	"LD" (Lord Darcy)
LORDS SPIRITUAL	Warham / Cranmer	"AC" (Archbishop of Canterbury)
	Fisher	"BR" (Bishop of Rochester)
	Gardiner	"BW" (Bishop of Winchester)
	Worcester	"BWo" (Bishop of Worcester)
	Hereford	"BH" (Bishop of Hereford)
	Lincoln	"BL" (Bishop of Lincoln)
	Durham	"BD" (Bishop of Durham)
FOREIGN POWERS	Charles	"E" (Emperor)
	Francis	"F" (France)
	Clement	"P" (Pope)
	Protestant Germans	"GS" (German States)

Patronage chits serve three purposes: (1) they enhance the voting power of persons who possess them; (2) they afford immunity from prosecution when held in sufficient number; and (3) they provide a source of victory points for certain characters.

Voting Power

Each player has one vote by virtue of his/her seat in parliament. In addition, each chit held at the time of voting increases a player's vote count by one (all chits count equally regardless of origin). The burgess for Maldon, for example, with two chits in her possession, casts three votes. The chit-bearing lords give away their chits (or some of them) in hopes of influencing the votes of M.Ps, and thus of augmenting their own voting power, for a chit cast by a lord adds only one vote to that lord's tally; but a chit given away, and then voted as the lord directs, brings at least two votes in support of the lord's position—the chit itself, plus the seat-vote of the M.P. (plus any other chits that an M.P. might possess, all cast together and in support of the lord). Hence lords have cause to circulate their chits.

Some chits are not transferable, however. These represent the stationary patronage that goes with a title. Thomas Howard, for example, has four stationary patronage chits; he has four not because his seat is worth four, but because as Duke of Norfolk he can command the certain votes of four other parliamentarians, not present in the game but presumed to be his loyal allies (parliament was a body of about 400). In every case, the number of stationary patronage chits of in-game patrons determines the number of transferable patronage chits. Thus Howard has four transferable chits to go with his four stationary patronage chits; plus he has the one vote belonging to his seat, for a total of nine votes—five of which stay always with him, four of which he is free to distribute to others to be cast as votes by their recipients. Howard's total might rise above nine, if Howard is the recipient of royal patronage (Henry or Anne) or of patronage from abroad. Royal/foreign chits may be kept by their original recipients or handed on to others. Royal/foreign chits, however, are doubly insecure, since if redistributed, they have two patrons able to recall them.

In the event that a recipient, called a client, fails to vote as the patron directs (perhaps because the client has chits from other sources making opposite demands), the patron can reclaim the chit and give it to another.

Here is a breakdown of the patronage, transferable and stationary, and of the minimum vote count (stationary patronage plus seat-vote) of the lords. The royals, Henry and Anne, and several of the foreign powers also have patronage for distribution; but they cast no votes since they are not in the game.

Faction	Patrons	Transferable Patronage	Stationary Patronage	Minimum Votes
ROYALS	Henry	15		
	Anne	5		
TEMPORAL LORDS	More	2	2	3
	Howard	4	4	5
	Brandon	3	3	4
	Boleyn	2	2	3
	Shrewsbury	1	1	2
	Darcy	1	1	2
SPIRITUAL LORDS	Warham / Cranmer	2	2	3
	Fisher	1	1	2
	Gardiner	1	1	2
	Worcester	1	1	2
	Hereford	1	1	2
	Lincoln	1	1	2
	Durham	1	1	2
FOREIGN POWERS	Charles	2		
	Francis	1		
	Clement	1		
	Protestant Germans	1		

The 21 characters who start the game, plus the royals and the foreign powers, have 44 transferable patronage chits in all (i.e., there are 44 poker chips on the table). Stationary patronage chits number 19, for a total of 63. To these 63 chits, which are also votes, 21 more votes are added, representing the seat-votes of the 21 characters. The new total then is 84. **But in order to give fair representation to the forces of tradition, an extra 35 votes are added to the conservative side, bringing the final total to 119** (an approximate number only, since different patrons, with different patronage, come and go, and since all roles might not be in use.) Success of the reform agenda causes the 35-vote bonus to decline slightly with each new parliamentary session.

Those players with chits are responsible for keeping track of the persons to whom the chits are distributed (and for remembering the initials of their own insignia), and recipients of chits are responsible for bringing the chits with them to class. Chits not in the classroom afford no benefits and effectively do not exist; clients prone to forgetfulness lessen their voting power and sacrifice the protection from prosecution that chits can provide. Also, chits should be visible for all to see—arrayed on the table like so many "Monopoly" properties—since to be in the service of a higher-up is to be a higher-up oneself, relative to others.

IMMUNITY

In sufficient number, patronage chits can protect a person from prosecution for heresy or attainder for treason. A commoner is immune from prosecution with five transferable patronage chits; a lord needs eight. Chits, however, must be in the accused person's possession at the time charges are filed, not collected subsequent to the filing so as to forestall a trial.

Several characters can score victory points with the patronage chits they have collected; and many more characters, having a sufficiency of chits, can safeguard a victory seemingly won from suddenly disappearing.

Voting Procedures

Voting is usually done by voice and in sequence, beginning with the Lord Chancellor and the lords temporal, moving to the archbishop and the lords spiritual, and concluding with the Speaker of the House and the knights of the shire, followed by the burgesses. This one-by-one, around-the-table system is needed because the vote count varies with the person, because the votes cast are many and their tabulation difficult, and because patrons require time to signal their clients and to check upon their compliance. Also, voting slowly and in rank adds an appropriate formality to the process. In a few cases, often at the king's direction, secret ballots are allowed.

Embassies Abroad

The most common instance of secret balloting occurs when parliamentarians are dispatched on diplomatic assignments. Seven parliamentarians belong to a quasi-diplomatic corps, and during the course of the game, the king might elect to send groups of them on embassies abroad. The purpose is not diplomacy, as such; it merely is to permit certain persons certain opportunities to act on any indeterminacy that may be present in their roles by casting written, secret ballots in advance of their departing the country (i.e., leaving the room).

Revenues

Some laws passed by parliament will require the collecting of taxes. Students should assume that £1,500,000 can be raised without grievous harm being done to any of England's social orders; also that each of the orders—clergy, nobility, commons—possesses a third of the total. Victory objectives are affected if any of the orders is made to pay more than its allotted £500,000.

Victory

Individuals, not groups, win or lose in this game—or they merely survive. Students win by achieving their victory objectives (or a majority of the victory points assigned—information provided to the gamemaster but withheld from the students lest in focusing on scorekeeping they neglect the larger issues of the game). They lose if some personal disaster befalls them (usually stipulated in the role description). They survive if they avoid the disaster but also score half or fewer of their victory points.

Papers

Role descriptions provide directions regarding the topics and timing of student papers. Often, though, these directions are phrased as suggestions rather than as commands. Several reasons explain the ambiguity: **(1) students are to write about 10 pages for the game**, but they may spread those pages over an undetermined number of papers; thus one student may write two five-page papers; another may write five two-page papers; (2) issue coverage can be accomplished by formal speeches at the podium or, if need be, by close questioning of other speakers and by cross-table debate; (3) the agenda is crowded, and a particular issue might never receive a hearing; or (4) a student might change roles before a particular issue ever comes up for a hearing; and (5) additional paper topics await assignment by faction leaders to their followers; when given out, these new assignments might alter student plans. All of which means that students must themselves decide—at least to some degree—what to write on and how much to write. (See "Class Sessions" below.)

Grades

Written work accounts for two-thirds of a student's grade; one-third is given to participation—i.e., speeches from the podium (graded higher if spoken and not read) and cross-table debate, plus caucusing, negotiating, and strategizing, to the extent that these activities are known to the instructor. It is the instructor's option whether to affix a bonus grade for winning and (possibly) a penalty grade for losing.

Class Sessions

Sessions of the class may not correspond to sessions of the parliament. There were seven sessions of the Reformation Parliament, each running for weeks at a time before adjourning temporarily. Whether one class meeting will be sufficient to accomplish the work of one parliamentary session is uncertain. Assignments and instructions inside role descriptions are based on parliamentary sessions; it is incumbent on the Lord Chancellor and Speaker of the House to make clear to all which parliamentary session is taking place. Conceivably, in the same class meeting, one parliamentary session could end and another session begin. In cases where the legislative agenda seems stalled, the gamemaster will decide whether the time has come to declare the start of a new session of parliament.

Many issues will come up in the course of parliamentary debates. Most of these are listed below and in the order of likely occurrence—although the order is only approximate, as is the assignment of issues to parliamentary sessions. Some issues will unfold over several sessions (e.g., supremacy, divorce), and so their placement in the order indicates nothing more than the moment of likely resolution—again approximate because parliamentary leaders have some latitude in setting the agenda, because other issues, embedded in the role descriptions, press for attention and because stuff happens. Those issues printed in **bold** are elements of the English Reformation.

Session # 1 (1529)	Wolsey **Anticlericalism** Repudiation of Royal Debts
Session # 2 (1531)	**Praemunire** Poor Relief Enclosures **Lutheranism**
Session # 3 (1532)	**Supremacy of State Over Church**
Session # 4 (1533)	**Independence of England from Rome** **Divorce**
Session # 5 (winter 1534)	**Arrests of Fisher and More** Alliances Defense Tax
Session # 6 (fall 1534)	Court Jurisdictions Privy Chamber Exploration
Session # 7 (1536)	**Dissolution of the Monasteries** Princely Character and Advice-Giving

Issues are not quite the same thing as laws. Issues are best thought of as ends, laws as the means of attaining those ends. The core issues of the English Reformation are divorce, supremacy, and independence; the first is realized by a decision in Convocation, the latter two by such legislative acts as *Supplication*, *Submission*, *Supremacy* on the one hand and by *Annates* and *Appeals* on the other. Many of the laws that will be considered by the game parliament are the actual laws of the period. In the course of debate, some of these laws will likely undergo modification, perhaps even radical alteration. Also, some issues (e.g., exploration) will require that students draft laws of their own. All role descriptions identify the principal laws composing the reform agenda and indicate how characters feel about the legislation. Students, beginning with this information, are to proceed then to the "Schedule of Major Legislation," where the order of passage of laws and brief descriptions of content can be found. Fuller descriptions, explaining context and purpose, are provided by the selection titled "Reform Legislation," and students are expected to go there next; finally, students should turn to the texts of the laws themselves—modernized and redacted, with important provisions and action passages underlined—provided under "Statutes of the Reformation Parliament" (all of the above are in Appendix A). These laws need not be read until the time of their proposal in parliament.

The schedule of laws, resolutions, and petitions given below represents the actual work of the Reformation Parliament/Convocation. This schedule should be generally respected regarding reform legislation proper (printed in **bold**, with an asterisk [*] preceding the most essential pieces). Some repackaging and economizing might be in order since certain acts were revisited and revised (e.g., the *Submission of Clergy* [done once as a resolution of Convocation and once as an act of parliament—the second is not critical]; the *Supremacy Act* [done conditionally by Convocation, then absolutely by parliament—both are important]; the *Restraint of Annates Act* [done conditionally by parliament then absolutely by parliament—the second need not be passed]; the *Act of Succession* and the *Oath of Succession* [done twice because the former failed to include the latter—the two can be presented as one]). Laws not connected to the Reformation (e.g., poor relief—also done twice) can be proposed at any time or not proposed at all. Parliamentary leaders should not suppose, therefore, that class sessions can be mapped out in exact accordance with either the issues list above or the lawmaking schedule below.

Students whose papers propose legislation for consideration by parliament should focus primarily on the issues at stake (e.g., the harm/the benefit of monastic life). Additionally, students should refer to (but not replicate) the text of the law, if provided in the Game Book, and note its principal requirements or those they wish to have implemented. A text so referenced is the starting point. The proposer of the legislation, perhaps acting on suggestions in her role description, is free to alter some provisions of the law (e.g., more restrictions on the clergy, more generous support for the poor), and of course debate in parliament may alter the law still further. Absent such changes, however, the ordinary presumption is that the law passed by parliament is the same law as that contained in Appendix A of the Game Book.

Schedule of Major Legislation of the Reformation Parliament/Convocation

The titles of laws in this "Schedule of Major Legislation" are shortened versions of the titles found under "Statutes of the Reformation Parliament." No texts exist of decisions taken in Convocation.

SESSION #1 (NOVEMBER 1529)

Last Wills and Testaments Act—restrictions on probate fees charged by clergy

Mortuaries Act—restrictions on burial fees charged by clergy

Plurality of Benefices and Residence Act—restrictions on clerical benefices and on clerical non-residency

Cancellation of Royal Debts Act—monies loaned to king by subjects converted into a grant

SESSION #2 (JANUARY–MARCH 1531)

*Conditional Supremacy Resolution—recognition by CONVOCATION of Henry's supremacy over the church of England "as far as the law of Christ allows"

Beggars and Vagabonds Act I—permission to beg in restricted areas

Royal Pardon Act(s)—forgiveness granted clergy and laity charged with praemunire

SESSION #3 (JANUARY–MAY 1532)

*Conditional Restraint of Annates Act—cessation of payments to Rome by newly appointed bishops and archbishops; implementation delayed a year at king's discretion

*Supplication Against the Ordinaries—petition by COMMONS to have legislative and judicial powers of Convocation curtailed

*Submission of Clergy Resolution—legislative power yielded by CONVOCATION

SESSION #4 (FEBRUARY–APRIL 1533)

Act in Restraint of Appeals—prohibition of appeals to Rome of law cases originating in England, in particular Henry's nullity suit; England declared an empire with all rights pertaining thereto

Divorce Judgment—marriage to Catherine ruled invalid by CONVOCATION; marriage to Anne ruled valid

SESSION #5 (JANUARY–MARCH 1534)

Submission of Clergy Act—parliamentary codification of previous submission by Convocation

Absolute Restraint of Annates Act—immediate cessation of all annates; royal nomination of bishops, with praemunire penalties for ecclesiastics refusing to elect

Dispensations and Peter's Pence Act—archbishop of Canterbury made source of dispensations from canon law; abolition of payments by householders to Rome

Act of Succession—succession settled on heirs of Anne Boleyn, the lawful queen

SESSION #6 (NOVEMBER 1534)

Supremacy Act—legal expression given to the king's ecclesiastical powers

Oath of Succession—exact wording of oath (oath referred to, but not included in, Succession Act)

Treasons Act—malicious speech against the monarchy proscribed

Grant of Subsidy Act—defense tax

SESSION #7 (FEBRUARY–APRIL 1536)

Enclosure Act—half of profits of land converted from tillage to pasture to be given to king

Beggars and Vagabonds Act II—some public responsibility for relief of poor

Dissolution of the Monasteries Act—suppression of smaller houses

Court of Augmentations of the Revenues of the King's Crown Act—creation of revenue
  court, its officers, their duties and perquisites

SPECIAL SESSION (MAY 1536)

Issues undisclosed.

Significant Characters of the Period

Thomas Audley (1488–1544). Speaker of the House of Commons (1529–1532); later Lord Chancellor (1532–1544)

Anne Boleyn (1501 or 1507–1536). Henry's second wife (1533–1536); executed on charges of adultery

Thomas Boleyn, Earl of Wiltshire and Ormonde (1477–1539). Father of Anne; Lord Privy Seal and a member of the Privy Council

Catherine of Aragon (1480–1536). Wife of Henry's brother, Arthur, then wife of Henry (1509–1533); aunt of Charles V

Charles Brandon, Duke of Suffolk (1484–1545). Youthful companion of Henry and husband of his sister, Mary Tudor (briefly queen of France); Privy Council co-president

Lorenzo Campeggio (1472–1539). Cardinal and papal envoy to England (1528–1535); member of Lords as bishop of Salisbury

Eustace Chapuys (1489–1556). Emperor's ambassador to England (1529–1546); leading member of the Catherine of Aragon faction

Charles V (1500–1556). King of Spain (1516) and Holy Roman Emperor (1519) (grandson of Maximillian); crowned emperor by pope in 1530

Clement VII (1475–1534). Giuilo de'Medici; pope (1523–1534)

Thomas Cranmer (1489-1556). Archbishop of Canterbury (1533-1553), succeeding Warham; chief architect of Henry's divorce

Thomas Cromwell (1485–1540). Secretary to Wolsey; member of Commons; member of Privy Council; Henry's principal minister after More and the driving force behind the English Reformation

Jean du Bellay (1491–1543). French ambassador; friend of the Boleyns

Elizabeth (1533–1603). Daughter of Henry and Anne Boleyn; queen 1558–1603

Desiderius Erasmus (1466–1536). Dutch humanist; author of *The Praise of Folly, Colloquies, Education of a Christian Prince, Enchiridion*; friend of More

Simon Fish (?–1531). Anticlerical pamphleteer; author of *A Supplication for the Beggars*

John Fisher (1469–1535). Bishop of Rochester (1504–1535); chancellor of Cambridge University; executed by Henry (1535)

Henry Fitzroy, Duke of Richmond (1519–1536). Henry's illegitimate son by Elizabeth Blount

Edward Fox (mid 1490s–1538). Co-author of *Collectanea satis copiosa* (or *King's Book*), which made the case for Henry's divorce; reform bishop (1535–1538)

Francis I (1494–1547). King of France (1515–1547)

Stephen Gardiner (1483-1555). Bishop of Winchester (1531-1551) and leading Privy Council member after fall of Wolsey; out of favor himself for resisting the *Supplication Against the Ordinaries* petition (1532)

Henry VIII (1491–1547). King of England (1509–1547)

Edward Hall (1498–1547). Member of Commons (burgess for Wenlock in Shropshire) and principal native historian of the period (*The Triumphant Reigne of Kyng Henry the VIII*)

Thomas Howard, Duke of **Norfolk** (1473–1554). Privy Council co-president; Lord Treasurer (1524-1547); supreme peer; uncle of Anne Boleyn

Hugh Latimer (1485?–1555). Unorthodox preacher patronized by Anne Boleyn; reform bishop (1535–1539); executed for heresy during Mary's reign

Edward Lee (1482–1544). Archbishop of York succeeding Wolsey (1531–1544); member of Privy Council and supporter of Henry

John Longland (1573–1547). Scholarly bishop close to the king and changing with the times

Martin Luther (1483–1546). Augustinian monk who in protest over the sale of indulgences initiated the reformation of the church, known in Catholic circles as the Protestant Revolution; author of over 500 publications

Mary (1516–1558). Daughter of Henry and Catherine of Aragon; queen 1553–1558; returned England temporarily to the Catholic religion; nicknamed by her opponents "Bloody Mary"

Thomas More (1478–1535). Author of *Utopia* (1516); Privy Council member (1517–1532); knight and Under-Treasurer of Exchequer (1521-1525); Lord Chancellor (1529–1532); imprisoned (April 1534), then executed (July 1535) for refusing to take the oath of succession

Paul III (1468–1549). Alessandro Farnese; pope (1534–1549)

Reginald Pole (1500–1556). Henry's cousin; cardinal (1536–); enemy of Cromwell; author of *De Unitate Ecclesiastica*, a book attacking Henry and the Reformation; archbishop of Canterbury during Mary's reign

Richard Rich (1496–1567). Lawyer and one-time steward of Thomas More; Lord Chancellor in later years

Christopher St. German (1460?–1540). Common lawyer and proponent of equity law; author of *Dialogue between Doctor and Student*, *New Additions* (to previous work), *Treatise Concerning the Division between the Spirituality and the Temporality*; not a member of parliament but a source of Cromwell's reform legislation

Jane Seymour (1508–1537). Henry's third wife and the mother of his only legitimate son, Edward (king Edward VI, 1547–1553)

Thomas Starkey (1498–1538). Cromwell propagandist; author of *An Exhortation to the People Instructing Them to Unity and Obedience*

John Stokesley (1475–1539). Bishop of London (1530–1539)

Margaret Tudor (1489–1541). Older sister of Henry; queen of Scotland (1502–1513)

Mary Tudor (1496–1533). Younger sister of Henry; queen of France (1515); duchess of Suffolk (1515–1533)

Cuthbert Tunstall (1474–1559). Conservative bishop; friend of More and Catherine

William Tyndale (1494–1536). Leading English follower of Luther; translator of the New Testament; exile living in Antwerp; condemned for heresy and executed

Polydore Vergil (1470–1555). Papal tax collector resident in England; historian of the period, with influence on Edward Hall

William Warham (1450–1532). Lord Chancellor (1504–1515); archbishop of Canterbury (1504–1532); chancellor of Oxford University

Thomas Wolsey (1475?–1530). Archbishop of York (1514–1530) (and of lesser episcopates); cardinal, Lord Chancellor, and Keeper of the Great Seal (1515–1529); papal legate (1518–1529); Henry's chief minister until removed from office on charges of praemunire (1529); arrested the following year on charges of treason, but died before being imprisoned in the Tower of London

Appendix A: Documents and Supplementary Texts

MARSILIUS OF PADUA,, *DEFENDER OF THE PEACE* (1324)

[From the Marsilius of Padua, *Defensor Pacis*. Trans. Alan Gewirth (New York: Columbia University Press, 1956); reprinted with permission of the publisher]

I.17.1–7

DISCOURSE ONE

Chapter XVII: On the numerical unity of the supreme government of the city or state, and the necessity for that unity; whence there appears also the numerical unity of the city or state itself, and of each of its primary parts or offices

1. We must now discuss the unity of the ruler or government. To begin with, let us say that in a single city or state there must be only a single government; or if there is more than one government in number or in species, as seems expedient in large cities and especially in a state (*regno*) taken in its first sense, then there must be among them one in number which is supreme, to which all the other governments are reduced, by which they are regulated, and which corrects any errors arising in them.

2. Now I maintain, with respect to this supreme government alone, that it must necessarily be one in number, not many, if the state or city is to be rightly ordered. And I say the same with regard to the ruler, not that the ruler is to be one in number with respect to person but rather with respect to office. For there may be some supreme, well-tempered government which is one in number, but in which more than one man rules; such are the aristocracy and the polity, of which we spoke in Chapter VIII. These several men, however, are numerically one government with respect to office, because of the numerical unity of every action, judgment, sentence or command forthcoming from them. For no such action can emerge from any one of them separately, but only from the common decree and consent of them all or of their weightier part, in accordance with the laws established on such matters. And it is because of such numerical unity of the action thus forthcoming from them that the government is and is called one in number, whether it be ruled by one man or by many. Such unity of action is not, however, required in any of the other offices or parts of the state; for in each of them there can and must be forthcoming separately, from the diverse individuals in them, many actions similar or diverse in species. Indeed, such unity of action in these offices would be unbearable and harmful to both the community and to the individuals.

3. Such being the meaning of the numerical unity of the government or ruler, we wish to prove that the government or ruler in the city or state is to be only one in number, or, if

more than one, that the supreme government of them all is to be only one in number, not more. We shall demonstrate this first as follows. If there were several governments in the city or state, and they were not reduced or ordered under one supreme government, then the judgment, command, and execution of matters of benefit and justice would fail, and because men's injuries would therefore be unavenged the result would be fighting, separation, and finally the destruction of the city or state. But this consequence is the evil which is most to be avoided; and that it is a consequence of the given antecedent, that is, of a plurality of governments, can be clearly shown. For, in the first place, transgressors of the laws cannot reasonably be brought to justice unless they are called before the ruler for examination of the charges against them. But if we assume a plurality of governments not reduced to some one supreme government, as our opponent says, then no one called before the ruler will be able sufficiently to obey the summons. For suppose, as frequently happens, that because of some transgression of the law a man is called by several rulers not ordered one below another, to answer charges at the same time. One ruler is bound and able to summon the accused man for the same reason as the other ruler; and the man who is summoned is bound to appear before one of the rulers, lest he be regarded as being in contempt, for the same reason as before the other ruler, or rulers, if there be more than two. Either, therefore, he will appear before all the rulers at once, or before none of them, or else before a certain one and not before the other or others. But he will not appear before all the rulers at one and the same time, since this is impossible by nature and by art, for the same body cannot be in different places at the same time, or reply or speak at the same time to many persons who are perhaps asking different questions at the same time. Moreover, even though it is impossible, let us assume that the person summoned does appear before several rulers, and is silent or replies to different questions at the same time. Yet he will perhaps be convicted by one ruler and be acquitted by another, of the same crime; or if convicted by both, with different penalties. Hence he will be both required and not required to make amends; or if required by both, it will be to such a degree by one, and to a greater or lesser degree by another, and thus both to such a degree and not to such a degree. Hence he will either do contradictory things at the same time, or else will make no amends at all. For he must obey one ruler's command for the same reason as another's. He has no more reason for appearing before one ruler than before the other or others. If, however, he appears before one of them, ignoring the others, and is perhaps absolved by him of civil guilt and punishment, he will nevertheless be convicted by the others for contempt. Therefore the man summoned will neither appear before all the rulers at once nor be able properly to appear before a certain one and not before another. The only remaining course, consequently, is for the man who is summoned to appear before no ruler at all; therefore justice will be incapable of being done in his case. It is impossible, therefore, for the city or state to have a plurality of such governments not subordinated to one another, if civil justice and benefit are to be conserved.

4. Moreover, if there were a plurality of such governments, the common utility would be completely disturbed. For the rulers must frequently command the assemblage of the citizens, especially of those who have leisure, to inquire into and to decide matters relating to the common benefit, or to avoid harmful impending dangers such as are presented by external or internal enemies who intend to oppress the community and to take away its freedom. Now the citizens or subjects who must obey the command of one

ruler to assemble at a certain place and time must for the same reason obey the command of another ruler to assemble at the place and time which he selects; and each ruler might select the same time but different places; and again, what one of the rulers wishes to propose may perhaps be different from what the other wants. But it does not seem possible to be in different places at the same time, or to have different aims at the same time.

5. Again, from this there would result the division and opposition of the citizens, their fighting and separation, and finally the destruction of the state, for some of the citizens would wish to obey one government, and some another. There would also be strife between the governments themselves because one of them would want to be superior to the other; in addition, the governments would war against the citizens who refused to be subject to them. Moreover, when the rulers disagreed or quarreled among themselves, since they would lack a superior judge, the above-mentioned scandals would also arise.

6. Again, if this plurality of governments is assumed, one of the greatest effects of human reason and art will be useless and superfluous. For all the civil utility which would be had from many supreme governments can be perfectly had through one government or one supreme government without the harms resulting from a plurality of them.

7. Moreover, if such a plurality is assumed, no state or city will be one. For states are one, and are called one, because of the unity of the government to which and by which all the other parts of the state are ordered, as will appear also from what follows. And again there will be no order of the parts of the city or state, since they will be ordered to no first part, because they are required to be subject to none, as is clear from the previous arguments. And there will be a confusion both of them and of the whole state; for each man will choose for himself whatever office he wishes, one or more, with no one regulating or separating such offices. So many are the evils which would follow upon this that it is difficult or impossible to enumerate them all.

I.19.7–9, 11–13

Chapter XIX: On the efficient causes of the tranquillity and intranquillity of the city or state, and on that singular cause which disturbs states in an unusual way; and on the connection between the first discourse and the second

7. And so, having thus repeated and made somewhat clear the origin of ecclesiastic ministers, and the efficient cause of their office, we must now note further that among the aforesaid apostles of Christ there was one named Simon, also called Peter, who first received from Christ the promise of the authority of the keys, as it is said in Augustine's gloss on the sixteenth chapter of Matthew, on that statement of Christ: "And I will give unto thee the keys of the kingdom of heaven." The gloss says: "He who avowed before the others," that is, that Jesus Christ is the true son of God, "is given the keys ahead of the others," that is, before the others. And after Christ's passion, resurrection, and ascent

into heaven, this apostle came to Antioch, and was there made bishop by the people, as is shown by his history. From that city, as the aforesaid history says, he went to Rome for an undetermined reason concerning which there are diverse views. At Rome he became bishop over the Christian faithful, and finally on account of his profession and preaching of Christ, he was beheaded, and with him at that same time and place the apostle Paul was also, according to the afore-mentioned history.

8. Because of the prerogative which this disciple or apostle seemed to have over the others, inasmuch as he was given the keys before the others through the afore-mentioned words of the Scripture and certain other words spoken to him alone by Christ, which will also be mentioned below, some of the bishops who succeeded him in the apostolic or episcopal seat at Rome, especially after the time of the Roman emperor Constantine, declare and assert that they are over all the other bishops and priests in the world, with respect to every kind of jurisdictional authority. And some of the more recent Roman bishops make this claim not only with regard to bishops and priests, but even with regard to all the rulers, communities, and individuals in the world, although they do not apply it equally or express it so explicitly with regard to all the others as they do with regard to the ruler they call emperor of the Romans and all the provinces, cities, and individual persons subject to him. And yet in truth, the singular expression of dominion or coercive jurisdiction over this ruler seems to have taken its form and origin from a certain edict and gift which certain men say that Constantine made to St. Sylvester, Roman pontiff.

9. But because that gift or privilege did not state this clearly, or because it perhaps expired on account of later events, or even because, while being valid with regard to the other governments in the world, the force of that privilege or concession did not extend to the government of the Romans in all their provinces, later bishops of the Romans therefore assumed for themselves this universal coercive jurisdiction over the whole world under another all-embracing title, "plenitude of power," which they assert was granted by Christ to St. Peter and to his successors in the episcopal seat of Rome, as vicars of Christ. For Christ, as they truly say, was "king of kings and lord of lords," and of all persons and things; yet from this there does not follow what they wish to infer, as will appear with certainty in our subsequent discussions. The meaning of this title among the Roman bishops, therefore, is that just as Christ had plenitude of power and jurisdiction over all kings, princes, communities, groups and individuals, so too do those who call themselves vicars of Christ and of St. Peter have this plenitude of coercive jurisdiction, limited by no human law.

11. In this way, then, have the Roman bishops entered upon these affairs. First, under the guise of seeking peace among the Christian believers, they have excommunicated certain men who are unwilling to obey their decrees. Then they impose on them penalties both real and personal, more harshly against those who are less able to resist their power, such as communities and individuals among the Italians, whose state, divided and wounded in almost all its parts, can more easily be oppressed; but more mildly against those, like kings and rulers, whose resistance and coercive power they fear. On these latter, however, they are gradually creeping up in the attempt to usurp their jurisdictions, not daring to invade them all at once. Hence their stealthy double-dealing has hitherto been concealed even from the Roman rulers and the peoples subject to them. For the

Roman bishops have gradually seized one jurisdiction after another, especially when the imperial seat was vacant; so that now they finally say that they have total coercive temporal jurisdiction over the Roman ruler. Most recently and most obviously, the present bishop has written that he has supreme jurisdiction over the ruler of the Romans, both in the Italian and the German provinces, and also over all the lesser rulers, communities, groups, and individuals of the aforesaid provinces, of whatever dignity and condition they may be, and over all their fiefs and other temporalities. This bishop openly ascribes to himself the power to give and transfer their governments, as all can clearly see from certain writings of this bishop, which he calls "edicts" or "sentences."

12. This wrong option of certain Roman bishops, and also perhaps their perverted desire for rulership, which they assert is owed to them because of the plentitude of power given to them, as they say, by Christ—this is that singular cause for which we have said produces the intranquillity or discord of the city or state. For it is prone to creep up on all states, as we said in our introductory remarks, and by its hateful action it has for a long time distressed the Italian state, and has kept and still keeps it from tranquillity or peace, by preventing with all its force the appointment or institution of the ruler, the Roman emperor, and his functioning in the said empire. From the lack of this function, which is the just regulation of civil acts, there readily emerge injuries and contentions, and these, if not measured by a standard of justice or law because of the absence of the measurer, cause fights, whence there have resulted the separation of the citizens and finally the destruction of the Italian polities or cities, as we have said. With this opinion, therefore, and perhaps also with what we have called a desire for ruling, the Roman bishop strives to make the Roman ruler subject to him in coercive or temporal jurisdiction, whereas that ruler neither rightly ought to be, as we shall clearly show below, nor wishes to be subject to him in such judgment. From this there has arisen so much strife and discord that it cannot be extinguished without great effort of the souls and bodies and expenditure of wealth.

For the office of coercive rulership over any individual, of whatever condition he may be, or over any community or group, does not belong to the Roman or any other bishop, priest, or spiritual minister, as such, as has been demonstrated in Chapters XV and XVII of this discourse. And this was what Aristotle held with respect to the priesthood in any law or religion, when he said in the fourth book of the *Politics*: "Hence not all those who are elected or chosen by lot are to be regarded as rulers. Consider the priests in the first place. These must be regarded as different from the political rulers," etc. "And of the superintendent functions," that is, offices "some are political," etc. And a little below he adds: "And other offices are economic."

13. Since this pernicious pestilence, which is completely opposed to all the peace and happiness of man, could well infect with a disease of the same corrupt root the other states of faithful Christians throughout the world, I consider it supremely necessary to repel it, as I said in my introductory remarks. This is to be done first by tearing away the mask of the afore-mentioned false opinion, as the root of the past and future evils; and then by checking, through external action if necessary, its ignorant or unjust patrons or expositors and stubborn defenders. To these tasks all men are obligated who have the knowledge and ability to thwart this evil; and those who neglect or omit them on

whatever grounds are unjust, as Tully attested in the treatise *On Duties*, Book I, Chapter V, when he said: "There are two kinds of injustice: one, of those men who inflict it; the other, of those who do not drive away the injury from those upon whom it is inflicted, if they can." See, then, according to this notable statement of Tully, that not only those who inflict injury on others are unjust, but also those who, while having the knowledge and ability to prevent men from inflicting injury on others, do not do so. For every man is obligated to do this for another by a certain quasi-natural law, the duty of friendship and human society. And lest I myself, by knowingly transgressing this law, be called unjust at least to myself, I propose to drive away this pestilence from my brethren, the Christian believers, first by teaching, and then by external action so far as I may be able. For, as I seem indubitably to see, there has been given to me from above the power to discern and unmask the sophism which has sustained in the past, and by which they still strive to sustain, the wrong opinion, and perhaps also the perverted desire, of certain former Roman bishops and of the present one with his accomplices. It is this opinion and desire which is the parent of all the scandals mentioned above.

II.2.1–3 (first three sentences), 4–5, 7–8

DISCOURSE TWO

Chapter II: On the distinction of the meanings of the words or terms which compose the questions to be decided

1. Before entering upon our proposed discussion, we shall distinguish the meanings of the words which we shall use in the principal questions, lest the many meanings of these words cause the doctrines which we wish to set forth to become ambiguous and confused. For as it is said in the first chapter of the *Refutations*: "Those who are ignorant of the force of names misreason both in their own discussions and when listening to others." The words or terms whose many meanings we wish to distinguish are these: "church," "judge," "spiritual," and "temporal"; for the purpose of our inquiry is to know whether it pertains to the Roman or any other bishop, priest, deacon, or group of them, who are usually called "churchmen," to be coercive judges over temporal or spiritual affairs, or both, or whether they are such judges over neither of these.

2. And so, in pursuit of these aims, let us say that this term "church" is a word used by the Greeks, signifying among them, in those writings which have come down to us, an assembly of people contained under one regime. Aristotle used it in this sense when he said, in the *Politics*, Book II, Chapter 10: "All men share the ecclesia."

Among the Latins, this word according to colloquial and familiar usage means, in one of its senses, a temple or house in which the believers worship together and most frequently invoke God. For thus the Apostle spoke of the "church" in the first epistle to the Corinthians, Chapter 11: "Have you not houses to eat and to drink in? or despise ye the church of God?" Whereon the gloss according to Augustine: "Despise ye the church of God, that is, the house of prayer?", and a little below he adds: "daily usage has brought it about that one does not say 'to go forth or take refuge in the church' unless one goes or takes refuge in a certain place and building."

In another sense this word "church" means all the priests or bishops, deacons, and others who minister in the temple or the church taken in the preceding sense. And according to this meaning, only clergymen or ministers are commonly called persons of the church or churchmen.

Again in another sense, and especially among the moderns, this word "church" means those ministers, priests or bishops and deacons, who minister in and preside over the metropolitan or principal church. This usage was long since brought about by the church of the city of Rome, whose ministers and overseers are the Roman pope and his cardinals. Through custom they have brought it about that they are called the "church" and that one says the "church" has done or received something when it is these men who have done or received or otherwise ordained something.

3. But the word "church" has also another meaning which is the truest and most fitting one of all, according to the first imposition of the word an the intention of these first imposers, even though this meaning is not so familiar nor in accord with modern usage. According to this signification, the "church" means the whole body of the faithful who believe in and invoke the name of Christ, and all the parts of this whole body in any community, even the household. And this was the first imposition of this term and the sense in which it was customarily used among the apostles and in the primitive church . . .

4. Now we must proceed to distinguish the meanings of the words "temporal" and "spiritual." Beginning with that which is better known to us, let us say that this term "temporal" in one of its more familiar senses refers to all corporeal things, natural and artificial, except man, which are in any way in man's power and are ordered toward his use, needs, and pleasures in and for the status of worldly life. In this way, also, more generally, "temporal" customarily refers to all that which begins and ends in time. For these things, as it is written in the fourth book of the *Physics*, properly are and are said to be in time.

In another sense, "temporal" refers to every human habit, action, or passion, whether in oneself or directed toward another by man for a purpose of this world or of the present life.

Less universally, this word "temporal" refers to those human actions and passions which are voluntary and transient, resulting in benefit or harm to someone other than the agent. It is with these actions and passions that the makers of human laws are mainly concerned.

5. Now I wish to distinguish the meanings or senses of the term "spiritual." In one sense it refers to all incorporeal substances and their actions.

In another sense it refers to every immanent action or passion of man's cognitive or appetitive power. In this meaning, too, certain actions of corporeal things on the senses of animals are usually called spiritual and immaterial, such as the idols or phantasms and species of things, which are in some way the soul's means of knowing; in this class some place the actions of sensible things even on inanimate substances, like the generation of light and similar things.

Again, and more pertinently, this word "spiritual" refers to the divine law, and the teaching and learning of the commands and counsels in accordance with it and through it. Under this signification also come all ecclesiastic sacraments and their effects, all divine grace, all theological virtues, and the gifts of the Holy Spirit ordering us toward eternal life. For it was in this way, and appropriately, that the Apostle used this word in the epistle to the Romans, Chapter 15, and in the first epistle to the Corinthians, Chapter 9, when he said: "If we have sown unto you spiritual things, is it a great matter if we reap your carnal things?" Whereon the gloss according to Ambrose: "Spiritual things, that is, those things which vivify your spirit, or which were given by the Holy Spirit, namely, the word of God, and the mystery of the kingdom of the heavens."

Moreover, in another sense this word is used for any voluntary human action of passion, whether in oneself or directed toward another, which is done for the purpose of meriting a blessed life in the future world. Such are the contemplation of God, love of God, and of one's neighbors, abstinence, mercy, meekness, prayer, offerings for piety or divine worship, hospitality, pilgrimage, castigation of one's own body, contempt for and flight from worldly and carnal pleasures, and generally all similar actions and passions done for the aforesaid purpose.

Again, this word refers, although not so properly as in the second and third sense, to the temple or the church taken in its second sense; and to all the utensils and ornaments which serve therein for divine worship.

Most recently of all, very unsuitably and improperly, certain men tend this word to signify the voluntary transient actions and omissions of priests or bishops, deacons, and other temple ministers, which are for the benefit or harm of someone other than the agent for the status of worldly life.

Again, and even more improperly, these men extend the same word to signify their possessions and temporal goods, mobile and immobile, as well as certain proceeds of these which they call tithes, so that under cover of this word they may be exempted from the regulation of the civil laws and rulers.

7. The same view must also undoubtedly be held concerning certain actions of priests, bishops, and deacons. For not all their acts are or should be called spiritual; on the contrary, many of them are civil, contentious, and carnal or temporal. For these men can lend at interest, deposit, buy, sell, strike, kill, steal, commit adultery, rob with violence, betray, deceive, bear false witness, defame, fall into heresy, and commit other outrages, crimes, and contentious acts such as are perpetrated also by non-priests. Hence it is appropriate to ask them whether such acts as these, of which we have said they are capable, are spiritual or should be so called by anyone of sound mind. And it is clear that the answer is no, but rather carnal and temporal. Hence the Apostle, in the first epistle to the Corinthians, Chapter 3, speaking to all men about such actions, said: "For whereas

there is among you envying and contention, are you not carnal and walk you not according to man?" Since, therefore, undoubted experience demonstrates that from the afore-mentioned acts and other similar ones there arise envying and contentions among priests, both among themselves and toward laymen, it is manifest that such acts of priests are carnal or temporal and should not in truth be called spiritual.

A sign that what we have said is true, even according to the views of clergymen, is that the Roman pontiffs, to settle such contentions, have given forth many human ordinances, which they call "decretals," and before these there were laws of the Roman rulers dealing with the same acts. For the deacons and priests or bishops can and do perform many voluntary transient actions which redound to the benefit or harm and injury of someone else for and in the status of the present life. And therefore the human law must be the measure of such actions, as was said in Chapter XV of Discourse I, and as will be said still more pertinently in Chapter VIII of this discourse.

8. It now remains to distinguish the meanings of the word "judge" and "judgment," which signifies the action of the judge. For these are among the terms which have many meanings, and that multiplicity introduces ambiguity which impedes the determination of questions. In one sense, "judge" means anyone who discerns or knows, especially in accordance with some theoretic or practical habit; and so the word "judgment" means such men's knowledge or discernment. In this sense, the geometer is a judge, and judges concerning figures and their attributes; and the physician judges concerning the healthy and the sick, and the prudent man concerning what should be done and what should be avoided, and the housebuilder concerning how to build houses. Thus, every knower or expert is called a judge, and judges about things which can be known or done by him. It was in this sense that Aristotle used these words in the *Ethics*, Book I, Chapter I, when he said: "Everyone judges well the things which he knows, and is a good judge of them."
In another sense this word "judge" means the man who has the science of political or civil law, and who is usually called an "advocate," although in many provinces, and particularly in Italy, he is called a "judge."

In a third sense, this word "judge" means the ruler, and "judgment" means the sentence of the ruler who has the authority to judge concerning the just and beneficial in accordance with the laws or customs, and to command and execute through coercive forces the sentences made by him. In this sense, a certain book is called Judges, being one part of the holy canon or Bible. It was in this sense, too, that Aristotle spoke of the judge or ruler in the *Rhetoric*, Book I, Chapter I, when he said: "But the magistrate and the judge make judgments concerning the present and the determinate." So too, referring to the judgment of the ruler, he continues: "They," that is, the magistrate or judge, "are often involved in personal likes and dislikes, so that they cannot see the truth sufficiently well, but instead have regard in their judgments to their own pleasure and displeasure."

There are perhaps other meanings of the above words; we think, however, that we have indicated those which are more familiar and more necessary for our proposed inquiry.

Chapter III: On the canonic statements and other arguments which seem to prove that coercive rulership belongs to bishops or priests as such, even without the grant of the human legislator, and that the supreme of all such rulerships belongs to the Roman bishop or pope

10. Following upon these, it is fitting to adduce some quasi-political arguments which might perhaps lead men to fancy and believe the aforesaid conclusion. The first of these arguments is as follows. As the human body is to the soul, so is the ruler of bodies to the ruler of souls. But the body is subject to the soul with respect to rule. Therefore too the ruler of bodies, the secular judge, must be subject to the rule of the judge or ruler of souls, and especially of the first of them all, the Roman pontiff.

11. Again, another argument from almost the same root: As corporeals are to spirituals, so is the ruler of corporeals to the ruler of spirituals. But it is certain that corporeals are by nature inferior and subject to spirituals. Therefore the ruler of corporeals, the secular judge, must be subject to the ruler of spirituals, the ecclesiastic judge.

12. Moreover, as end is to end, and law to law, and legislator to legislator, so is the judge or ruler in accordance with one of these to the judge or ruler in accordance with the other. But the end toward which the ecclesiastic judge, the priest or bishop, directs, the law by which he directs, and the maker of that law, are all superior to and more perfect than the end, the law, and the maker to which and by which the secular judge directs. Therefore the ecclesiastic judge, bishop or priest, and especially the first of them all, is superior to every secular judge. For the end toward which the ecclesiastic judge directs is eternal life; the law by which he directs is divine; and its immediate maker is God, in whom neither error nor malice can lodge. But the end toward which the secular judge aims to direct is sufficiently of this worldly life; the law by which he directs is human; and the immediate maker of this law is man or men, who are subject to error and malice. Therefore, the latter are inferior to and less worthy than the former. Therefore, too, the secular judge, even the supreme one, is inferior to and less worthy than the ecclesiastic judge, the supreme priest.

13. Moreover, a person or thing is absolutely more honorable than another when the action of that first person or thing is absolutely more honorable than the action of the second. But the action of the priest or bishop, the consecration of the blessed body of Christ, is the most honorable of all the actions which can be performed by man in the present life. Therefore, any priest is more worthy than any non-priest. Since, therefore, the more worthy should not be subject to the less worthy, but rather above it, it seems that the secular judge should not be above the priest in jurisdiction, but rather subordinate to him, and especially to the first of them all, the Roman pontiff.

Chapter IV: On the canonic Scriptures, the commands, counsels, and examples of Christ and of the saints and approved doctors who expounded the evangelic law, whereby it is clearly demonstrated that the Roman or any other bishop or priest, or clergyman, can by virtue of the words of Scripture claim or ascribe to himself no coercive rulership or contentious jurisdiction, let alone the supreme jurisdiction over any clergyman or layman; and that, by Christ's counsel and example, they ought to refuse such rulership, especially in communities of the faithful, if it is offered to them or bestowed on them by someone having the authority to do so; and again, that all bishops, and generally all persons now called clergymen, must be subject to the coercive judgment or rulership of him who governs by the authority of the human legislator, especially where this legislator is Christian

3. Therefore for the present purpose it suffices to show, and I shall first show, that Christ himself came into the world not to dominate men, nor to judge them by judgment in the third sense, nor to wield temporal rule, but rather to be subject as regards the status of the present life; and moreover, that he wanted to and did exclude himself, his apostles and disciples, and their successors, the bishop or priests, from all such coercive authority or worldly rule, both by his example and by his words of counsel or command. I shall also show that the leading apostles, as Christ's true imitators, did this same thing and taught their successors to do likewise; and moreover, that both Christ and the apostles wanted to be and were continuously subject in property and in person to the coercive jurisdiction of the secular rulers, and that they taught and commanded all others, to whom they preached or wrote the law of truth, to do likewise, under pain of eternal damnation. Then I shall write a chapter on the power or authority of the keys which Christ gave to the apostles and their successors in office, bishops and priests, so that it may be clear what is the nature, quality, and extent of such power, both of the Roman bishop and of the others. For ignorance on this point has hitherto been and still is the source of many questions and damnable controversies among the Christian faithful, as was mentioned in the first chapter of this discourse.

4. And so in pursuit of these aims we wish to show that Christ, in his purposes or intentions, words, and deeds, wished to exclude and did exclude himself and the apostles from every office of rulership, contentious jurisdiction, government or coercive judgment in the world. This is first shown clearly beyond any doubt by the passage in the eighteenth chapter of the gospel of John. For when Christ was brought before Pontius Pilate, vicar of the Roman ruler in Judaea, and accused of having called himself king of the Jews, Pontius asked him whether he had said this, or whether he did call himself a king, and Christ's reply included these words, among others: "My kingdom is not of this world," that is, I have not come to reign by temporal rule or dominion, in the way in which worldly kings reign. And proof of this was given by Christ himself through an evident sign when he said: "If my kingdom were of this world, my servants would certainly fight, that I should not be delivered to the Jews," as if to argue as follows: If I had come into this world to reign by worldly or coercive rule, I would have ministers for this rule, namely, men to fight and to coerce transgressors, as the other kings have; but I do not have such ministers, as you can clearly see. Hence the interlinear gloss: "It is

clear that no one defends him." And this is what Christ reiterates: "But now my kingdom is not from hence," that is, the kingdom about which I have come to teach.

9. It now remains to show that not only did Christ himself refuse rulership or coercive judgment in this world, whereby he furnished an example for his apostles and disciples and their successors to do likewise, but also he taught by words and showed by example that all men, both priests and non-priests, should be subject in property and in person to the coercive judgment of the rulers of this world. By his word and example, then Christ showed this first with respect to property, by what is written in the twenty-second chapter of Matthew. For when the Jews asked him: "Tell us therefore, what dost thou think? Is it lawful to give tribute to Caesar, or not?" Christ, after looking at the coin and its inscription, replied: "Render therefore to Caesar the things that are Caesar's, and to God the things that are God's." Whereon the interlinear gloss says, "that is, tribute and money." And on the words: "Whose image and inscription is this?" Ambrose wrote as follows: "Just as Caesar demanded the imprinting of his image, so too does God demand that the soul be stamped with the light of his countenance." Note, therefore, what it was that Christ came into the world to demand. Furthermore, Chrysostom writes as follows: "When you hear: 'Render to Caesar the things that are Caesar's,' know that he means only those things which are not harmful to piety, for if they were, the tribute would be not to Caesar but to the devil." So, then, we ought to be subject to Caesar in all things, so long only as they are not contrary to piety, that is, to divine worship or commandment. Therefore, Christ wanted us to be subject in property to the secular ruler. This too was plainly the doctrine of St. Ambrose, based upon the doctrine of Christ, for in his epistle against Valentinian, entitled *To the People*, he wrote: "we pay to Caesar the things that are Caesar's, and to God the things that are God's. That the tribute is Caesar's is not denied."

II.6.1, 4, 7, 9, 12

Chapter VI: On the authority of the priestly keys, and what kind of power the priest or bishop has in excommunication

1. We must next show what power and authority and what kind of judgment over the believers Christ wanted to grant, and did in fact grant, to these same apostles and their successors by virtue of the words of the holy Scripture. Among the passages which seem to have the most explicit bearing on this question are Christ's words to Peter in Matthew, Chapter 16, when he said: "I will give unto thee the keys of the kingdom of heaven"; also Christ's words to all the apostles, in Matthew, chapter 18, and John, Chapter 20: "Whatsoever ye shall bind on earth, shall be bound in heaven"; and: "Whoseoever sins ye remit, they are remitted unto them," etc. For it was from these words especially that the opinion and title of plentitude of power, which the Roman bishop ascribes to himself, drew its origin.

4. But first we must note that, in the soul of him who commits a mortal sin, guilt is generated and the divine grace which had been bestowed on him is destroyed. This guilt binds the sinner to a debt of eternal damnation for the status of the future life. If he persists in this guilt, he is cut off from the society of the faithful in this world by a certain form of correction called, among the Christian faithful, "excommunication." And on the other hand we must note that by repenting of his sin and by making an external confession to the priest—both of which, together and separately, are called by the name "penance"—the sinner obtains a three-fold benefit: first, he is cleansed of his internal guilt and the grace of God is restored in him; second, he is absolved from the debt of eternal damnation to which his guilt had bound him; and third, he is reconciled to the church, that is, he is or should be reunited to the society of the faithful. To accomplish these things, then, in the sinner, namely, to loose him from or bind him to guilt or the debt of eternal damnation, which has to be done somehow by the power of the keys granted to the priest, as will be said below, is to minister the sacrament of penance.

7. However, as we said above, God requires that the penitent have the intention of confessing his sins to the priest at the very first opportunity, just as the Master says in Book IV, Distinction 17, Chapter IV, where he asks "whether it is sufficient to confess one's sins to God alone," and decides, by the authorities of the Scripture, that the answer is in the negative, if a priest be available. But if a priest be not available, it is sufficient to have made a confession to God alone, but always with the intention of confessing if one can. And Richard, agreeing with the Master, also held this view in his book mentioned above, and from his discussion in various chapters it is concluded that before all ministry on the part of the priest, God removes the guilt from the persons who is truly penitent, that is, contrite, about his sin, and frees him from the debt of eternal death, but under the condition that he must then confess his crime to a priest at the first opportunity. This condition the Master calls the "firm intention" of confessing one's sins, when a priest was available. And the Master reached the same conclusion in Book IV, Distinction 18, Chapters V and VI, answering therewith the reasonable question as to why the action or office of the priest is required in penance, if God alone, before all ministry on the priest's part, wipes out the guilt and the debt of eternal damnation. Said the Master: "Amid such great diversity," for both the saints and the doctors seemed to disagree on this point, although they do not in truth disagree, "what must be held? This much we can well say and think, that God alone cancels and retains sins. And yet he bestows upon the church," that is, the priests, who in one sense are called the church, as was seen in Chapter II of this discourse, "the power of binding and loosing. But he binds and looses in one way, and the church," that is, the priests, "in another. For he by himself so cancels the sin, that he cleanses the soul of its internal stain, and relieves it from the debt of eternal death. This power, however, he did not grant to the priests, but he gave them the power of binding and loosing, that is, of showing men to be loosed or bound." In this passage, the Master set forth for what purpose the office or ministry of the priest is required in penance, and then he went on to clarify it:

> Hence the Lord himself first restored the leper to health and then he sent him to the priests, by whose judgment it was to be shown that the leper was cleansed. Thus too he sent Lazarus, who had already been brought to life, to his disciples to be loosed, for although one may be loosed in the eyes of god, yet in the eyes [that

is, in the knowledge] of the church one is not regarded as being loosed except through the judgment of the priest. Hence in loosing or retaining sins the ecclesiastic priest acts and judges just as the rabbi once did with regard to those who had been contaminated with leprosy, which signifies sin.

This view is reiterated towards the close of Chapter VI, and is confirmed by the authority of Jerome. On the passage in Matthew, Chapter 16: "And I shall give unto thee the keys of the kingdom of heaven," Jerome writes: "the evangelic priests have the right and duty which rabbis once had under the law in the treatment of lepers. They cancel or retain sins when they judge and show that these sins have been cancelled or retained by God." Hence, "in Leviticus lepers are commanded to show themselves to the priests, who do not make them leprous or clean, but discern who are clean and who are unclean." For this reason, therefore, is the priest's office required for the penitent, namely in order to show, in the eyes of the church, whose sins God has retained or cancelled.

9. From these authorities of the saints, the Master, and Richard, it is thus clear that God alone removes the guilt and the debt of eternal damnation from the truly penitent sinner, without any prior or concomitant action on the part of the priest, as was shown above. Of this I also wish to give an infallible demonstration in accordance with the Scripture and the words of the saints and teachers. For it is God alone who cannot be ignorant as to whose sin it is to be pardoned and whose retained; and it is God alone who neither is affected by vicious emotions nor renders unjust judgments over anyone. But such is not the case with the church or the priest, whoever he be, even the Roman bishop. For anyone of these priests and bishops may sometimes err, or be swayed by vicious emotions, or both; as a result, if a truly penitent person who duly intended to confess, or had even actually confessed, were not forgiven his sin or guilt and his debt of eternal damnation because of the priest's ignorance, malice, or both, then Christ's evangelic promise, which is an object of faith, that he would give rewards of eternal glory to the good and the punishment of Gehenna to the wicked, would frequently come to naught. Hence, suppose, as frequently occurs, that some sinner has falsely and wrongly made a confession of his sins, and as a result, due to the priest's ignorance, malice, or both, he has received absolution and benediction; or suppose, as also frequently occurs, that some other person has properly and adequately confessed his sins to the priest, and has been refused absolution and benediction due to the priest's ignorance, malice, or both. Are then the sins of the first, the one who made a false confession, canceled, and those of the second, the true penitent, retained? This question must firmly and undoubtedly be answered in the negative. And hence on the words of John, Chapter 20: "Receive ye the Holy Ghost, and whosoever sins ye remit," etc., Chrysostom wrote as follows: "For neither the priest, nor the angel or archangel, can accomplish anything in those things which have been given by God. The priest gives indeed his benediction and his hand; for it is not just that those who come to the faith should be harmed through another's malice with respect to the symbols of our salvation." And on the words of Matthew, Chapter 16: "And I shall give unto thee the keys of the kingdom of heaven," etc., Jerome wrote in the same vein, as follows: "Some men, not understanding this passage, adopt the supercilious attitude of the Pharisees, thinking that they can condemn the harmless and acquit the harmful, when with God it is not the sentence of the priests but rather the lives of the accused parties that are inquired into." To these words the Master, in Distinction

18, Chapter VI, adds this noteworthy statement: "Thus it is here clearly shown that God does not (always) follow the judgment of the church, which sometimes judges with malice and ignorance"; "of the church," that is, of the priests in it. And in Chapter VIII the Master adds: "For sometimes he who is sent out," that is, he is judged to be outside the church by the priest, "is within; and he who is outside," that is, in accordance with the truth, "is seen to be kept within," namely, by the false judgment of the priests.

12. With regard to the above, in order that it may be known to whom belongs the power of excommunication, and in what way, we must note that in excommunication, the accused is judged as to his punishment for the status of his future life, by a certain judgment which will be discussed more explicitly in Chapter IX of this discourse; and also a grave penalty is inflicted on him for the status of the present life, in that he is publicly defamed and the company of other persons is forbidden to him. Hence too he is deprived of civil communion and benefits. And although the infliction of the first penalty, on a person who is undeservedly smitten, does no harm for the status of the future life, because "God does not always follow the judgment of the church," that is, of the priests, namely, when they judge someone unjustly, as was sufficiently shown above; yet a person who was thus unjustly smitten by the priest would be harmed more gravely for the status of the present life, because he is defamed and deprived of civil association. And for this reason it must be said that although the words and actions of the priest are required to promulgate such a judgment, yet it does not pertain to some one priest alone or to a group of priests alone to give a coercive judgment and command about who is to be excommunicated or acquitted. But the appointment of such a judge—that is, one who is to summon, examine, and judge the accused person, and acquit him or condemn him to be thus publicly defamed or cut off from the company of the faithful—pertains to the whole body of the faithful in that community in which the defendant is to be judged by such a judgment, or to the superior of that whole body, or to a general Council. However, the examination of the imputed crime, as to whether or not it be such as merits excommunication, ought to be made by such a judge with the help of a group of priests or of a determinate number of the more experienced from among them, in accordance with the established laws or customs.

For the priest must discern or judge, by a judgment in the first sense, about the crimes for which, according to the evangelic law, a person must be cut off from the company of the faithful lest he infect others; just as a physician or a group of physicians has to judge, by a judgment in the first sense, about the bodily diseases for which a diseased person such as a leper, must be separated from the company of others lest he infect hem. And again, the crime must be such as can by sure testimony be proved to have been committed by someone. Consequently, just as it does not pertain to any physician or group of physicians to make a judgment or to appoint a judge having coercive power to expel lepers, but rather this pertains to the whole body of faithful citizens or to the weightier part of them, as was demonstrated in Chapter XV of Discourse I, so too in the community of the faithful it pertains to no one priest or group of priests to make a judgment or to appoint a judge having coercive power to expel persons from the company of the community because of a disease of the soul, such as a notorious crime, although such a judgment ought to emerge from the counsel of the priests, inasmuch as they are held to know the divine law wherein are determined the crimes because of which the criminal must be denied the society of the crimeless believers. "For the lips of the priest shall keep knowledge, and they shall seek the law at his mouth," from Malachi, Chapter 2.

But whether the person who is charged with such a crime has committed it, must be judged not by the bishop or priest alone but by the whole body of the faithful in that community, or by that body's superior, as we have said, or by a judge whom it has appointed for this purpose, either a priest or non-priest; but the judgment must be based upon the proofs which are brought forth. And if the defendant be convicted by witnesses, and the crime be such as merits excommunication—which is the only question on which it is necessary to sand by the judgment of the college of the priests or of the sounder part thereof—then the sentence of excommunication must be pronounced upon the criminal by the afore-mentioned judge appointed for this purpose by the whole body of the faithful in that community, and this sentence must be executed by the command of the judge and the words of the priest, insofar as it affects the criminal for the status of the future life also.

II.10.1, 8

Chapter 10: On the coercive judge of heretics, namely to whom it pertains to judge heretics in this world, to correct them, to inflict on them penalties in person and in property, and to exact and dispose of these penalties

1. Concerning what we have said doubts may well arise. For if only the ruler by the legislator's authority has jurisdiction over all forms of compulsion in the present life, through coercive judgment and the infliction and exaction of penalties in property and in person, as was shown above, then it will pertain to this ruler to make coercive judgments over heretics or other infidels or schismatics, and to inflict, exact, and dispose of the penalties in property and in person. But this seems inappropriate. For it might seem that it pertains to the same authority to inquire into a crime and to judge and correct the crime; but since it pertains to the priest, the presbyter or bishop, and to no one else, to discern the crime of heresy, it would seem to follow that the coercive judgment or correction of this and similar crimes also pertains to the priest or bishop alone. Moreover, the judging and punishing of a criminal might seem to pertain to the person against whom or against whose law the criminal has sinned. But this person is the priest or bishop. For he is the minister or judge of divine law, against which essentially the heretic, schismatic, or other infidel sins, whether this sinner be a group or an individual. It follows, therefore, that this judgment pertains to the priest, and not to the ruler. And this clearly seems to be the view of St. Ambrose in his first epistle to the Emperor Valentinian; but since he seems to adhere to this view throughout the whole epistle, I have omitted to quote from it for the sake of brevity.

8. Therefore, the judgment over heretics, schismatics, and other infidels, and the power to coerce them, to exact temporal punishment from them, and to assign the pecuniary mulcts to oneself or to the community, and not to anyone else, belongs only to the ruler by authority of the human legislator, and not to any priest or bishop, even though it be divine law which is sinned against. For although the latter is indeed a law in its relation

to men in and for the status of the present life, yet it is not law in the last sense as having coercive power over anyone in this world; this is evident from the preceding chapter and Chapter V of this discourse. It is, however, a law in the third sense, as was made clear in Chapter X of Discourse I. And the priests are its judges, in the first sense of "judge," in this world, and they have no coercive power, as was shown in Chapter V of this discourse and in the preceding chapter by the words of the Apostle, Ambrose, Hilary, and Chrysostom. For if the priests were coercive judges or rulers over heretics because the latter sin against the discipline of which the priests are the teachers and the performers of certain operations upon others in accordance with it, then in similar fashion the gold smith would be coercive judge and ruler over the counterfeiter of golden works, which is quite absurd; similarly too the physician would coerce those who act wrongly with respect to the art of medicine; and there would be as many rulers as there are functions or offices of the state against which it is possible to sin. But the impossibility or uselessness of this multiplicity of rulers was shown in Chapter XVII of Discourse I. For persons who committed such sins against the offices of the state would not on that account be coerced or punished, unless something else intervened, namely, a command of human law or of the legislator. For if such sins were not prohibited by human law, then those who committed them would not be punished.

II.11.2 (first sentence), 3 (first 2 sentences), 4, 6–7

Chapter XI: On some signs, testimonies, and examples from both canonic and human writings, which show the truth of the conclusions reached in Chapters IV, V, VIII, IX, and X of this discourse with regard to the status of bishops and of priests generally, and why Christ separated their status, that of poverty, from the status of rulers

2. But Christ separated the office of priests or bishops from that of rulers; yet if he had wanted to, he could have exercised both the status of ruler and the office of priest, and he could have ordained that the apostles do likewise. . . .

3. See, then, that the status of poverty and contempt for the world is that which befits every perfect man, especially the disciple and successor of Christ in the pastoral office; indeed, it is almost necessary for the man who must urge upon others contempt for the world, if he wishes to succeed in his teaching or preaching. For if such a person who teaches those whom he addresses to spurn riches and governmental office, nevertheless himself possesses and thirsts for these things, then he manifestly refutes his own words by his actions. . . .

4. For they who are teachers or pastors of others, and who possess such riches, do more to destroy men's faith and devotion by their contrary deeds and examples than they do to strengthen them by their words, for these latter are manifestly contradicted by their deeds, which men heed more than they do words. And it is greatly to be feared that the evil examples furnished by these men's deeds will finally make the faithful give up all hope of the future world. For what almost all the ministers of the church do—the bishops or priests and the other clergymen, but most obviously those who occupy the greater thrones

of the church—is such that they seem in no way to believe in God's future judgment in the other world. For if the future just judgment of God in the world to come is indeed believed in by most of the Roman pontiffs and their cardinals and other priests or bishops, who have been given the care of men's souls and put in charge of distributing ecclesiastic temporal goods to the poor, and similarly by all the rest, deacons and clergy, then by what conscience in accordance with God—let them answer, I beg—do they seize or steal, at every opportunity, all the temporal goods they can, which devout believers have bequeathed for the sustenance of gospel ministers and other poor persons, and donate or bequeath them to their relatives, or to any other persons not in need, obviously despoiling the poor thereby? And again—let them answer, I beg—by what conscience in accordance with the Christian religion do they consume the goods of the poor on so many unnecessary things—horses, estates, banquets, and other vanities and pleasures, open and concealed—when, according to the Apostle in the first epistle to Timothy, last chapter, they ought to be content with food and shelter for the ministering of the gospel?

6. But rather than attempt to enumerate every one of their corrupt practices, which would be impossible or at any rate very difficult, we shall make a general statement concerning the acts of almost all priests or bishops and other ministers of the temple. Invoking Christ's judgment if we lie, we testify before him that these bishops and almost all other priests in modern time practice in almost every instance the opposites of the gospel teachings whose observance they preach to others. For they have a burning desire for pleasures, vanities, temporal possessions, and secular rulership, and they pursue and attain these objectives with all their energies, not by rightful means, but by wrongdoing, hidden and open. And yet Christ and his true imitators the apostles spurned these things and taught other men to spurn them, especially if they are to preach before others the gospel of contempt for worldly things.

7. For if Christ had wanted to, if he had thought it proper for a preacher, he could have held the status of ruler in this world and could similarly have suffered in that status. But he fled to the mountain in order to reject and to teach the rejection of such a status, as we showed above in Chapter IV of this discourse from John, Chapter 6. For not this status befits men who preach contempt for it, but rather the status of subjects and of humble men, such as both Christ and his apostles held in this world. On the other hand, the status of external poverty and humility does not befit the ruler, for he should have a status which good subjects will respect and bad ones fear, and through which he will be able to use coercion, if necessary, upon rebellious transgressors of the laws; this he could not well do if he held the status of poverty and humility. And for this reason the preacher's office does not befit the ruler. For if the ruler were to urge upon the people the status of poverty and humility and if he were to counsel turning the other cheek when smitten, and giving a cloak to the stealer of one's tunic rather than suing him, such counsels would not readily be believed when spoken by the ruler, because by the status which befits him and which he bears he would deny his own words. Moreover, it would be inappropriate for the ruler to give and observe such counsels. For inasmuch as it is his function to punish wrongdoers even when those who suffer wrong do not demand that such punishment be given; it follows that if he were to preach that injuries should be forgiven he would furnish wrongdoers with an opportunity for further crime, and persons who were offended or wronged would come to question or to lose faith in the enforcement of

justice. This was why Christ, who always disposed all things for the best, wanted the offices of ruler and priest not to be joined in the same person, but rather to be separated. And this seems to be the explicit conviction of St. Bernard in his treatise addressed to Pope Eugene, *On Consideration*, Book II, Chapter 4, where he writes as follows: "Go, then, if you dare, and usurp either the apostolate if you are a lord or lordship if you are an apostle. You are plainly prohibited from having both. If you wish to have both at once, you shall lose both. In any case, do not think you are excepted from the number of those about whom God complained in these words: They have reigned, but not by me: they have been princes, and I knew not."

II.13.11–14, 22–23 (first two sentences), 26, 28 (first paragraph), 29–32

Chapter XIII: On the status of supreme poverty, which is usually called evangelical perfection; and that this status was held by Christ and his apostles

11. Having set forth these premises, we now enter more fully upon our main task. We say first that the existence of poverty or of poor persons is almost self-evident, and is found in many passages of Scripture, from which it will suffice to quote one, in Mark, Chapter 12, where Christ says: "Verily I say unto you, that this poor widow hath cast more in than all of them."

12. Next I show similarly by Scripture that poverty is meritorious as a means towards eternal life, for the Truth has said, in Luke, Chapter 6: "Blessed be the poor: for yours is the kingdom of God," that is, you merit it, for in this life no one except Christ is actually blessed, but rather merits it.

13. And from this it necessarily follows that poverty is a virtue, if one becomes habituated thereto by many acts of thus willing to lack temporal goods; or else poverty is an act which is productive of a virtue or elicited from a virtue; for everything which is meritorious is a virtue or an act of virtue. Again, every counsel of Christ pertains essentially to virtue; but poverty is such a counsel, as is sufficiently clear from Matthew, Chapter 5 and 19, and from many other passages of the evangelic Scripture.

14. From this it necessarily follows that the poverty to which we here refer as a virtue is that voluntary poverty which was defined in the third and fourth senses of poverty given above. For there is no virtue or deed of virtue without choice, and there is no choice without consent, as is sufficiently clear from the second and third books of the *Ethics*. This can be confirmed by Matthew, Chapter 5, where Christ said: "Blessed are the poor in spirit," by "spirit" meaning will or consent, although some of the saints interpret "spirit" to mean pride, which interpretation is not, however, very appropriate, inasmuch as there immediately follow in the same chapter these words: "Blessed are the meek." But whatever be the interpretation of this passage, there is no doubt, according to the views of the saints, that if poverty is deserving of the kingdom of heavens as Christ says, it must be not primarily the external lack of temporal goods, but an internal habit of the mind, whereby one freely wishes to be lacking in such goods for the sake of Christ.

Whence on the words in Luke, Chapter 6: "Blessed are the poor," etc., Basil writes: "Not everyone who is oppressed by poverty is blessed. For there are many persons who are poor in means, but most avaricious in desire, and these are not saved by their poverty, but damned by their desire. For nothing which is involuntary can be blessed, since every virtue is marked by free will." Poverty, then, is a meritorious virtue, and consequently voluntary. But external lack is not in itself a virtue, inasmuch as it does not lead to salvation without the proper desire; for a person might be lacking in temporal goods under coercion and against his will, and yet would be condemned because of his inordinate desire for these goods. This was also the view of the Apostle on the subject, when in II Corinthians, Chapter 8, he said: "For if there be first a willing mind, it is accepted according to that a man hath"—"accepted," that is, meritorious.

22. Moreover, I say that the highest mode or species of this virtue is the explicit vow of the wayfarer, whereby for the sake of Christ he renounces and wishes to be deprived of and to lack all acquired legal ownership, both in private and in common, or the power to claim and to prohibit another from temporal things (called "riches") before a coercive judge. And by this vow, also, the wayfarer wishes, for the sake of Christ, to be deprived of and to lack, both in private and in common, all power, holding, handling or use of temporal things over and above what is necessary quantitatively and qualitatively for his present subsistence. Nor does he wish at one time to have such goods, however lawfully they may come to him, in an amount sufficient to supply several of the future needs or necessities either of himself alone or of himself together with a determinate other person or persons in common. Rather, he wishes to have at one time only what is necessary for a single need, as the immediate actual and present need of food and shelter; but with this sole exception, that the person who takes this vow should be in such place, time, and personal circumstances that he can acquire for himself, on each successive day, a quantity of temporal things sufficient to supply his aforesaid individual need, but only one at a time, not more. This mode or species of meritorious poverty is the status which is considered to be necessary for evangelical perfection, as will clearly be seen from what follows. And this mode of meritorious poverty, or this status of a person who does not have possessions in private (in the third sense) or even in common with another (in the sense "common" which is opposed to the above sense of "private"), we shall henceforth, for the sake of brevity, call "supreme poverty," and the person who wishes to have this status we shall call, in keeping with the custom of theologians, "perfect."

23. That this mode of meritorious poverty is the supreme one can be shown from this, that through it all the other meritorious counsels of Christ are observed. For in the first place, men give up by a vow all the temporal things which it is possible for a wayfarer to give up; secondly, most of the impediments to divine charity are removed for those who take this vow; thirdly, they are put in condition to endure many secular passions, humiliations, and hardships, and are willingly deprived of many secular pleasures and vanities; and in a word, they are put in the best condition to observe all the commands and counsels of Christ. . . .

26. Furthermore, that through this mode of meritorious poverty, which we have called the supreme mode, all the commands and counsels of Christ can be observed to the highest degree, will be apparent to anyone who reads the gospel, especially the chapters

we have indicated. For how can a person who has chosen to endure such poverty be avaricious or proud, incontinent or intemperate, ambitious, pitiless, unjust, timid, slothful, or jealous; why should he be mendacious or intolerant, for what reason malevolent toward others? On the contrary, he who has put himself in this condition seems to have an open door to all the virtues, and also the serene fulfillment of all the commands and counsels. This is so plain to anyone who considers it that I omit the proof, for the sake of brevity.

28. Now when we said that the perfect person is not allowed to provide for himself for the morrow, we did not mean that if anything remained from his lawful daily acquisitions, he ought to throw it away and in no manner save it, but that he ought to save it only with the firm intention of properly distributing it to any poor person or persons he met who were more needy than he. Whence in Luke, Chapter 3: "He that hath two coats, let him impart to him that hath none: and he that hath meat, let him do likewise"; understanding by "two coats" and "meat" that which remains over and above one's own present needs. . . .

29. And from this it is clear that they are wrong who say that perfection is attained by vowing to accept nothing for distribution to the poor who are weak or otherwise incapable of acquiring for themselves the necessities of life. For, as is clear from II Corinthians, Chapters 8 and 9, the Apostle acquired goods with this purpose, and there is no doubt that he did so lawfully and meritoriously. And this is also apparent from the gloss on the words in John, Chapter 21: "Feed my sheep," etc. But since the matter is quite evident, I omit to quote these passages, for the sake of brevity.

30. From our above description of supreme poverty it also necessarily follows that the perfect person neither can nor ought to save or keep in his power any real estate, like house or field, unless he has the firm intention of giving it away as soon as he can, or exchanging it for money or for something else which can immediately and conveniently be distributed to the poor. For since house or field could not as such be conveniently distributed to the poor with out incurring the difficulty of giving too much to some and too little to others, we must follow the counsel of Christ, and do what he advised when he said, in Matthew, Chapter 19, Luke, Chapter 8, and Mark, Chapter 10: "Go and sell." Nor did Christ say: give to the poor everything that you have; nor did he say: Throw away everything that you have; but rather he said: "Go and sell," for by selling the distribution of wealth can be more conveniently made. Such too was the counsel of the apostles and those to whom they gave this counsel followed it out, wishing to distribute their goods to the poor conveniently. Whence in Acts, Chapter 4: "for as many as were possessors of land or houses sold them, and bought the prices of the things that were sold. And the distribution was made unto every man according as he had need."

31. From the above it is also apparent that no perfect person can acquire the ownership (in the first, second, or third senses) of any temporal thing, as we have proved above from Matthew, Chapter 5, and Luke, Chapter 6. And we have confirmed this through the Apostle in I Corinthians, Chapter 6; and we made it sufficiently clear by the words of Augustine and the gloss on that scriptural passage. Since the matter is evident, I have omitted to quote these passages for the sake of brevity.

32. Nor should we pay attention to the argument that perfect men may lawfully save real estate in order to distribute the annual income thereof to the poor. For it is more meritorious because of love of Christ and pity for one's neighbor to distribute at once to the poor both the real estate and the income thereof, rather than the latter alone; and besides, it is more meritorious to give away the real estate alone rather than its income alone. For in this way help can be given to many poor and needy persons at once, who might perhaps through want become ill or die before the income became available, or commit an act of violence, theft, or some other evil. Again, a person who kept the real estate might die before the time when the income was distributed, and thus he would never have the merit therefrom that he could have had.

Entirely the same view must be held with respect to any kind of chattels, which similarly, when thus kept, naturally affect to an inordinate degree the desire of the person who holds them. But if the virtue here considered is believed to be charity, as some seem to think, then undoubtedly this mode of charity, that is, with supreme poverty, is more perfect than having private or common ownership of a temporal thing, as is plain from the preceding reasonings.

II.15.4 (first sentence), 5 (first two sentences), 6–7

Chapter XV: On the differentiation of the priestly office according to its essential and accidental, separable and inseparable authority; and that no priest is inferior to a bishop in essential, but only in accidental dignity

4. Now with respect to this priestly character, whether one or many, which we have said to be the power of performing the sacrament of the eucharist or of consecrating Christ's body and blood, and the power of binding and loosing men from sins, which character we shall henceforth call the "essential" or "inseparable authority" of the priest insofar as he is a priest, to me it seems likely that this character is the same kind among all priests, and that the Roman or any other bishop has no more of it than has any simple priest. . . .

5. The more clearly to grasp this, we must not overlook the fact that these names "priest" and "bishop" were in the primitive church synonymous, although they were applied to the same man by virtue of different properties. For the name "priest" (*presbyter*) was applied to a man by virtue of his age, as being an elder; "bishop" (*episcopus*) was applied to him by virtue of his dignity or care over others, as being an overseer. . . .

6. But because the number of priests had markedly increased after the days of the apostles, the priests, in order to avoid scandal and schism, elected one of their number to guide and direct the others in the exercise of the ecclesiastic office and service, in the distribution of offerings, and in the proper arrangement of other matters, lest the household and service of the temples be disturbed because of conflicting desires, by each man's acting according to his own pleasure, and sometimes wrongly. Through later custom this priest, who was elected to regulate the other priests, retained for himself

alone the name of "bishop," as being an overseer, because he supervised not only the faithful people (for which reason all priests were in the primitive church called bishops), but also his fellow priests; and hence, antonomastically, the overseer later kept for himself alone the name "bishop," while the others retained the simple name "priest."

7. But the aforesaid election or appointment made by man does not give to the person thus elected any greater essential merit or priestly authority or power, but only a certain power with regard to the ordering of the household in God's house or temple: namely, the power to direct and regulate the other priests, deacons, and officials, in the same way that the prior is today given power over monks. This power is not coercive unless the authority for such coercion shall have been granted by the human legislator to the person thus elected, as was demonstrated in Chapters IV and VIII of this discourse, and as will appear more fully in the following chapter; nor does this power bestow any other, intrinsic dignity or authority on the person elected. This is similar to the way in which soldiers at war elect the captain, who in ancient times was called "commander" (*praeceptor*) or "imperator" (although this name "imperator" was transferred to a certain kind of royal monarchy, the highest of all, and the word is now used in this sense). In this way, too, the deacons elect one of their number to be archdeacon, who is by this election given no essential merit or holy order greater than that of the diaconate, but only such human power as we have mentioned, to direct and regulate the other deacons. Hence the Roman bishop has no more essential priestly authority than has any other bishop, just as St. Peter had no more such authority than the other apostles. For they all received this same authority equally and immediately from Christ, as was shown above by the authority of Jerome writing on the words in Matthew, Chapter 16: "And I will give unto thee the keys of the kingdom of heaven," and as will be more fully shown in the following chapter.

II.16.5 (first two sentences), 6 (first two sentences), 9, 12, 15 (first sentence)

Chapter XVI: On the equality of the apostles in each office or dignity bestowed on them immediately by Christ. Whence is proved what was said in the preceding chapter concerning the equality of all their successors; and how all the bishops are alike successor of every apostle

5. A sign that what we have said is true, is that St. Peter is in the Scripture found to have assumed no special authority over the other apostles, but rather to have maintained equality with them. For he assumed for himself no authority to settle questions relating to the preaching of the gospel, with respect to doctrine; but these questions were settled through common deliberation of the apostles and of other more learned believers, and not by Peter or any other apostle alone. . . .

6. It was by the congregation of learned believers, therefore, that deliberations were conducted, and questions settled, and elections made, and documents written; and on this congregation's authority rested the validity of what was thus determined and

commanded. For the congregation of the apostles was of greater authority than was Peter or any other apostle alone. . . .

9. Moreover, just as we read that Peter was elected bishop at Antioch by the multitude of believers, not needing the confirmation of the other apostles, so too did the other apostles become administrators of other provinces without any knowledge, appointment, or consecration on the part of Peter, for they had been sufficiently consecrated by Christ. Consequently, it must similarly be held that the successors of these apostles needed no confirmation by the successors of Peter; indeed, many of the successors of the other apostles were duly elected and appointed as bishops, and piously ruled their provinces, without appointment or confirmation by the successors of Peter. And this practice was thus legitimately maintained until about the time of the emperor Constantine, who gave to the bishop and church of Rome a certain preeminence and authority over all the other churches, bishops, and priests in the world. And that Peter and the other apostles were thus equal was shown by the Apostle in Galatians, Chapter 2, when he wrote: "They," James, Peter, and John, "gave to me and Barnabas the right hands of fellowship; that we should go unto the heathen, and they unto the circumcision"—" the right hands of fellowship," and therefore, "of equality," as has been sufficiently shown above by the gloss according to Augustine, although the Apostle's statement on this point is so clear that it does not need the gloss. We have also proved this point through Jerome's epistle to Evander, which says that all bishops, "whether at Rome or" elsewhere, "are of the same priesthood" and "of the same merit" or power bestowed immediately by Christ.

12. But even if the apostles had chosen St. Peter to be their bishop or leader because of his age and his greater acquired holiness, as is maintained in a decree of the pope Anacletus, contained in the *Codex* of Isidore, as follows: "The other apostles received honor and power in equal fellowship with him," Peter, "and wanted him to be their leader"; even if this were true, it would not follow that his successors in the Roman or some other seat, if he was bishop elsewhere, have this priority over the successors of the other apostles, unless they have been elected to such leadership by the successors of those others; for some of the successors of the other apostles have been of greater virtue than some of Peter's successors, although properly, every bishop is alike the successor of every apostle in office, though not in territory. Again, why would this priority belong more to Peter's successors at Rome than to those at Antioch or Jerusalem or elsewhere, if he was bishop in many cities?

15. That the above-mentioned outmoded claims (for they will perhaps be seen to be more outmoded and unthinkable, if not false) are heard is all the more surprising because it can be proved by the certain testimony of the Scripture that the Roman bishops are, without reference to province and people, the successors of Paul rather than of Peter, especially in the episcopal seat at Rome; and again (which will appear even more surprising), because it cannot be directly proved through the Scripture that the Roman bishops are particular successors of St. Peter in virtue of being assigned to a certain seat or province, but by this criterion it is rather the bishops at Antioch who are St. Peter's successors. . . .

II.26.4–5, 7–8, 13 (first 2 sentences), 14 (last three sentences), 16 (first paragraph), 19 (second to fourth paragraphs)

Chapter XXVI: How the Roman bishop has used this plenary power and primacy still more particularly with regard to the Roman ruler and empire

4. These assumptions, or rather presumptions, were occasioned (superfluously, let me add) by a certain devoutness, among other things. For some of the Roman rulers after the time of Constantine wished to give friendly notice of their election to the Roman pontiffs, in order that by paying to Christ in the person of the pontiffs this special request, they might obtain from him through their meditation greater blessings and grace for their guidance of the empire; and likewise, in order to solemnize and herald their inauguration and to obtain more of God's grace, some Roman rulers had their royal crown placed on their heads by the Roman pontiffs. But who will say that such coronation gives any greater authority to the Roman pontiff over the Roman ruler than to the archbishop of Rheims over the king of the Franks? For such solemnities do not bestow authority; they only signify that authority is had or that it has been bestowed. But from this respect which was so willingly paid by the Roman rulers in their simplicity, not to say foolishness, the Roman pontiffs, who too frequently seek what is not theirs, have developed a custom, or rather abuse, of calling their commendation and benediction of an elected person their confirmation of his election. The Roman rulers of old did not see what harmful intent underlay this mode of designation, and so the Roman pontiffs continued to use it, at first secretly, but now openly, to mean that no person, regardless of how duly he has been elected king of the Romans, is to be called king, or to have or exercise the authority of the Roman king, unless he shall have been approved by the Roman bishop. And this approval consists in the mere will of the Roman bishop alone, as he says, inasmuch as he recognizes no one on earth who is superior or equal to him in such judgment, nor is he obliged in this or in any other matter to follow the counsel of his brethren, called the cardinals, although he may use it; but through his plentitude of power he can, so he says, do precisely the opposite of what his cardinals advise, if he so wills.

5. But in this matter the Roman bishop, as is his custom, draws a conclusion which is false and bad from premises which are true and good. For from the fact that the Roman ruler in his devoutness has voluntarily paid respect to the Roman bishop, by giving him notice of his election and asking for his benediction and mediation with God, it does not follow that the election of the Roman ruler depends upon the will of the Roman bishop. For this would be none other than to destroy the Roman government and to prevent forever the election of the Roman ruler. For if the authority of an elected king depends solely upon the will of the Roman bishop, then the office of the electors is entirely an empty one, inasmuch as the man whom they elect is not king, nor is he to be so called, nor can he exercise any kingly authority, until he is confirmed by that bishop's will or authority, which he calls the "apostolic seat"; indeed (what is very oppressive even to hear, let alone endure) the elected person will not even be allowed to draw from the revenues of the empire enough for his daily subsistence, without leave by this bishop. Hence, so far as the granting of authority to the king is concerned, what will his election by the princes amount to other than a nomination, since their designation of him will depend upon the will solely of one other man? For this much authority could be granted

to the Roman king by seven barbers or blind men. I say this not in contempt of the electors but in derision of the man who wants to deprive them of their due authority. For he is ignorant of what is the force and meaning of an election, and why its authority depends upon the weightier part of those who have the right to elect; and he also cannot depend solely on the will of some one man, if it is to be reasonably instituted, but that it depends solely upon the legislator over whom the ruler is to be instituted, or upon those to whom this legislator has granted such authority, as we have demonstrated with certainty in Chapters XII and XIII of Discourse I.

7. Again, to claim for himself the authority to confirm the elected Roman king, and to decree that without such confirmation no one is or is to be called king, or is to perform the kingly functions—this is none other that to prohibit forever the effective appointment and inauguration of the Roman ruler and to reduce the Roman government to total slavery to the Roman bishop. For this bishop will not approve or confirm any elected king of the Romans, if he does not wish to, since he asserts that he is superior to everyone and is subordinate to no group or individual. But he will never wish to confirm anyone, for before doing so he intends to exact from the elected king certain oaths and agreements, among others an oath whereby the Roman emperor swears fealty to the bishop and asserts that he is subject to the bishop in temporal coercive jurisdiction. And the latter also wants the elected king to promise and swear to uphold the bishop's unjust and unlawful seizures of certain provinces. But since the royal majesty cannot with a clear conscience take and fulfill such unlawful oaths at the same time as the lawful oath, which he takes upon his inauguration, to preserve the liberties of the empire, no elected king will ever take such unlawful oaths or make such promises to the Roman or any other pontiff, unless he is softer than a woman and is clearly perjuring himself in taking such oaths or making such promises. Consequently, no elected king will ever be inaugurated as king of the Romans or be entitled to speak for the empire, if the royal or imperial authority of those who are elected depends upon the Roman bishop; for this bishop will both in word and in deed oppose and prevent the royal accession as long as he possibly can, notwithstanding the utter viciousness of such action in seeking what does not belong to him.

8. But this leads to something even more gravely injurious and unbearably harmful to all rulers, communities, and individual subject to the Roman empire. For since the Roman bishop asserts that during a vacancy in the imperial seat he succeeds the Roman emperor in office, it necessarily follows that he has the authority to compel all princes and other imperial feudatories to take oaths of fealty to him, and besides this the authority to demand and to exact from them taxes and other forms of tribute, both such as the Roman rulers customarily received and also exceptional taxes which this bishop has wished to pretend are owed to him through the plentitude of power which he claims for himself; and also this bishop will have the authority, during an imperial vacancy, to bestow rulership, fiefs, and other rights which the Roman ruler can bestow when a prince has died without leaving male heirs, or for some other reason. Moreover, and this is the most injurious and harmful of all, during an imperial vacancy, which, as we have said, the Roman bishop will strive to make permanent, all rulers, communities, groups and individuals subject to the Roman empire will be compelled to bring their civil suits, real and personal, to the court of the Roman bishop by appeal or by delation, and to undergo

civil judgment at his hands. And no ruler, community, or judge subject to the Roman empire will be able to command the execution of any civil sentence, for those whom their sentences condemn will always appeal from them to the court of the Roman bishop. But if subjects of the Roman empire refuse to obey this bishop, or to be subject to him in the aforesaid ways, just as they are not obliged to, he will incessantly, viciously, and shamelessly persecute them by his so-called sentences of anathematization, malediction, excommunication, indictment for heresy, and interdict, and finally he will confiscate their temporal goods, granting these goods to whoever can steal them; also he will give pardons (although empty and false ones) to all those who incur any guilt or condemnation for persecuting or even killing the men who refuse to obey him, as well as their subjects or adherents, and he will absolve these men's subjects from their oaths of fealty, although to do this is heretical.

13. And in addition to these horrible evils, this bishop perpetrates a new kind of iniquity whose heretical viciousness is only too obvious. For he stirs up rebellion against the afore-mentioned catholic ruler by issuing various diabolic (although he calls them "apostolic") statements releasing this ruler's subjects and adherents from the oaths of fealty whereby they had been and in truth still are bound to him, and proclaiming these annulments everywhere through agents who hope that the bishop will reward them by giving them church offices and benefices. . . .

14. . . . And he incessantly strives to stir up such conflicts in order that the weaker of the two opposing parties may be forced to beg him for help and to undergo his lordship. For although he wears a mask of piety and mercifulness, and seems at times to protect the weak and to give them more material aid when they chance to be wrongly oppressed, yet he does this only when he is sure that those who need and implore his help will undergo his secular lordship or rulership thereafter; for he hopes that in this way both opposing parties, through their mutual violence and hatred, will be finally compelled to come under his power. And hence men must guard against all quarrels and actions which may make it necessary to seek this bishop's support, since the final outcome is loss of liberty and the slavery of those who receive such support.

16. But now we come to what is the most vicious and most gravely harmful of all the acts of this present Roman bishop [pope John XXII]: an iniquitous practice which we have briefly mentioned above, and which no one who desires to cling to the law of love can pass over in silence. I refer to those acts of his whereby he brings about the eternal confusion and destruction of "all Christ's sheep," who says were entrusted to him that he might feed them with salutary doctrine. For again putting "good for evil and light for darkness," he has issued oral and written pronouncements "absolving from all guilt and punishment" every soldier, in cavalry or infantry, that has waged war at a certain time against those Christian believers who maintain steadfast and resolute subjection and obedience to the Roman ruler; and by himself or through others this Roman bishop has issued oral and written proclamations making it lawful to attack in any way, to rob and even to kill these faithful subjects, as being "heretics" and "rebels" against the cross of Christ. And, what is horrible to hear, this bishop declares that such action is just as pleasing in God's sight as is fighting the heathen overseas, and he has this declaration published far and wide by the false pseudo-brethren who thirst for ecclesiastic office. To

those whom physical disability prevents from participating in such criminal action, he grants a similar fallacious pardon if they have up to that some time gotten others to perpetrate these outrages in their place or if they have paid to his vicious collectors a sufficient sum for this purpose. But no one should doubt that, according to the catholic religion, this empty and ridiculous pardon is utterly worthless, nay, harmful, to men who fight in such a cause. Nevertheless, by vocally granting something that is not in his power, the bishop dupes simple men into carrying out his impious desires, or rather he seduces and misleads them to the eternal perdition of their souls. For when men, unjustly invading and attacking a foreign land, disturb the peace and quiet of innocent believers, and, even though they well know that their victims are true catholics, nevertheless rob and kill them because they are defenders of their own country and loyal to their true and legitimate ruler, then such aggressors are fighters not for Christ but for the devil. For they commit rapine, arson, theft, homicide, fornication, adultery and practically every other type of crime. And hence it is indubitably certain that the proper desert of such men is not pardon but rather prosecution and punishment by eternal damnation. And yet they are misled into perpetrating these crimes by the words and writings of the very man who calls himself (although he is not) Christ's vicar on earth. . . .

19. . . . And this is the singular cause, quite hidden in its origin, of civil war or discord—that cause which it has been our intention from the very outset to reveal. For many believers, misreasoning because of the confusing of divine Scriptures and human writings, have been led to believe that the Roman bishop and his clergymen, called cardinals, can make any decrees they like over the believers, and that divine law binds all men to obey their decrees, and that those who transgress them will be eternally damned. But that this is not true, nor even close to the truth, but rather manifestly the opposite of the truth, we have with certainly proved above especially in Chapters XII and XIII of Discourse I, and in Chapter XXI, paragraph 8, of this discourse.

This too is the cause, as we said in our prefatory remarks, of the travails under which the Italian state has long been laboring, and is still laboring. Extremely contagious, this cause is prone to creep up on all other cities and states; it has already infected them all to some extent, and unless stopped, it will finally infect them totally, just as it has the Italian state.

It will therefore be well for all rulers and peoples, acting through a general Council to be called in the way we have said, to forbid and prohibit completely the use of this title by the Roman bishop or by anyone else, lest otherwise people be misled because of the custom of listening to falsehoods; and the bishop's power of bestowing and distributing ecclesiastic offices and temporal goods or benefices must also be revoked, because he abuses this power and thus causes the ruin of the bodies and the damnation for the souls of Christian believers. Such revocation is a duty which divine law makes binding upon all men who have jurisdiction, especially kings; for they have been instituted for the purpose of making judgments and doing justice, and their failure to do this in the present instance cannot be excused, because they well know what scandal arises from such neglect. And as for the Roman bishop and his successors, as well as all other priests, deacons, and spiritual ministers (and may God be witness over my soul and body that I address these words to them not as enemies but rather as fathers and brothers in Christ), let them strive to imitate Christ and the apostles by completely renouncing secular rulership and the ownership of temporal goods. For, as I have plainly proved, and as I have warned them before all men, in accordance with the teaching of Christ and the apostles, these bishops and priests are sinners; and as a herald of the truth I have tried to lead them back to the path of truth through the harmony of the divine Scriptures and human writings, so that they, and especially the Roman bishop, who seems to have strayed most from the true path, may beware of that "indignation of almighty God and of the apostles Peter and Paul" with which this bishop in particular very often threatens others.

NICCOLÒ MACHIAVELLI, *THE PRINCE* (1513)

[from *Harvard Classics*, ed., Charles Eliot (New York: P.F. Collier and Son, 1910)]

Chapter VI

Of New Princedoms which a Prince Acquires with his Own Arms and by Merit

Let no man marvel if in what I am about to say concerning Princedoms wholly new, both as regards the Prince and the form of Government, I cite the highest examples. For since men for the most part follow in the footsteps and imitate the actions of others, and yet are unable to adhere exactly to those paths which others have taken, or attain to the virtues of those whom they would resemble, the wise man should always follow the roads that have been trodden by the great, and imitate those who have most excelled so that if he cannot reach their perfection, he may at least acquire something of its savour. Acting in this like the skillful archer, who seeing that the object he would hit is distant, and knowing the range of his bow, takes aim much above the destined mark; not designing that his arrow should strike so high, but that flying high it may alight at the point intended.

I say, then, that in entirely new Princedoms where the Prince himself is new, the difficulty of maintaining possession varies with the greater or less ability [virtue] of him who acquires possession. And, because the mere fact of a private person rising to be a Prince presupposes either merit [virtue] or good fortune, it will be seen that the presence of one or other of these two conditions lessens, to some extent, many difficulties. And yet, he who is less beholden to Fortune has often in the end the better success; and it may be for the advantage of a Prince that, from his having no other territories, he is obliged to reside in person in the State which he has acquired.

Looking first to those who have become Princes by their merit and not by their good fortune, I say that the most excellent among them are Moses, Cyrus, Romulus, Theseus, and the like. And though perhaps I ought not to name Moses, he being merely an instrument for carrying out the Divine commands, he is still to be admired for those qualities [that grace] which made him worthy to converse with God. But if we consider Cyrus and others who have acquired or founded kingdoms, they will all be seen to be admirable. And if their actions and the particular institutions of which they were the authors be studied, they will be found not to differ from those of Moses, instructed though he was by so great a teacher. Moreover, on examining their lives and actions, we shall see that they were debtors to Fortune for nothing beyond the opportunity which enabled them to shape things as they pleased, without which the force [virtue] of their spirit would have been spent in vain; had the capacity for turning it to account been wanting. It was necessary, therefore, that Moses should find the children of Israel in bondage in Egypt, and oppressed by the Egyptians, in order that they might be disposed to follow him, and so escape from their servitude. It was fortunate for Romulus that he found no home in Alba, but was exposed at the time of his birth, to the end that he might become king and founder of the City of Rome. It was necessary that Cyrus should find the Persians discontented with the rule of the Medes, and the Medes enervated and effeminate from a prolonged peace. Nor could Theseus have displayed his great qualities had he not found the Athenians disunited and dispersed. But while it was their opportunities that made these men fortunate, it was their own merit [virtue] than enabled them to recognize these opportunities and turn them to account, to the glory and prosperity of their country.

They who come to the Princedom, as these did, by virtuous paths, acquire with difficulty, but keep with ease. The difficulties which they have in acquiring arise mainly from the new laws and institutions which they are forced to introduce in founding and securing their government. And let it be noted that there is no more delicate matter to take in hand, nor more dangerous to conduct, nor more doubtful in its success, than to set up as a leader in the introduction of changes. For he who innovates will have for his enemies all those who are well off under the existing order of things, and only lukewarm supporters in those who might be better off under the new. This lukewarm temper arises partly from the fear of adversaries who have the laws on their side, and partly from the incredulity of mankind, who will never admit the merit of anything new, until they have seen it proved by the event. The result, however, is that whenever the enemies of change make an attack, they do so with all the zeal of partisans, while the others defend themselves so feebly as to endanger both themselves and their cause.

But to get a clearer understanding of this part of our subject, we must look whether these innovators can stand alone, or whether they depend for aid upon others; in other words, whether to carry out their ends they must resort to entreaty, or can prevail by force. In the former case they always fare badly and bring nothing to a successful issue; but when they depend upon their own resources and can employ force, they seldom fail. Hence it comes that all armed Prophets have been victorious, and all unarmed Prophets have been destroyed.

For besides what has been said, it should be borne in mind that the temper of the multitude is fickle, and that while it is s easy to persuade them of a thing, it is hard to fix them in that persuasion. Wherefore, matters should be so ordered that when men no longer believe of their own accord, they may be compelled to believe by force. Moses, Cyrus, Theseus, and Romulus could never have made their ordinances be observed for any length of time had they been unarmed, as was the case, in our own days, with the Friar Girolamo Savonarola, whose new institutions came to nothing so soon as the multitude began to waver in their faith; since he had not the means to keep those who had been believers steadfast in their belief, or to make unbelievers believe.

Such persons, therefore, have great difficulty in carrying out their designs; but all their difficulties are on the road, and may be overcome by courage. Having conquered these, and coming to be held in reverence, and having destroyed all who were jealous of their influence, they remain powerful, safe, honoured, and prosperous.

To the great examples cited above, I would add one other, of less note indeed, but assuredly bearing some proportion to them, and which may stand for all others of a like character. I mean the example of Hiero the Syracusan. He from a private station rose to be Prince of Syracuse, and he too was indebted to Fortune only for his opportunity. For the Syracusans being oppressed, chose him to be their Captain, which office he so discharged as deservedly to be made their King. For even while a private citizen his merit was so remarkable that one who writes of him says, he lacked nothing that a King should have save the Kingdom. Doing away with the old army, he organized a new, abandoned existing alliances and assumed new allies, and with an army and allies of his own, was able on that foundation to build what superstructure he pleased; having trouble enough in acquiring, but none in preserving what he had acquired.

Chapter VII

Of New Princedoms Acquired by the Aid of Others and By Good Fortune

They who from a private station become Princes by mere good fortune, do so with little trouble, but have much trouble to maintain themselves. They meet with no hindrance on their way, being carried as it were on wings to their destination, but all their difficulties overtake them when they alight. Of this class are those on whom States are conferred either in return for money, or through the favour of him who confers them; as it happened to many in the Greek cities of Ionia and the Hellespont to be made Princes by Darius, that they might hold these cities for his security and glory; and as happened in the case of those Emperors who, from privacy, attained the Imperial dignity by corrupting the army. Such Princes are wholly dependent on the favour and fortunes of those who have made them great, than which supports none could be less stable or secure; and they lack both the knowledge and the power that would enable them to maintain their position. They lack the knowledge, because unless they have great parts and force of character, it is not to be expected that having always lived in a private station they should have learned how to command. They lack the power, since they cannot look for support from attached and faithful troops. Moreover, States suddenly acquired, like all else that is produced and that grows up rapidly, can never have such root or hold as that the first storm which strikes them shall not overthrow them; unless, indeed, as I have said already, they who thus suddenly become Princes have a capacity for learning quickly how to defend what Fortune has placed in their lap, and can lay these foundations after they rise which by others are laid before.

Of each of these methods of becoming a Prince, namely, by merit [virtue] and by good fortune, I shall select and instance from times within my own recollection, and shall take the cases of Francesco Sforza and Cesare Borgia. By suitable measures and singular ability, Francesco Sforza rose from privacy to be Duke of Milan, preserving with little trouble what it cost him infinite effort to gain. On the other hand, Cesare Borgia, vulgarly spoken of as Duke Valentino, obtained his Princedom through the favorable fortunes of his father, and with these lost it, although, so far as in him lay, he used every effort and practiced every expedient that a prudent and able [virtuous] man should, who desires to strike root in a State given him by the arms and fortune of another. For, as I have already said, he who does not lay his foundations at first, may, if he be of great parts, succeed in laying them afterwards, though with the inconvenience to the builder and risk to the building. And if we consider the various measures taken by Duke Valentino, we shall perceive how broad were the foundations he had laid whereon to rest his future power.

These I think it not superfluous to examine, since I know not what lessons I could teach a new Prince, more useful than the example of his actions. And if the measures taken by him did not profit him in the end, it was through no fault of his, but from the extraordinary and extreme malignity of Fortune.

In this effort to aggrandize the Duke his son, Alexander VI had to face many difficulties, both immediate and remote. In the first place, he saw no way to make him Lord of any State which was not a State of the Church, while, if he sought to take for him a State belonging to the church, he knew that the Duke of Milan and the Venetians would withhold their consent; Faenza and Rimini being already under the protection of the latter. Further, he saw that the arms of Italy, and those most especially of which he might have availed himself, were in the hands of men who had reason to fear his aggrandizement, that is, of the Orsini, the Colonnesi, and their followers. These therefore he could not trust. It was consequently necessary that the existing order of things should be changed, and the States of Italy thrown into confusion, in order that he might safely make himself master of some parts of them; and this became easy for him when he found that the Venetians, moved by other causes, were plotting to bring the French once more into Italy. This design he accordingly did not oppose, but furthered by annulling the first marriage of the French King.

King Louis therefore came into Italy at the instance of the Venetians, and with the consent of Pope Alexander, and no sooner was he in Milan than the Pope got troops from him to aid him in his enterprise against Romagna, which Province, moved by the reputation of the French arms, at once submitted. After thus obtaining possession of Romagna, and after quelling the Colonnesi, Duke Valentino was desirous to follow up and extend his conquests. Two causes, however, held him back, namely, the doubtful fidelity of his own forces, and the waywardness of Frances. For he feared that the Orsini, of whose arms he had made use, might fail him, and not merely prove a hindrance to further acquisitions, but take from him what he had gained, and that the King might serve him the same turn. How little he could count on the Orsini was made plain when, after the capture of Faenza, he turned his arms against Bologna, and saw how reluctantly they took part in that enterprise. The King's mind he understood, when, after seizing on the Dukedom of Urbino, he was about to attack Tuscany; from which designs Louis compelled him to desist. Whereupon the Duke resolved to depend no longer on the arms or fortune of others. His first step, therefore, was to weaken the factions of the Orsini and Colonnesi in Rome. Those of their following who were of good birth, he gained over by making them his own gentlemen, assigning them a liberal provision, and conferring upon them commands and appointments suited to their rank; so that in a few months their old partisan attachments died out, and the hopes of all rested on the Duke alone.

He then awaited an occasion to crush the chiefs of the Orsini, for those of the house of Colonna he had already scattered, and a good opportunity presenting itself, he turned it to the best account. For when the Orsini came at last to see that the greatness of the Duke and the Church involved their ruin, they assembled a council at Magione in the Perugian territory, whence resulted the revolt of Urbino, commotions in Romagna, and an infinity of dangers to the Duke, all of which he overcame with the help of France. His credit thus restored, the Duke trusting no longer either to the French or to any other foreign aid, that he might not have to confront them openly, resorted to stratagem, and was so well able to dissemble his designs, that the Orsini, through the mediation of Signor Paolo (whom he failed not to secure by every friendly attention, furnishing him with clothes, money, and horses), were so won over as to be drawn in their simplicity into his hands at Sinigalia. When the leaders were thus disposed of, their followers made his friends, the Duke had laid sufficiently good foundations for his future power, since he held all Romagna together with the Dukedom of Urbino, and had ingratiated himself with the entire population of these States, who now began to see that they were well off.

And since this part of his conduct merits both attention and imitation, I shall not pass it over in silence. After the Duke had taken Romagna, finding that it had been ruled by feeble Lords, who thought more of plundering than correcting their subjects, and gave them more cause for division than for union, so that the country was overrun with robbery, tumult, and every kind of outrage, he judged it necessary, with a view to render it peaceful and obedient to his authority, to provide it with a good government. Accordingly he set over it Messer Remiro d'Orco, a stern and prompt ruler, who being entrusted with the fullest powers, in a very short time, and with much credit to himself, restored it to tranquility and order. But afterwards apprehending that such unlimited authority might become odious, the Duke decided that it was no longer needed, and established in the center of the Province a civil Tribunal, with an excellent President, in which every town was represented by its advocate. And knowing that past severities had generated ill-felling against himself, in order to purge the minds of the people and gain their good-will, he sought to show them that any cruelty which had been done had not originated with him, but in the harsh disposition of his minister. Availing himself of the pretext which this afforded, he one morning caused Remiro to be beheaded [to be cut in two pieces] and exposed in the market place of Cesena with a block and bloody axe [knife] by his side. The barbarity of which spectacle at once astounded and satisfied the populace.

But, returning to the point whence we diverged, I say that the Duke, finding himself fairly strong and in a measure secured against present dangers, being furnished with arms of his own choosing and having to a great extent got rid of those which, if left near him, might have caused him trouble, had to consider, if he desired to follow up his conquests, how he was to deal with France, since he saw he could expect no further support from King Louis, whose eyes were at last opened to his mistake. He therefore began to look about for new alliances, and to waver in his adherence to the French, then occupied with their expedition into the kingdom of Naples against the Spaniards, at that time laying siege to Gaeta; his object being to secure himself against France; and in this he would soon have succeeded had Alexander lived.

Such was the line he took to meet present exigencies. As regards the future, he had to apprehend that a new Head of the Church might not be his friend, and might even seek to deprive him of what Alexander had given. This he thought to provide against in four ways. First by exterminating all who were of kin to those Lords whom he had despoiled of their possessions, that they might not become instruments in the hands of a new Pope. Second, by gaining over all the Roman nobles, so as to be able with their help to put a bridle, as the saying is, in the Pope's mouth. Third, by bringing the College of Cardinals, so far as he could, under his control. And fourth, by establishing his authority so firmly before his father's death, as to be able by himself to withstand the shock of a first onset.

Of these measures, at the time when Alexander died, he had already effected three, and had almost carried out the fourth. For of the Lords whose possessions he had usurped, he had put to death all whom he could reach, and very few had escaped. He had gained over the Roman nobility, and had the majority in the College of Cardinals on his side.

As to further acquisitions, his design was to make himself master of Tuscany. He was already in possession of Perugia and Piombino, and had assumed the protectorship of Pisa, on which city he was about to spring; taking no heed of France, as indeed he no longer had occasion, since the French had been deprived of the kingdom of Naples by the Spaniards under circumstances which made it necessary for both nations to buy his friendship. Pisa taken, Lucca and Siena would soon have yielded, partly through jealousy of Florence, partly through fear, and the position of the Florentines must then have been desperate.

Had he therefore succeeded in these designs, as he was succeeding in that very year in which Alexander died [1503], he would have won such power and reputations that he might afterwards have stood alone, relying on his own strength and resources, without being beholden to the power and fortune of others. But Alexander died five years from the time he first unsheathed the sword, leaving his son with the State of Romagna alone consolidated, with all the rest unsettled, between two powerful hostile armies, and sick almost to death. And yet such were the fire and courage [virtue] of the Duke, he knew so well how men must either be conciliated or crushed, and so solid were the foundations he had laid in that brief period, that had these armies not been upon his back, or had he been in sound health, he must have surmounted every difficulty.

How strong his foundations were may be seen from this, that Romagna waited for him for more than a month; and that although half dead, he remained in safety in Rome, where though the Baglioni, the Vitelli, and the Orsini came to attack him, they met with no success. Moreover, since he was able if not to make whom he liked Pope, at least to prevent the election of any whom he disliked, had he been in health at the time when Alexander died, all would have been easy for him. But he told me himself on the day on which Julius II was created, that he had foreseen and provided for everything else that could happen on his father's death, but had never anticipated that when his father died he too should be at death's-door.

Taking all these actions of the Duke together, I can find no fault with him; nay, it seems to me reasonable to put him forward, as I have done, as a pattern for all such as rise to power by good fortune and the help [arms] of others. For with his great spirit and high aims he could not act otherwise than he did, and nothing but the shortness of his father's life and his own illness prevented the success of his designs. Whoever, therefore, on entering a new Princedom, judges it necessary to rid himself of enemies, to conciliate friends, to prevail by force or fraud, to make himself feared yet not hated by his subjects, respected and obeyed by his soldiers, to crush those who can or ought to injure him, to introduce changes in the old order of things, to be at once severe and affable, magnanimous and liberal, to do away with a mutinous army and create a new one, to maintain relations with Kings and Princes on such a footing that they must see it for their interest to aid him, and dangerous to offend, can find no brighter example than in the actions of this Prince.

The one thing for which he may be blamed was the creation of Pope Julius II, in respect of whom he chose badly. Because, as I have said already, though he could not secure the election he desired, he could have prevented any other; and he ought never to have consented to the creation of any one of those Cardinals whom he had injured, or who on becoming Pope would have reason to fear him; for fear is as dangerous an enemy as resentment. Those whom he had offended were, among others, San Pietro ad Vincula [Guiliano della Rovere—Julius II], Colonna [Giovanni Colonna], San Giorgio [Raffaelo Riario], and Ascanio [Ascanio Sforza]; all the rest, excepting [Georges] d'Amboise [bishop of Rouen] and the Spanish Cardinals (the latter from their connexion and obligations, the former from the power he derived through his relations with the French Court), would on assuming the Pontificate have had reason to fear him. The Duke, therefore, ought, in the first place, to have laboured for the creation of a Spanish Pope; failing in which, he should have agreed to the election of d'Amboise but never to that of San Pietro ad Vincula. And he deceives himself who believes that with the great, recent benefits cause old wrongs to be forgotten.

The Duke, therefore, erred in the part he took in this election; and his error was the cause of his ultimate downfall.

Chapter VIII

Of Those Who by Their Crimes Come to Be Princes

But since from privacy a man may also rise to be a Prince in one or other of two ways, neither of which can be referred wholly either to merit [virtue] or to fortune, it is fit that I notice them here, though one of them may fall to be discussed more fully in treating of Republics.

The ways I speak of are, first, when the ascent to power is made by paths of wickedness and crime; and second, when a private person becomes ruler of his country by the favour of his fellow-citizens. The former method I shall make clear by two examples, one ancient, the other modern, without entering further into the merits of the matter, for these, I think, should be enough for any one who is driven to follow them.

Agathocles the Sicilian came, not merely from a private station, but from the very dregs of the people, to be King of Syracuse. Son of a potter, through all the stages of his fortunes he led a foul life. His vices, however, were conjoined with so great vigour [virtue] both of the mind and body, that becoming a soldier, he rose through the various grades of the service to be Praetor of Syracuse. Once established in that post, he resolved to make himself Prince, and to hold by violence and without obligation to others the authority which had been spontaneously entrusted to him. Accordingly, after imparting his design to Hamilcar, who with the Carthaginian armies was at that time waging war in Sicily, he one morning assembled the people and senate of Syracuse as though to consult with them on matters of public moment, and on a preconcerted signal caused his soldiers to put to death all the senators and the wealthiest of the commons. These being thus got rid of, he assumed and retained possession of the sovereignty without opposition on the part of the people; and although twice defeated by the Carthaginians, and afterwards besieged, he was able not only to defend his city, but leaving a part of his forces for its protection, to invade Africa with the remainder, and so in short time to raise the siege of Syracuse, reducing the Carthaginians to the utmost extremities, and compelling them to make terms whereby they abandoned Sicily to him and confined themselves to Africa.

Whoever examines this man's actions and achievements will discover little or nothing in them which can be ascribed to Fortune, seeing, as has already been said, that it was not through favour of any, but by the regular steps of the military service, gained at the cost of a thousand hardships and hazards, he reached the princedom which he afterwards maintained by so many daring and dangerous enterprises. Still, to slaughter fellow-citizens, to betray friends, to be devoid of honour, pity, and religion, cannot be counted as merits [virtue], for these are means which may lead to power, but which confer no glory. Wherefore, if in respect of the valour [virtue] with which he encountered and extricated himself from difficulties, and the constancy of his spirit in supporting and conquering adverse fortune, there seems no reason to judge him inferior to the greatest captains that have ever lived, his unbridled cruelty and inhumanity, together with his countless crimes, forbid us to number him with the greatest men; but, at any rate, we cannot attribute to Fortune or to merit [virtue] what he accomplished without either.

In our own times, during the papacy of Alexander VI, Oliverotto of Fermo, who some years before had been left an orphan, and had been brought up by his maternal uncle Giovanni Fogliani, was sent while still a lad to serve under Paolo Vitelli, in the expectation that a thorough training under that commander might qualify him for high rank as a soldier. After the death of Paolo, he served under his brother Vitellozo, and in a very short time, being of a quick wit, hardy and resolute, he became one of the first soldiers of his company. But thinking it beneath him to serve under others, with the countenance of the Vitelleschi and the connivance of certain citizens of Fermo who preferred the slavery to the freedom of their country, he formed the design to seize on that town.

He accordingly wrote to Giovanni Fogliani that after many years of absence from home, he desired to see him and his native city once more, and to look a little into the condition of his patrimony; and as his one endeavour had been to make himself a name, in order that his fellow-citizens might see that his time had not been mis-spent, he proposed to return honourably attended by a hundred horsemen from among his own friends and followers; and he begged Giovanni graciously to arrange for his reception by the citizens of Fermo with corresponding marks of distinction, as this would be creditable not only to himself, but also to the uncle who had brought him up.

Giovanni accordingly, did not fail in any proper attention to his nephew, but caused him to be splendidly received by his fellow-citizens, and lodged him in his house; where Oliverotto having passed some days, and made the necessary arrangements for carrying out his wickedness, gave a formal banquet, to which he invited his uncle and all the first men of Fermo. When the repast and the other entertainments proper to such an occasion had come to an end, Oliverotto artfully turned the conversation to matters of grave interest, by speaking of the greatness of Pope Alexander and Cesare his son, and of their enterprises; and when Giovanni and the others were replying to what he said, he suddenly rose up, observing that these were matters to be discussed in a more private place, and so withdrew to another chamber; whither his uncle and all the other citizens followed him, and where they had no sooner seated themselves, than soldiers rushing out from places of concealment put Giovanni and all the rest to death.

After this butchery, Oliverotto mounted his horse, rode through the streets, and besieged the chief magistrate in the palace, so that all were constrained by fear to yield obedience and accept a government of which he made himself the head. And all who from being disaffected were likely to stand in his way, he put to death, while he strengthened himself with new ordinances, civil and military, to such purpose, that for the space of a year during which he retained the Princedom, he not merely kept a firm hold of the city, but grew formidable to all his neighbours. And it would have been as impossible to unseat him as it was to unseat Agathocles, had he not let himself be overreached by Cesare Borgia on the occasion when, as has already been told, the Orsini and Vitelli were entrapped at Sinigaglia; where he too being taken, one year after the commission of his parricidal crime, was strangled along with Vitellozzo whom he had assumed for his master in villainy as in valour [virtue].

It may be asked how Agathocles and some like him, after numberless acts of treachery and cruelty, have been able to live long in their own country in safety, and to defend themselves from foreign enemies, without being plotted against by their fellow-citizens, whereas, many others, by reason of their cruelty, have failed to maintain their position even in peaceful times, not to speak of the perilous times of war. I believe that this results from cruelty being well or ill employed. Those cruelties we may say are well employed, if it be permitted to speak well of things evil, which are done once for all under the necessity of self-preservation, and are not afterwards persisted in, but so far as possible modified to the advantage of the governed. Ill-employed cruelties, on the other hand, are those which from small beginnings increase rather than diminish with time. They who follow the first of these methods, may, by the grace of God and man, find, as did Agathocles, that their condition is not desperate; but by no possibility can the others maintain themselves.

Hence we may learn the lesson that on seizing a state, the usurper would make haste to inflict what injuries he must, at a stroke, that he may not have to renew them daily, but be enabled by their discontinuance to reassure men's minds, and afterwards win them over by benefits. Whosoever, either through timidity or from following bad counsels, adopts a contrary course, must keep the sword always drawn, and can put no trust in his subjects, who suffering from continued and constantly renewed severities, will never yield him their confidence. Injuries, therefore, should be inflicted all at once, that their ill savour being less lasting may the less offend; whereas, benefits should be conferred little by little, so that they may be more fully relished.

But, before all things, a Prince should so live with his subjects that no vicissitude of good or evil fortune shall oblige him to alter his behaviour; because, if a need to change come through adversity, it is then too late to resort to severity; while any leniency you may use will be thrown away, for it will be seen to be compulsory and gain you no thanks.

Chapter IX

Of the Civil Princedom

I come now to the second case, namely, of the leading citizen who, not by crimes or violence, but by the favour of his fellow-citizens is made Prince of his country. This may be called a Civil Princedom, and its attainment depends not wholly on merit [virtue], nor wholly on good fortune, but rather on what may be termed a fortunate astuteness. I say that the road to this Princedom lies either through the favour of the people or of the nobles. For in every city are to be found these two opposed humours having their origin in this, that the people desire not to be domineered over or oppressed by the nobles, while the nobles desire to oppress and domineer over the people. And from these two contrary appetites there arises in cities one of three results, a Princedom, or Liberty, or License. A Princedom is created either by the people or by the nobles, according as one or other of these factions has occasion for it. For when the nobles perceive that they cannot withstand the people, they set to work to magnify the reputation of one of their number, and make him their Prince, to the end that under his shadow they may be enabled to indulge their desires. The people, on the other hand, when they see that they cannot make head against the nobles, invest a single citizen with all their influence and make him Prince, that they may have the shelter of his authority.

He who is made Prince by the favour of the nobles, has greater difficulty to maintain himself than he who comes to the Princedom by aid of the people, since he finds many about him who think themselves as good as he, and whom, on that account, he cannot guide or govern as he would. But he who reaches the Princedom by the popular support, finds himself alone, with none, or but a very few about him who are not ready to obey. Moreover, the demands of the nobles cannot be satisfied with credit to the Prince, nor without injury to others, while those of the people well may, the aim of the people being more honourable than that of the nobles, the latter seeking to oppress, the former not to be oppressed. Add to this, that a Prince can never secure himself against a disaffected people, their number being too great, while he may against a disaffected nobility, since their number is small. The worst that a Prince need fear from a disaffected people is, that they may desert him, whereas when the nobles are his enemies he has to fear not only that they may desert him, but also that they may turn against him; because, as they have greater craft and foresight, they always choose their time to suit their safety, and seek favour with the side they think will win. Again, a Prince must always live with the same people, but need not always live with the same nobles, being able to make and unmake these from day to day, and give and take away their authority at his pleasure.

But to make this part of the matter clearer, I say that as regards the nobles there is this first distinction to be made. They either so govern their conduct as to bind themselves wholly to your fortunes, or they do not. Those who so bind themselves, and who are not grasping, should be loved and honoured. As to those who do not so bind themselves, there is this further distinction. For the most part they are held back by pusillanimity and a natural defect of courage, in which case you should make use of them, and of those among them more especially who are prudent, for they will do you honour in prosperity, and in adversity give you no cause for fear. But where they abstain from attaching themselves to you of set purpose and for ambitious ends, it is a sign that they are thinking more of themselves than of you, and against such men a Prince should be on his guard, and treat them as though they were declared enemies, for in his adversity they will always help to ruin him.

He who became a Prince through the favour of the people should always keep on good terms with them; which is easy for him to do, since all they ask is not to be oppressed. But he who against the will of the people is made a Prince by the favour of the nobles, must, above all things, seek to conciliate the people, which he readily may by taking them under his protection. For since men who are well treated by one whom they expected to treat them ill, feel more beholden to their benefactor, the people will at once become better disposed to such a Prince when he protects them, than if he owed his Princedom to them.

There are many ways in which a Prince may gain the good-will of the people, but, because these vary with circumstances, no certain rule can be laid down respecting them, and I shall, therefore, say no more about them. But this is the sum of the matter, that it is essential for a Prince to be on a friendly footing with his people, since, otherwise, he will have no resource in adversity. Nabis, Prince of Sparta, was attacked by the whole hosts of Greece, and by a Roman army flushed with victory, and defended his country and crown against them; and when danger approached, there were but few of his subjects against whom he needed to guard himself, whereas had the people been hostile, this would not have been enough.

And what I affirm let no one controvert by citing the old saw that *"he who builds on the people builds on mire,"* for that may be true of a private citizen who presumes on his favour with the people, and counts on being rescued by them when overpowered by his enemies or by the magistrates. In such cases a man may often find himself deceived, as happened to the Gracchi in Rome, and in Florence to Messer Giorgio Scali. But when he who builds on the people is a Prince capable of command, of a spirit not to be cast down by ill-fortune, who, while he animates the whole community by his courage and bearing, neglects no prudent precaution, he will not find himself betrayed by the people, but will be seen to have laid his foundations well.

The most critical juncture for Princedoms of this kind, is at the moment when they are about to pass from the popular to the absolute form of government; and as these Princes exercise their authority either directly or through the agency of the magistrates, in the latter case their position is weaker and more hazardous, since they are wholly in the power of those citizens whom the magistracies are entrusted, who can, and especially in difficult times, with the greatest ease deprive them of their authority, either by opposing, or by not obeying them. And in times of peril it is too late for a Prince to assume to himself an absolute authority, for the citizens and subjects who are accustomed to take their orders from the magistrates, will not when dangers threaten take them from the Prince, so that at such seasons there will always be very few in whom he can trust. Such Princes, therefore, must not build on what they see in tranquil times when the citizens feel the need of the State. For then every one is ready to run, to promise, and, danger of death being remote, even to die for the State. But in troubled times, when the State has need of its citizens, few of them are to be found. And the risk of the experiment is greater in that it can only be made once. Wherefore, a wise Prince should devise means whereby his subjects may at all times, whether favourable or adverse, feel the need of the State and of him, and then they will always be faithful to him.

Chapter XV

Of the Qualities in Respect of Which Men, and Most of All Princes, Are Praised or Blamed

It now remains for us to consider what ought to be the conduct and bearing of a Prince in relation to his subjects and friends. And since I know that many have written on this subject, I fear it may be thought presumptuous in me to write of it also; the more so, because in my treatment of it I depart from the views that others have taken.

But since it is my object to write what shall be useful to whosoever understands it, it seems to me better to follow the real truth of things than an imaginary view of them. For many Republics and Princedoms have been imagined that were never seen or known to exist in reality. And the manner in which we live, and that in which we ought to live, are things so wide asunder, that he who quits the one to betake himself to the other is more likely to destroy than to save himself; since any one who would act up to a perfect standard of goodness in everything, must be ruined among so many who are not good. It is essential, therefore, for a Prince who desires to maintain his position, to have learned how to be other than good, and to use or not to use his goodness as necessity requires.

Laying aside, therefore, all fanciful notions concerning a Prince, and considering those only that are true, I say that all men when they are spoken of, and Princes more than others from their being set so high, are characterized by some one of those qualities which attach either praise or blame. Thus one is accounted liberal, another miserly (which word I use, rather than avaricious, to denote the man who is too sparing of what is his own, avarice being the disposition to take wrongfully what is another's); one is generous, another greedy; one cruel, another tender-hearted; one is faithless, another true to his word; one effeminate and cowardly, another high-spirited and courageous; one is courteous, another haughty; one impure, another chaste; one simple, another crafty; one firm, another facile; one grave, another frivolous; one devout, another unbelieving; and the like. Every one, I know, will admit that it would be most laudable for a Prince to be endowed with all the above qualities that are reckoned good; but since it is impossible for him to possess or constantly practice them all, the conditions of human nature not allowing it, he must be discreet enough to know how to avoid the infamy of those vices that would deprive him of his government, and, if possible, be on his guard also against those which might not deprive him of it; though if he cannot wholly restrain himself, he may with less scruple indulge in the latter. He need never hesitate, however, to incur the reproach of those vices without which his authority can hardly be preserved; for if he well consider the whole matter, he will find that there may be a line of conduct having the appearance of virtue, to follow which would be his ruin, and that there may be another course having the appearance of vice, by following which his safety and well-being are secured.

Chapter XVI

Of Liberality and Miserliness

Beginning, then, with the first of the qualities above noticed, I say that it may be a good thing to be reputed liberal, but, nevertheless, that liberality without the reputation of it is hurtful; because, though it be worthily and rightly used, still if it be not known, you escape not the reproach of its opposite vice. Hence, to have credit for liberality with the world at large, you must neglect no circumstance of sumptuous display; the result being, that a Prince of a liberal disposition will consume his whole substance in things of this sort, and, after all, be obliged, if he would maintain his reputation for liberality, to burden his subjects with extraordinary taxes, and to resort to confiscations and all the other shifts whereby money is raised. But in this way he becomes hateful to his subjects, and growing impoverished is held in little esteem by any. So that in the end, having by his liberality offended many and obliged few, he is worse of than when he began, and is exposed to all his original dangers. Recognizing this, and endeavouring to retrace his steps, he at once incurs the infamy of miserliness.

A Prince, therefore, since he cannot without injury to himself practice the virtue of liberality so that it may be known, will not, if he be wise, greatly concern himself though he be called miserly. Because in time he will come to be regarded as more and more liberal, when it is seen that through his parsimony his revenues are sufficient; that he is able to defend himself against any who make war on him; that he can engage in enterprises against others without burdening his subjects; and thus exercise liberality towards all from whom he does not take, whose number is infinite, while he is miserly in respect of those only to whom he does not give, whose number is few.

In our own days we have seen no Princes accomplish great results save those who have been accounted miserly. All others have been ruined. Pope Julius II, after availing himself of his reputation for liberality to arrive at the Papacy, made no effort to preserve that reputation when making war on the King of France, but carried on all his numerous campaigns without levying from his subjects a single extraordinary tax, providing for the increased expenditure out of his long-continued savings. Had the present King of Spain [Ferdinand] been accounted liberal, he never could have engaged or succeeded in so many enterprises.

A Prince, therefore, if he is enabled thereby to forbear from plundering his subjects, to defend himself, to escape poverty and contempt, and the necessity of becoming rapacious, ought to care little though he incur the reproach of miserliness, for this is one of those vices which enable him to reign.

And should any object that Caesar by his liberality rose to power, and that many others have been advanced to the highest dignities from their having been liberal and so reputed, I reply, 'Either you are already a Prince or you seek to become one; in the former case liberality is hurtful, in the latter it is very necessary that you be thought liberal; Caesar was one of those who sought the sovereignty of Rome; but if after obtaining it he had lived on without retrenching his expenditure, he must have ruined the Empire.' And if it be further urged that many Princes reputed to have been most liberal have achieved great things with their armies, I answer that a Prince spends either what belongs to himself and his subjects, or what belongs to others; and that in the former case he ought to be sparing, but in the latter ought not to refrain from any kind of liberality. Because for a Prince who leads his armies in person and maintains them by plunder, pillage, and forced contributions, dealing as he does with the property of others this liberality is necessary, since otherwise he would not be followed by his soldiers. Of what does not belong to you or to your subjects you should, therefore, be a lavish giver, as were Cyrus, Caesar, and Alexander; for to be liberal with the property of others does not take from your reputation, but adds to it. What injures you is to give away what is your own. And there is no quality so self-destructive as liberality; for while you practice it you lose the means whereby it can be practiced, and become poor and despised, or else, to avoid poverty, you become rapacious and hated. For liberality leads to one or other of these two results, against which, beyond all others, a Prince should guard.

Wherefore it is wiser to put up with the name of being miserly, which breeds ignominy, but without hate, than to be obliged, from the desire to be reckoned liberal, to incur the reproach of rapacity, which breeds hate as well as ignominy.

Chapter XVII

Of Cruelty and Clemency, and Whether It Is Better to Be Loved or Feared

Passing to the other qualities above referred to, I say that every Prince should desire to be accounted merciful and not cruel. Nevertheless, he should be on his guard against the abuse of this quality of mercy. Cesare Borgia was reputed cruel, yet his cruelty restored Romagna, united it, and brought it to order and obedience; so that if we look at things in their true light, it will be seen that he was in reality far more merciful than the prince of Florence, who, to avoid the imputation of cruelty, suffered Pistoja to be torn to pieces by factions.

A Prince should therefore disregard the reproach of being thought cruel where it enables him to keep his subjects united and obedient. For he who quells disorder by a very few signal examples will in the end be more merciful than he who from too great leniency permits things to take their course and so to result in rapine and bloodshed; for these hurt the whole State, whereas the severities of the Prince injure individuals only.

And for a new Prince, of all others, it is impossible to escape a name for cruelty, since new States are full of dangers. Wherefore Virgil, by the mouth of Dido, excuses the harshness of her reign on the plea that it was new, saying:

> 'A fate unkind, and newness in my reign
> Compel me thus to guard a wide domain.'

Nevertheless, the new Prince should not be too ready of belief, nor too easily set in motion; nor should he himself be the first to raise alarms; but should so temper prudence with kindliness that too great confidence in others shall not throw him off his guard, nor groundless distrust render him insupportable.

And here comes in the question whether it is better to be loved rather than feared, or feared rather than loved. It might perhaps be answered that we should wish to be both; but since love and fear can hardly exist together, if we must choose between them, it is far safer to be feared than loved. For of men it may generally be affirmed that they are thankless, fickle, false, studious to avoid danger, greedy of gain, devoted to you while you are able to confer benefits upon them, and ready, as I said before, while danger is distant, to shed their blood, and sacrifice their property, their lives, and their children for you; but in the hour of need they turn against you. The Prince, therefore, who without otherwise securing himself builds wholly on their professions is undone. For the friendships which we buy with a price, and do not gain by greatness and nobility of character, though they be fairly earned are not made good, but fail us when we have occasion to use them.

Moreover, men are less careful how they offend him who makes himself loved than him who makes himself feared. For love is held by the tie of obligation, which, because men are a sorry breed, is broken on every whisper of private interest; but fear is bound by the apprehension of punishment which never relaxes its grasp.

Nevertheless a Prince should inspire fear in such a fashion that if he does not win love he may escape hate. For a man may very well be feared and yet not hated, and this will be the case so long as he does not meddle with the property or with the women of his citizens and subjects. And if constrained to put any to death, he should do so only when there is manifest cause or reasonable justification. But, above all, he must abstain from the property of others. For men will sooner forget the death of their father than the loss of their patrimony. Moreover, pretexts for confiscation are never to seek [lacking], and he who has once begun to live by rapine always finds reasons for taking what is not his; whereas reasons for shedding blood are fewer, and sooner exhausted.

But when a Prince is with his army, and has many soldiers under his command, he must needs disregard the reproach of cruelty, for without such a reputation in its Captain, no army can be held together or kept under any kind of control. Among other things remarkable in Hannibal this has been noted, that having a very great army, made up of men of many different nations and brought to fight in a foreign country, no dissension ever arose among the soldiers themselves, nor any mutiny against their leader, either in his good or in his evil fortunes. This we can only ascribe to the transcendent [inhuman] cruelty, which, joined with numberless great qualities [virtues], rendered him at once venerable and terrible in the eyes of his soldiers; for without this reputation for cruelty these other virtues would not have produced the like results.

Unreflecting writers, indeed, while they praise his achievements, have condemned the chief cause of them; but that his other merits [virtues] would not by themselves have been so efficacious we may see from the case of Scipio, one of the greatest Captains, not of his own time only but of all times of which we have record, whose armies rose against him in Spain from no other cause than his too great leniency in allowing them a freedom inconsistent with military strictness. With which weakness Fabius Maximus taxed him in the Senate House, calling him the corrupter of the Roman soldiery. Again, when the Locrians were shamefully outraged by one of his lieutenants, he neither avenged them, nor punished the insolence of his officer; and this from the natural easiness of his disposition. So that it was said in the Senate by one who sought to excuse him, that there were many who knew better how to refrain from doing wrong themselves than how to correct the wrong-doing of others. This temper, however, must in time have marred the name and fame even of Scipio, had he continued in it, and retained his command. But living as he did under the control of the Senate, this hurtful quality was not merely disguised, but came to be regarded as a glory.

Returning to the question of being loved or feared, I sum up by saying, that since his being loved depends upon his subjects, while his being feared depends upon himself, a wise Prince should build on what is his own, and not on what rests with others. Only, as I have said, he must do his utmost to escape hatred.

Chapter XVIII

How Princes Should Keep Faith

Every one understands how praiseworthy it is in a Prince to keep faith, and to live uprightly and not craftily. Nevertheless, we see from what has taken place in our own days that Princes who have set little store by their word, but have known how to overreach men by their cunning, have accomplished great things, and in the end got the better of those who trusted to honest dealing.

Be it known, then, that there are two ways of contending, one in accordance with the laws, the other by force; the first which is proper to men, the second to beasts. But since the first method is often ineffectual, it becomes necessary to resort to the second. A Prince should, therefore, understand how to use well both the man and the beast. And this lesson has been covertly taught by the ancient writers, who relate how Achilles and many others of the old Princes were given over to be brought up and trained by Chiron the Centaur; since the only meaning of their having for instructor one who was half man and half beast is, that it is necessary for a Prince to know how to use both natures, and that the one without the other has no stability.

But since a Prince should know how to use the beast's nature wisely, he ought of beasts to choose both the lion and the fox; for the lion cannot guard himself from the toils, nor the fox from wolves. He must therefore be a fox to discern toils, and a lion to drive off wolves.

To rely wholly on the lion is unwise; and for this reason a prudent Prince neither can nor ought to keep his word when to keep it is hurtful to him and the causes which lead him to pledge it are removed. If all men were good, this would not be good advice, but since they are dishonest and do not keep faith with you, you, in return, need not keep faith with them; and no prince was ever at a loss for plausible reasons to cloak a breach of faith. Of this numberless recent instances could be given, and it might be shown how many solemn treaties and engagements have been rendered inoperative and idle through want of faith in Princes, and that he who was best known to play the fox has had the best success.

It is necessary, indeed, to put a good colour on this nature, and to be skilful in simulating and dissembling. But men are so simple, and governed so absolutely by their present needs, that he who wishes to deceive will never fail in finding willing dupes. One recent example I will not omit. Pope Alexander VI had no care or thought but how to deceive, and always found material to work on. No man ever had a more effective manner of asseverating, or made promises with more solemn protestations, or observed them less.

It is not essential, then, that a Prince should have all the good qualities which I have enumerated above, but it is most essential that he should seem to have them; I will even venture to affirm that if he has and invariably practices them all, they are hurtful, whereas the appearance of having them is useful. Thus, it is well to seem merciful, faithful, humane, religious, and upright, and also to be so; but the mind should remain so balanced that were it needful not to be so, you should be able and know how to change to the contrary.

And you are to understand that a Prince, and most of all a new Prince, cannot observe all those rules of conduct in respect whereof men are accounted good, being often forced, in order to preserve his Princedom, to act in opposition to good faith, charity, humanity, and religion. And there is no virtue [quality] which it is more necessary for him to seem to possess than this last; because men in general judge rather by the eye than by the hand, for every one can see but few can touch. Every one sees what you seem, but few know what you are, and these few dare not oppose themselves to the opinion of many who have the majesty of the State to back them up.

Moreover, in the actions of all men, and most of all Princes, where there is no tribunal to which we can appeal, we look to results. Wherefore if a Prince succeeds in establishing and maintaining his authority, the means will always be judged honourable and be approved by every one. For the vulgar are always taken by appearances and by results, and the world is made up of the vulgar, the few only finding room when the many have no longer ground to stand on.

A certain Prince of our own days, whose name it is as well not to mention, is always preaching peace and good faith, although the mortal enemy of both; and both, had he practiced them as he preaches them, would, oftener than once, have lost him his kingdom and authority.

Chapter XIX

That a Prince Should Seek to Escape Contempt and Hatred

Having now spoken of the chief of the qualities above referred to, the rest I shall dispose of briefly with these general remarks, that a Prince, as has already in part been said, should consider how he may avoid such courses as would make him hated or despised; and that whenever he succeeds in keeping clear of these, he has performed his part, and runs no risk though he incur other infamies.

A Prince, as I have said before, sooner becomes hated by being rapacious and by interfering with the property and with the women of his subjects, than in any other way. From these, therefore, he should abstain. For so long as neither their property nor their honour is touched, the mass of mankind live contentedly, and the Prince has only to cope with the ambition of a few, which can in many ways and easily be kept within bounds.

A Prince is despised when he is seen to be fickle, frivolous, effeminate, pusillanimous, or irresolute, against which defects he ought therefore most carefully to guard, striving so to bear himself that greatness, courage, wisdom, and strength may appear in all his actions. In his private dealings with his subjects his decisions should be irrevocable, and his reputation such that no one would dream of overreaching or cajoling him.

The Prince who inspires such an opinion of himself is greatly esteemed, and against one who is greatly esteemed conspiracy is difficult; nor, when he is known to be an excellent Prince and held in reverence by his subjects, will it be easy to attack him. For a Prince is exposed to two dangers, from within in respect of his subjects, and from without in respect of foreign powers. Against the latter he will defend himself with good arms and good allies, and if he have good arms he will always have good allies; and when things are settled abroad, they will always be settled at home, unless disturbed by conspiracies; and even should there be hostility from without, if he has taken those measures, and has lived in the way I have recommended, and if he never abandons hope, he will withstand every attack; as I have said was done by Nabis the Spartan.

As regards his own subjects, when affairs are quiet abroad, he has to fear they may engage in secret plots; against which a Prince best secures himself when he escapes being hated or despised, and keeps on good terms with his people; and this, as I have already shown at length, is essential he should do. Not to be hated or despised by the body of his subjects, is one of the surest safeguards that a Prince can have against conspiracy. For he who conspires always reckons on pleasing the people by putting the Prince to death; but when he sees that instead of pleasing he will offend them, he cannot summon courage to carry out his design. For the difficulties that attend conspirators are infinite, and we know from experience that while there have been many conspiracies, few of them have succeeded.

He who conspires cannot do so alone, nor can he assume as his companions any save those whom he believes to be discontented; but so soon as you impart your design to a discontented man, you supply him with the means of removing his discontent, since by betraying you he can procure for himself every advantage; so that seeing on the one hand certain gain, and on the other a doubtful and dangerous risk, he must either be a rare friend to you, or the mortal enemy of his Prince, if he keep your secret.

To put the matter shortly, I say that on the side of the conspirator there are distrust, jealousy, and dread of punishment to deter him, while on the side of the Prince there are the laws, the majesty of the throne, the protection of friends and of the government to defend him; to which if the general goodwill of the people be added, it is hardly possible that any should be rash enough to conspire. For while in ordinary cases, the conspirator has ground for fear only before the execution of his villainy, in this case he has also cause to fear after the crime has been perpetrated, since he has the people for his enemy, and is thus cut off from every hope of shelter.

Of this, endless instances might be given, but I shall content myself with one that happened within the recollection of our fathers. Messer Annibale Bentivoglio, Lord of Bologna and grandfather of the present Messer Annibale, was conspired against and murdered by the Canneschi, leaving behind none belonging to him save Messer Giovanni, then an infant in arms. Immediately upon the murder, the people rose and put all the Canneschi to death. This resulted from the general goodwill with which the House of the Bentivogli was then regarded in Bologna; which feeling was so strong, that when upon the death of Messer Annibale no one was left who could govern the State, there being reason to believe that a descendant of the family (who up to that time had been thought to be the son of a smith), was living in Florence, the citizens of Bologna came there for him, and entrusted him with the government of their city; which he retained until Messer Giovanni was old enough to govern.

To be brief, a Prince has little to fear from conspiracies when his subjects are well disposed towards him; but when they are hostile and hold him in detestation, he has then reason to fear everything and every one. And well ordered States and wise Princes have provided with extreme care that the nobility shall not be driven to desperation, and that the commons shall be satisfied and contented; for this is one of the most important matters that a Prince has to look to.

Among the well ordered and governed Kingdoms of our day is that of France, wherein we find an infinite number of wise institutions, upon which depend the freedom and the security of the King, and of which the most important are the Parliament and its authority. For he who gave constitution to this Realm, knowing the ambition and arrogance of the nobles, and judging it necessary to bridle and restrain them, and on the other hand knowing the hatred, originating in fear, entertained against them by the commons, and desiring that they should be safe, was unwilling that the responsibility for this should rest on the King; and to relieve him of the ill-will which he might incur with the nobles by favouring the commons or with the commons by favouring the nobles, appointed a third party to be arbitrator, who without committing the King, might depress the nobles and uphold the commons. Nor could there be any better, wiser, or surer safeguard for the King and the Kingdom. And hence we may draw another notable lesson, namely, that Princes should devolve on others those matters that entail responsibility, and reserve to themselves those that relate to grace and favour. And again I say that a Prince should esteem the great, but must not make himself odious to the people.

Chapter XXV

What Fortune Can Effect in Human Affairs, and How She May Be Withstood

I am not ignorant that many have been and are of the opinion that human affairs are so governed by Fortune and by God, that men cannot alter them by any prudence of theirs, and indeed, have no remedy against them; and for this reason have come to think that it is not worth while to labour much about anything, but that they must leave everything to be determined by chance.

Often when I turn the matter over, I am in part inclined to agree with this opinion, which has had the readier acceptance in our own times from the great changes in things which we have seen, and every day see happen contrary to all human expectation. Nevertheless, that our free will be not wholly set aside, I think it may be the case that Fortune is the mistress of one half our actions, and yet leaves the control of the other half, or a little less, to ourselves. And I would liken her to one of those wild torrents which, when angry, overflow the plains, sweep away the trees and houses, and carry off soil from one bank to throw it down upon the other. Every one flees before them, and yields to their fury without the least power to resist. And yet, though this be their nature, it does not follow that in seasons of fair weather, men cannot, by constructing weirs and moles [dikes and dams], take such precautions as will cause them when again in flood to pass off by some artificial channel, or at least prevent their course from being so uncontrolled and destructive. And so it is with Fortune, who displays her might where there is no organized strength to resist her, and directs her onset where she knows that there is neither barrier nor embankment to confine her.

And yet if you look at Italy, which has been at once the seat of these changes and their cause, you will perceive that it is a field without embankment or barrier. For if, like Germany, France, and Spain, it had been guarded with sufficient skill, this inundation, if it ever came upon us, would have never wrought the violent changes which we have witnessed.

This I think enough to say generally touching resistance to Fortune. But confining myself more closely to the matter in hand, I note that one day we see a Prince prospering and the next day overthrown, without detecting any change in his nature or character. This, I believe, comes chiefly from a cause already dwelt upon, namely, that a Prince who rests wholly on Fortune is ruined when she changes. Moreover, I believe that he will prosper most whose mode of acting bests adapts itself to the character of the times; and conversely that he will be unprosperous, with whose mode of acting the times do not accord. For we see that men in these matters which lead to the end that each has before him, namely, glory and wealth, proceeded by different ways, one with caution, another with impetuosity, one with violence, another with subtlety, another with patience, another with its contrary; and that by one or other of these different courses each may succeed.

Again, of two who act cautiously, you shall find that one attains his end, the other not, and that two of different temperament, the one cautious, the other impetuous, are equally successful. All which happens from no other cause than that the character of the times accords or does not accord with their methods of acting. And hence it comes, as I have already said, that two operating differently arrive at the same result, and two operating similarly, the one succeeds and the other not. On this likewise depends the vicissitudes of Fortune. For if to one who conducts himself with caution and patience, time and circumstances are propitious, so that his method of acting is good, he goes on prospering; but if these changes he is ruined, because he does not change his method of acting.

For no man is found so prudent as to know how to adapt himself to these changes, both because he cannot deviate from the course to which nature inclines him, and because, having always prospered while adhering to one path, he cannot be persuaded that it would be well for him to forsake it. And so when the occasion requires the cautions man to act impetuously, he cannot do so and is undone; whereas, had he changed his nature with time and circumstances, his fortune would have been unchanged.

Pope Julius II proceeded with impetuosity in all his undertakings, and found time and circumstances in such harmony with his mode of acting that he always obtained a happy result. Witness his first expedition against Bologna, when Messer Giovanni Bentivoglio was yet living. The Venetians were not favourable to the enterprise; nor was the King of Spain. Negotiations respecting it with the King of France were still open. Nevertheless, the Pope with his wonted hardihood and impetuosity marched in person on the expedition, and by this movement brought the King of Spain and the Venetians to a check, the latter through fear, the former from his eagerness to recover the entire Kingdom of Naples; at the same time, he dragged after him the King of France, who, desiring to have the Pope for an ally in humbling the Venetians, on finding him already in motion saw that he could not refuse him his soldiers without openly offending him. By the impetuosity of his movements, therefore, Julius effected what no other Pontiff endowed with the highest human prudence could. For had he, as any other Pope would have done, put off his departure from Rome until terms had been settled and everything duly arranged, he never would have succeeded. For the King of France would have found a thousand pretexts to delay him, and the others would have menaced him with a thousand alarms. I shall not touch upon his other actions, which were all of a like character, and all of which had a happy issue, since the shortness of his life did not allow him to experience reverses. But if times had overtaken him, rendering a cautious line of conduct necessary, his ruin must have ensured, since he never could have departed from those methods to which nature inclined him.

To be brief, I say that since Fortune changes and men stand fixed in their old ways, they are prosperous so long as there is not congruity between them, and the reverve when there is not. Of course, however, I am well persuaded, that it is better to be impetuous than cautious. For Fortune is a woman who to be kept under must be beaten and roughly handled; and we see that she suffers herself to be more readily mastered by those who so treat her than by those who are more timid in their approaches. And always, like a woman, she favours the young, because they are less scrupulous and fiercer, and command her with greater audacity.

MARTIN LUTHER, *ADDRESS TO THE CHRISTIAN NOBILITY OF THE GERMAN NATION RESPECTING THE REFORMATION OF THE CHRISTIAN ESTATE* (1520)

[from *Harvard Classics*, ed., Charles Eliot (New York: P. F. Collier and Son, 1910)]

The Three Walls of the Romanists

The Romanists have, with great adroitness, drawn three walls round themselves, with which they have hitherto protected themselves, so that no one could reform them, whereby all Christendom has fallen terribly. Firstly, if pressed by the temporal power, they have affirmed and maintained that the temporal power has no jurisdiction over them, but, on the contrary, that the spiritual power is above the temporal. Secondly, if it were proposed to admonish them with the Scriptures, they objected that no one may interpret the Scriptures but the Pope. Thirdly, if they are threatened with a council, they pretend that no one may call a council but the Pope.

Thus they have secretly stolen our three rods, so that they may be unpunished, and entrenched themselves behind these three walls, to act with all the wickedness and malice, which we now witness. And whenever they have been compelled to call a council, they have made it of no avail by binding the princes beforehand with an oath to leave them as they were, and to give moreover to the Pope full power over the procedure of the council, so that it is all one whether we have many councils or no councils, in addition to which they deceive us with false pretences and tricks. So grievously do they tremble for their skin before a true free council; and thus they have overawed kings and princes, that these believe they would be offending God, if they were not to obey them in all such knavish, deceitful artifices.

Now may God help us, and give us one of those trumpets that overthrew the walls of Jericho, so that we may blow down these walls of straw and paper, and that we may set free our Christian rods for the chastisement of sin, and expose the craft and deceit of the devil, so that we may amend ourselves by punishment and again obtain God's favour.

(A) THE FIRST WALL

That the Temporal Power has no Jurisdiction over the Spirituality

Let us, in the first place, attack the first wall.

It has been devised that the Pope, bishops, priests, and monks are called the *spiritual estate*, princes, lords, artificers, and peasants are the *temporal estate*. This is an artful lie and hypocritical device, but let no one be made afraid by it, and that for this reason: that all Christians are truly of the spiritual estate, and there is no difference among them, save of office alone. As St. Paul says (I Corinthians 12), we are all one body, though each member does its own work, to serve the others. This is because we have one baptism, one Gospel, one faith, and are all Christians alike; for baptism, Gospel, and faith, these alone make spiritual and Christian people.

As for the unction by a pope or a bishop, tonsure, ordination, consecration, and clothes differing from those of laymen—all this may make a hypocrite or an anointed puppet, but never a Christian or a spiritual man. Thus we are all consecrated as priests by baptism, as St. Peter says: "ye are a royal priesthood, a holy nation" (I Peter 2:9); and in the book of Revelations: "and hast made us unto our God (by Thy blood) kings and priests" (Revelations 5:10). For, if we had not a higher consecration in us than pope or bishop can give, no priest could ever be made by the consecration of pope or bishop, nor could he say the mass, or preach, or absolve. Therefore the bishop's consecration is just as if in the name of the whole congregation he took one person out of the community, each member of which has equal power, and commanded him to exercise this power for the rest; in the same way as if ten brothers, co-heirs as king's sons, were to choose one from among them to rule over their inheritance, they would all of them still remain kings and have equal power, although one is ordered to govern.

And to put the matter even more plainly, if a little company of pious Christian laymen were taken prisoners and carried away to a desert, and had not among them a priest consecrated by a bishop, and were there to agree to elect one of them, born in wedlock or not, and were to order him to baptize, to celebrate the mass, to absolve, and to preach, this man would as truly be a priest, as if all the bishops and all the popes had consecrated him. That is why in cases of necessity every man can baptize and absolve, which would not be possible if we were not all priests. This great grace and virtue of baptism and of the Christian estate they have quite destroyed and made us forget by their ecclesiastical law. In this way the Christians used to choose their bishops and priests out of the community; these being afterwards confirmed by other bishops, without the pomp that now prevails. So was it that St. Augustine, Ambrose, Cyprian, were bishops.

Since, then, the temporal power is baptized as we are, and has the same faith and Gospel, we must allow it to be priest and bishop, and account its office an office that is proper and useful to the Christian community. For whatever issues from baptism may boast that it has been consecrated priest, bishop, and pope, although it does not beseem every one to exercise these offices. For, since we are all priests alike, no man may put himself forward or take upon himself, without our consent and election, to do that which we have all alike power to do. For, if a thing is common to all, no man may take it to himself without the wish and command of the community. And if it should happen that a man were appointed to one of these offices and deposed for abuses, he would be just what he was before. Therefore a priest should be nothing in Christendom but a functionary; as long as he holds his office, he has precedence of others; if he is deprived of it, he is a peasant or a citizen like the rest. Therefore a priest is verily no longer a priest after deposition. But now they have invented *characters indelebiles*,[1] pretend that a priest

---

[1] In accordance with a doctrine of the Roman Catholic Church, the act of ordination impresses upon the priest an indelible character, so that he immutably retains the sacred dignity of priesthood.

after deprivation still differs from a simple layman. They even imagine that a priest can never be anything but a priest—that is, that he can never become a layman. All this is nothing but mere talk and ordinance of human invention.

It follows, then, that between laymen and priests, princes and bishops, or, as they call it, between spiritual and temporal persons, the only real difference is one of office and function, and not of estate; for they are all of the same spiritual estate, true priests, bishops, and popes, though their functions are not the same—just as among priests and monks every man has not the same functions. And this, as I said above, St. Paul says (Romans 12; I Corinthians 12), and St. Peter (I Peter 2): "We, being many, are one body in Christ, and severally members one of another." Christ's body is not double or twofold, one temporal, the other spiritual. He is one Head, and He has one body.

We see, then, that just as those that we call spiritual, or priests, bishops, or popes, do not differ from other Christians in any other or higher degree but in that they are to be concerned with the word of God and the sacraments—that being their work and office—in the same way the temporal authorities hold the sword and the rod in their hands to punish the wicked and to protect the good. A cobbler, a smith, a peasant, every man, has the office and function of his calling, and yet all alike are consecrated priests and bishops, and every man should by his office or function be useful and beneficial to the rest, so that various kinds of work may all be united for the furtherance of body and soul, just as the members of the body all serve one another.

Now see what a Christian doctrine is this: that the temporal authority is not above the clergy, and may not punish it. This is as if one were to say the hand may not help, though the eye is in grievous suffering. Is it not unnatural, not to say unchristian, that one member may not help another, or guard it against harm? Nay, the nobler the member, the more the rest are bound to help it. Therefore I say, Forasmuch as the temporal power has been ordained by God for the punishment of the bad and the protection of the good, therefore we must let it do its duty throughout the whole Christian body, without respect of persons, whether it strikes popes, bishops, priests, monks, nuns or whoever it may be. If it were sufficient reason for fettering the temporal power that it is inferior among the offices of Christianity to the offices of priest or confessor, or to the spiritual estate—if this were so, then we ought to restrain tailors, cobblers, masons, carpenters, cooks, cellarmen, peasants, and all secular workmen, from providing the Pope or bishops, priests and monks, with shoes, clothes, houses or victuals, or from paying them tithes. But if these laymen are allowed to do their work without restraint, what do the Romanist scribes mean by their laws? They mean that they withdraw themselves from the operation of temporal Christian power, simply in order that they may be free to do evil, and thus fulfill what St. Peter said: "There shall be false teachers among you, . . . and in covetousness shall they with feigned words make merchandise of you" (2 Peter 2:1, etc.).

Therefore the temporal Christian power must exercise its office without let or hindrance, without considering whom it may strike, whether pope, or bishop, or priest: whoever is guilty, let him suffer for it.

Whatever the ecclesiastical law has said in opposition to this is merely the invention of Romanist arrogance. For this is what St. Paul says to all Christians: "Let every soul" (I presume including the popes) "be subject unto the higher powers; for they bear not the sword in vain: they serve the Lord therewith, for vengeance on evildoers and for praise to them that do well" (Romans 13:1–4). Also St. Peter: "Submit yourselves to every ordinance of man for the Lord's sake, . . . for so is the will of God" (I Peter 2:13, 15). He has also foretold that men would come who should despise government (2 Peter 2), as has come to pass through ecclesiastical law.

Now, I imagine, the first paper wall is overthrown inasmuch as the temporal power has become a member of the Christian body; although its work relates to the body, yet does it belong to the spiritual estate. Therefore it must do its duty without let or hindrance upon all members of the whole body, to punish or urge, as guilt may deserve, or need may require, without respect of pope, bishops, or priests, let them threaten or excommunicate as they will. That is why a guilty priest is deprived of his priesthood before being given over to the secular arm; whereas this would not be right, if the secular sword had not authority over him already by Divine ordinance.

It is, indeed, past bearing that the spiritual law should esteem so highly the liberty, life, and property of the clergy, as if laymen were not as good spiritual Christians, or not equally members of the Church. Why should your body, life, goods, and honour be free, and not mine, seeing that we are equal as Christians, and have received alike baptism, faith, spirit, and all things? If a priest is killed, the country is laid under an interdict2: why not also if a peasant is killed? Whence comes this great difference among equal Christians? Simply from human laws and inventions.

It can have been no good spirit, either, that devised these evasions and made sin to go unpunished. For if, as Christ and the Apostles bid us, it is our duty to oppose the evil one and all his works and words, and to drive him away as well as may be, how then should we remain quiet and be silent when the Pope and his followers are guilty of devilish works and words? Are we for the sake of men to allow the commandments and the truth of God to be defeated, which at our baptism we vowed to support with body and soul? Truly we should have to answer for all souls that would thus be abandoned and led astray.

Therefore it must have been the arch-devil himself who said, as we read in the ecclesiastical law, If the Pope were so perniciously wicked, as to be dragging souls in crowds to the devil, yet he could not be deposed. This is the accursed and devilish foundation on which they build at Rome, and think that the whole world is to be allowed to go to the devil rather than they should be opposed in their knavery. If a man were to escape punishment simply because he is above the rest, then no Christian might punish

---

2 By the *Interdict*, or general excommunication, whole countries, districts, or towns, or their respective rulers, were deprived of all the spiritual benefits of the Church, such as Divine service, the administering of the sacraments, etc.

another, since Christ has commanded each of us to esteem himself the lowest and the humblest (St. Matthew 18:4; St. Luke 9:48).

Where there is sin, there remains no avoiding the punishment, as St. Gregory says, We are all equal, but guilt makes one subject to another. Now let us see how they deal with Christendom. They arrogate to themselves immunities without any warrant from the Scriptures, out of their own wickedness, whereas God and the Apostles made them subject to the secular sword; so that we must fear that it is the work of antichrist, or a sign of his near approach.

(B) THE SECOND WALL

That no one may interpret the Scriptures but the Pope

The second wall is even more tottering and weak; that they alone pretend to be considered masters of the Scriptures; although they learn nothing of them all their life. They assume authority, and juggle before us with impudent words, saying that the Pope cannot err in matters of faith, whether he be evil or good, albeit they cannot prove it by a single letter. That is why the canon law contains so many heretical and unchristian, nay unnatural, laws; but of these we need not speak now. For whereas they imagine the Holy Ghost never leaves them, however unlearned and wicked they may be, they grow bold enough to decree whatever they like. But were this true, where were the need and use of the Holy Scriptures? Let us burn them, and content ourselves with the unlearned gentlemen at Rome, in whom the Holy Ghost dwells, who, however, can dwell in pious souls only. If I had not read it, I could never have believed that the devil should have put forth such follies at Rome and find a following.

But not to fight them with our own words, we will quote the Scriptures. St. Paul says, "If anything be revealed to another that sitteth by, let the first hold his peace " (I Corinthians 14:30). What would be the use of this commandment, if we were to believe him alone that teaches or has the highest seat? Christ Himself says, "And they shall be all taught of God." (St. John 6:45). Thus it may come to pass that the Pope and his followers are wicked and not true Christians, and not being taught by God, have no true understanding, whereas a common man may have true understanding. Why should we then not follow him? Has not the Pope often erred? Who could help Christianity, in case the Pope errs, if we do not rather believe another who has the Scriptures for him?

Therefore it is a wickedly devised fable—and they cannot quote a single letter to confirm it—that it is for the Pope alone to interpret the Scriptures or to confirm the interpretation of them. They have assumed the authority of their own selves. And though they say that this authority was given to St. Peter when the keys were given to him, it is plain enough that the keys were not given to St. Peter alone, but to the whole community. Besides, the keys were not ordained for doctrine or authority, but for sin, to bind or loose; and what they claim besides this from the keys is mere invention. But what Christ said to St. Peter: "I have prayed for thee that thy faith fail not" (St. Luke 22:32), cannot relate to the Pope, inasmuch as the greater part of the Popes have been without faith, as they are themselves forced to acknowledge; nor did Christ pray for Peter alone, but for all the Apostles and all

Christians, as He says, "Neither pray I for these alone, but for them also which shall believe on Me through their word" (St. John 17). Is not this plain enough?

Only consider the matter. They must needs acknowledge that there are pious Christians among us that have the true faith, spirit, understanding, word, and mind of Christ: why then should we reject their word and understanding, and follow a pope who has neither understanding nor spirit? Surely this were to deny our whole faith and the Christian Church. Moreover, if the article of our faith is right, "I believe in the holy Christian Church," the Pope cannot alone be right; else we must say, "I believe in the Pope of Rome," and reduce the Christian Church to one man, which is a devilish and damnable heresy. Besides that, we are all priests, as I have said, and have all one faith, one Gospel, one Sacrament; how then should we not have the power of faith? What becomes of St. Paul's words, "But he that is spiritual judgeth all things, yet he himself is judged of no man" (I Corinthians 2:15), and also, "we having the same spirit of faith"? (2 Corinthians 4:13). Why then should we not perceive as well as an unbelieving pope what agrees or disagrees with our faith?

By these and many other texts we should gain courage and freedom, and should not let the spirit of liberty (as St. Paul has it) be frightened away by the inventions of the popes; we should boldly judge what they do and what they leave undone by our own believing understanding of the Scriptures, and force them to follow the better understanding, and not their own. Did not Abraham in old days have to obey his Sarah, who was in stricter bondage to him than we are to any one on earth? Thus, too, Balaam's ass was wiser than the prophet. If God spoke by an ass against a prophet, why should He not speak by a pious man against the Pope? Besides, St. Paul withstood St. Peter as being in error (Galatians 2). Therefore it behooves every Christian to aid the faith by understanding and defending it and by condemning all errors.

(C) THE THIRD WALL

That no one may call a council but the Pope

The third wall falls of itself, as soon as the first two have fallen; for if the Pope acts contrary to the Scriptures, we are bound to stand by the Scriptures, to punish and to constrain him, according to Christ's commandment, "Moreover, if thy brother shall trespass against thee, go and tell him his fault between thee and him alone; if he shall hear thee, thou hast gained thy brother. But if he will not hear thee, then take with thee one or two more, that in the mouth of two or three witnesses every word may be established. And if he shall neglect to hear them, tell it unto the Church; but if he neglect to hear the Church, let him be unto thee as a heathen man and a publican" (St. Matthew 18:15–17). Here each member is commanded to take care for the other; much more then should we do this, if it is a ruling member of the community that does evil, which by its evil-doing causes great harm and offence to the others. If then I am to accuse him before the Church, I must collect the Church together. Moreover, they can show nothing in the Scriptures giving the Pope sole power to call and confirm councils; they have nothing but their own laws; but these hold good only so long as they are not injurious to Christianity and the laws of God. Therefore, if the Pope deserves punishment, these laws cease to bind us, since Christendom would suffer, if he were not punished by a council. Thus we read (Acts 15) that the council of the Apostles was not called by St. Peter, but by all the Apostles and the elders. But if the right to call it had lain with St. Peter alone, it would not have been a Christian council, but a heretical *conciliabulum*. Moreover, the most celebrated council of all—that of Nicaea—was neither called nor confirmed by the Bishop of Rome, but by the Emperor Constantine; and after him many other emperors have done the same, and yet the councils called by them were accounted most Christian. But if the Pope alone had the power, they must all have been heretical. Moreover, if I consider the councils that the Pope has called, I do not find that they produced any notable results.

Therefore when need requires, and the Pope is a cause of offence to Christendom, in these cases whoever can best do so, as a faithful member of the whole body, must do what he can to procure a true free council. This no one can do so well as the temporal authorities, especially since they are fellow-Christians, fellow-priests, sharing one spirit and one power in all things, and since they should exercise the office that they have received from God without hindrance, whenever it is necessary and useful that it should be exercised. Would it not be most unnatural, if a fire were to break out in a city, and every one were to keep still and let it burn on and on, whatever might be burnt, simply because they had not the mayor's authority, or because the fire perchance broke out at the mayor 's house? Is not every citizen bound in this case to rouse and call in the rest? How much more should this be done in the spiritual city of Christ, if a fire of offence breaks out, either at the Pope's government or wherever it may! The like happens if an enemy attacks a town. The first to rouse up the rest earns glory and thanks. Why then should not he earn glory that descries the coming of our enemies from hell and rouses and summons all Christians?

But as for their boasts of their authority, that no one must oppose it, this is idle talk. No one in Christendom has any authority to do harm, or to forbid others to prevent harm being done. There is no authority in the Church but for reformation. Therefore if the Pope wished to use his power to prevent the calling of a free council, so as to prevent the reformation of the Church, we must not respect him or his power; and if he should begin to excommunicate and fulminate, we must despise this as the doings of a madman, and, trusting in God, excommunicate and repel him as best we may. For this his usurped power is nothing; he does not possess it, and he is at once overthrown by a text from the Scriptures. For St. Paul says to the Corinthians "that God has given us authority for edification, and not for destruction" (2 Corinthians 10:8). Who will set this text at nought? It is the power of the devil and of antichrist that prevents what would serve for the reformation of Christendom. Therefore we must not follow it, but oppose it with our body, our goods, and all that we have. And even if a miracle were to happen in favour of the Pope against the temporal power, or if some were to be stricken by a plague, as they sometimes boast has happened, all this is to be held as having been done by the devil in order to injure our faith in God, as was foretold by Christ: "There shall arise false Christs and false prophets, and shall show great signs and wonders, insomuch that, if it were possible, they shall deceive the very elect" (St. Matthew 24:23); and St. Paul tells the Thessalonians that the coming of antichrist shall be "after the working of Satan with all power and signs and lying wonders" (2 Thesselonians 2:9).

Therefore let us hold fast to this: that Christian power can do nothing against Christ, as St. Paul says, "For we can do nothing against Christ, but for Christ" (2 Corinthians 13:8). But, if it does anything against Christ, it is the power of antichrist and the devil, even if it rained and hailed wonders and plagues. Wonders and plagues prove nothing, especially in these latter evil days, of which false wonders are foretold in all the Scriptures. Therefore we must hold fast to the words of God with an assured faith; then the devil will soon cease his wonders.

And now I hope the false, lying spectre will be laid with which the Romanists have long terrified and stupefied our consciences. And it will be seen that, like all the rest of us, they are subject to the temporal sword; that they have no authority to interpret the Scriptures by force without skill; and that they have no power to prevent a council, or to pledge it in accordance with their pleasure, or to bind it beforehand, and deprive it of its freedom; and that if they do this, they are verily of the fellowship of antichrist and the devil, and have nothing of Christ but the name.

MARTIN LUTHER, *ON THE BABYLONIAN CAPTIVITY OF THE CHURCH* (1520)

[from *Luther's Primary Works*, eds., Henry Wace and C. A. Buchheim (Philadelphia: Lutheran Publication Society, 1885)]

On the Lord's Supper

The third bondage of this same sacrament in that abuse of it—and by far the most impious—by which it has come about that at this day there is no belief in the Church more generally received or more firmly held than that the mass is a good work and a sacrifice. This abuse has brought in an infinite flood of other abuses, until faith in the sacrament has been utterly lost, and they have made this divine sacrament a mere subject of traffic, huckstering, and money-getting contracts. Hence communions, brotherhoods, suffrages, merits, anniversaries, memorials, and other things of that kind are bought and sold in the Church, and made the subjects of bargains and agreements; and the entire maintenance of priests and monks depends upon these things. . . .

Concerning the Sacrament of the Altar. To begin,—if we wish to attain safely and prosperously to the true and free knowledge of this sacrament, we must take the utmost care to put aside all that has been added by the zeal or the notions of men to the primitive and simple institution; such as vestments, ornaments, hymns, prayers, musical instruments, lamps, and all the pomp of visible things; and must turn our eyes and our attention only to the pure institution of Christ; and set nothing else before us but those very words of Christ, with which He instituted and perfected that sacrament, and committed it to us. In that word, and absolutely in nothing else, lies the whole force, nature, and substance of the mass. All the rest are human notions, accessory to the word of Christ; and the mass can perfectly well subsist and be kept up without them. Now the words in which Christ instituted this sacrament are as follows:—While they were at supper Jesus took bread, and blessed it, and broke it, and gave it to His disciplines, and said: "Take, eat; this is my body which is given for you." And He took the cup, and gave thanks, and gave it to them, saying: "Drink ye all of this; this cup is the New Testament in my blood, which is shed for you and for many for the remission of sins; do this in remembrance of me" . . . .

Let this then stand as a first and infallible truth, that the mass or Sacrament of the Altar is the testament of Christ, which He left behind Him at His death, distributing an inheritance to those who believe in Him. For such are His words: "This cup is the new testament in my blood." Let this truth, I say, stand as an immovable foundation, on which we shall erect all our arguments. You will see how we shall thus overthrow all the impious attacks of men on this sweetest sacrament. The truthful Christ, then, says with truth, that this is the new testament in His blood, shed for us. It is not without cause that I urge this; the matter is no small one, but must be received into the depths of our minds.

If then we enquire what a testament is, we shall also learn what the mass is; what are its uses, advantages, abuses. A testament is certainly a promise made by a man about to die, by which he assigns his inheritance and appoints heirs. Thus the idea of a testament implies, first, the death of the testator, and secondly, the promise of the inheritance, and the appointment of an heir. In this way Paul (Romans 4; Galatians 3, 4; Hebrews 9) speaks at some length of testaments. We also see this clearly in those words of Christ. Christ testifies of His own death, when he says: "This is my body which is given; this is my blood which is shed." He assigns and points out the inheritance, when He says: "For the remission of sins." And He appoints heirs when He says: "For you and for many;" that is, for those who accept and believe the promise of the testator; for it is faith which makes us heirs, as we shall see.

You see then that the mass—as we call it—is a promise of the remission of sins, made to us by God; and such a promise as has been confirmed by the death of the Son of God. For a promise and a testament only differ in this, that a testament implies the death of the promiser. A testator is a promiser who is about to die; and a promiser is, so to speak, a testator who is about to live. This testament of Christ was prefigured in all the promises of God from the beginning of the world; yea! whatsoever value the ancient promises had, lay in that new promise which was about to be made in Christ, and on which they depended. Hence the words, "agreement, covenant, testament of the Lord," are constantly employed in the Scriptures; and by these it was implied that God was about to die. "For where a testament is, there must also of necessity be the death of the testator." (Hebrews 9:16) God having made a testament, it was necessary that He should die. Now He could not die, unless He became a man; and thus in this one word "testament" the incarnation and the death of Christ are both comprehended.

From all this it is now self-evident what is the use, and what the abuse, of the mass; what is a worthy or an unworthy preparation for it. If the mass is a promise, as we have said, we can approach to it by no works, no strength, no merits, but by faith alone. For where we have the word of God who promises, there we must have faith on the part of man who accepts; and it is thus clear that the beginning of our salvation is faith, depending on the word of a promising God, who, independently of any efforts of ours, preserves us by His free and undeserved mercy, and holds out to us the word of His promise. "He sent His word and healed them." (Psalm 107:20.) He did not receive our works and so save us. First of all comes the word of God; this is followed by faith, and faith by love, which in its turn does every good work, because it worketh no evil, yea, it is the fulfilling of the law. There is no other way in which man can meet or deal with God but by faith. It is not man by any works of his, but God, who by His own promise is the author of salvation; so that everything depends, is contained, and preserved in the word of His power, by which He begot us, that we might be a kind of first-fruits of His creation.

Thus, when Adam was to be raised up after the fall, God gave him a promise, saying to the serpent: "I will place enmity between thee and the woman, and between thy seed and her seed; she shall bruise thy head, and thou shalt bruise her heel." In this word of promise, Adam with his posterity was, as it were, borne in the bosom of God, and preserved by faith in Him; waiting patiently for the woman who should bruise the head of the serpent, as God had promised. In this faith and waiting he died; not knowing when and how the promise would be accomplished, but not doubting that it would be accomplished. For such a promise, being the truth of God, preserves even in hell those who believe and wait for it. This promise was followed by another, made to Noah; the bow in the cloud being given as a sign of the covenant, believing in which he and his posterity found God propitious. After this, God promised to Abraham that in his seed all the kindreds of the earth should be blessed. This is that bosom of Abraham into which his posterity have been received. Lastly to Moses, and to the children of Israel, especially to David, God gave a most distinct promise of Christ; and thus at length revealed what had been the meaning of the promise made to them of old time.

Thus we come to the most perfect promise of all, that of the new Testament, in which life and salvation are freely promised in plain words, and are bestowed on those who believe the promise. Christ conspicuously distinguishes this testament from the old one, by calling it the " New Testament." The old testament given by Moses was a promise, not of remission of sins, nor of eternal blessings, but of temporal ones, namely, those of the land of Canaan; and by it no one could be renewed in spirit, and fitted to receive a heavenly inheritance. Hence it was necessary that, as a figure of Christ, an unreasoning lamb should be slain, in the blood of which the same testament was confirmed; thus, as is the blood, so is the testament; as is the victim, so is the promise. Now Christ says, "The new testament in my blood," not in another's, but in His own blood, by which grace is promised through the Spirit for the remission of sins, that we may receive the inheritance.

The mass then, as regards its substance, is properly nothing else than the aforesaid words of Christ, " Take, eat," etc. He seems to say:—"Behold, O man, sinner and condemned as thou art, out of the pure and free love with which I love thee, according to the will of the Father of mercies, I promise to thee in these words, antecedently to any merits or prayers of thine, remission of all thy sins, and eternal life. That thou mayest be most certain of this, my irrevocable promise, I will confirm it by my very death; I will give my body and shed my blood, and will leave both to thee, as a sign and memorial of this very promise. As often as thou shalt receive them, remember me; declare and praise my love and bounty to thee; and give thanks."

From this you see that nothing else is required for a worthy reception of the mass than faith, resting with confidence on this promise, believing Christ to be truthful in these words of His, and not doubting that these immeasurable blessings have been bestowed upon us. On this faith a spontaneous and most sweet affection of the heart will speedily follow, by which the spirit of the man is enlarged and enriched; that is, love, bestowed through the Holy Spirit on believers in Christ. Thus the believer is carried away to Christ, that bounteous and beneficent testator, and becomes altogether another and a new man. Who would not weep tears of delight, nay, almost die for joy in Christ, if he believed with unhesitating faith that this inestimable promise of Christ belongs to him? How can he fail to love such a benefactor, who of His own accord offers, promises, and gives the greatest riches and an eternal inheritance to an unworthy sinner, who has deserved very different treatment?

Our one great misery is this, that while we have many masses in the world, few or none of us recognise, consider, or apprehend the rich promises set before us in them. Now in the mass the one thing that demands our greatest, nay, our sole attention, is to keep these words and promises of Christ, which indeed constitute the mass itself, constantly before our eyes; that we should meditate on and digest them, and exercise, nourish, increase, and strengthen our faith in them by this daily commemoration. This is what Christ commands when He says, "Do this in remembrance of me." It is the work of an evangelist faithfully to present and commend that promise to the people and to call forth faith in it on their part. As it is—to say nothing of the impious fables of those who teach human traditions in the place of this great promise—how many are there who know that the mass is a promise of Christ? Even if they teach these words of Christ, they do not teach them as conveying a promise or a testament, and therefore call forth no faith in them . . . .

God (as I have said) never has dealt, or does deal, with men otherwise than by the word of promise. Again, we can never deal with God otherwise than by faith in the word of His promise. He takes no heed of our works, and has no need of them,—though it is by these we deal with other men and with ourselves;—but He does require to be esteemed by us truthful in His promises, and to be patiently considered as such, and thus worshipped in faith, hope, and love. And thus it is that He is glorified in us, when we receive and hold every blessing not by our own efforts, but from His mercy, promise, and gift. This is that true worship and service of God, which we are bound to render in the mass. But when the words of the promise are not delivered to us, what exercise of faith can there be? And without faith who can hope? who can love? without faith, hope, and love, what service can there be? There is no doubt therefore that, at the present day, the whole body of priests and monks, with their bishops and all their superiors, are idolaters, and living in a most perilous state, through their ignorance, abuse, and mockery of the mass, or sacrament, or promise of God.

It is easy for any one to understand that two things are necessary at the same time, the promise and faith. Without a promise we have nothing to believe; while without faith the promise is useless, since it is through faith that it is established and fulfilled. Whence we easily conclude that the mass, being nothing else than a promise, can be approached and partaken of by faith alone; without which whatever prayers, preparations, works, signs, or gestures are practised, are rather provocations to impiety than acts of piety. It constantly happens that when men have given their attention to all these things they imagine that they are approaching the altar lawfully; and yet, in reality, could never be more unfit to approach it, because of the unbelief which they bring with them. What a number of sacrificing priests you may daily see everywhere, who if they have committed some trifling error, by unsuitable vestments, or unwashed hands, or by some hesitation in the prayers, are wretched, and think themselves guilty of an immense crime! Meanwhile, as for the mass itself, that is, the divine promise, they neither heed nor believe it; yea, are utterly unconscious of its existence. O, unworthy religion of our age, the most impious and ungrateful of all ages!

There is then no worthy preparation for the mass, or rightful use of it, except faith, by which it is believed in as a divine promise. Wherefore let him who is about to approach the altar, or to receive the sacrament, take care not to appear before the Lord his God empty. Now he will be empty, if he has not faith in the mass, or New Testament; and what more grievous impiety can he commit against the truth of God than by this unbelief? As far as in him lies, he makes God a liar, and renders His promises idle. It will be safest then to go to the mass in no other spirit than that in which thou wouldst go to hear any other promise of God; that is, to be prepared, not to do many works, and bring many gifts, but to believe and receive all that is promised thee in that ordinance, or is declared to thee through the ministry of the priest as promised. Unless thou comest in this spirit, beware of drawing near; for thou wilt surely draw near unto judgment.

I have rightly said then, that the whole virtue of the mass consists in those words of Christ, in which He testifies that remission is granted to all who believe that His body is given and His blood shed for them. There is nothing then more necessary for those who are about to hear mass than to mediate earnestly and with full faith on the very words of Christ; for unless they do this, all else is done in vain. It is certainly true that God has ever been wont, in all His promises, to give some sign, token, or memorial of His promise; that it might be kept more faithfully and tell more strongly on men' s minds. Thus when He promised to Noah that the earth should not be destroyed by another deluge, He gave His bow in the cloud, and said that He would thus remember His covenant. To Abraham, when He promised that his seed should inherit the earth, He gave circumcision as a seal of the righteousness which is by faith. Thus to Gideon He gave the dry and the dewy fleece, to confirm His promise of victory over the Midianites. Thus to Ahaz He gave a sign through Isaiah, to confirm his faith in the promise of victory over the kings of Syria and Samaria. We read in the Scriptures of many such signs of the promises of God.

So too in the mass, that first of all promises, He gave a sign in memory of so great a promise, namely, His own body and His own blood in the bread and wine, saying, "Do this is remembrance of me." Thus in baptism He adds to the words of the promise the sign of immersion in water. Whence we see that in every promise of God two things are set before us, the word and the sign. The word we are to understand as being the testament, and the sign as being the sacrament; thus, in the mass, the word of Christ is the testament, the bread and wine are the sacrament. And as there is greater power in the word than in the sign, so is there greater power in the testament than in the sacrament. A man can have and use the word or testament without the sign or sacrament. "Believe," saith Augustine, "and thou hast eaten;" but in what do we believe except in the word of Him who promises? Thus I can have the mass daily, nay hourly; since, as often as I will, I can set before myself the words of Christ, and nourish and strengthen my faith in them; and this is in very truth the spiritual eating and drinking . . . .

There are two difficulties which are wont to beset us, and prevent our receiving the benefits of the mass. The one is, that we are sinners and unworthy, from our utter vileness, of such great blessings. The other is—even if we were worthy—the very greatness of the blessings themselves, which are such that weak nature cannot dare to seek or hope for them. Who would not be struck in the first place with amazement rather than with the desire for the remission of sins and eternal life, if he rightly estimates the greatness of the blessings which come through these—namely, the having God as his Father, and being a child of God, and heir of all good things? To meet this double weakness of nature, thou must take hold of the word of Christ, and fix thine eyes much more strongly on it, than on these cogitations of thine own infirmity. For the works of the Lord are great, and He is mighty to give, beyond all that we can seek or comprehend. Indeed, unless His works surpassed our worthiness, our capacity, our whole comprehension, they would not be divine. Thus too Christ encourages us, saying: "Fear not, little flock; for it is your Father's good pleasure to give you the kingdom." (Luke 12:32.) This incomprehensible exuberance of God's mercy, poured out on us through Christ, makes us, in our turn, to love Him above all things, to cast ourselves upon Him with the most perfect trust, to despise all things, and be ready to suffer all things for Him. Hence this sacrament has been rightly called the fountain of love.

Here we may draw an example from human affairs. If some very rich lord were to bequeath a thousand pieces of gold to any beggar, or even to an unworthy and bad servant, such a one would certainly demand and receive them confidently, without regard either to his own unworthiness or to the greatness of the legacy. If any one were to set these before him as objections, what do you think he would reply? He would certainly answer: "What is that to you? It is not by my deserving, nor by any right of my own, that I receive what I do receive. I know that I am unworthy of it, and that I am receiving much more than I deserve; nay, I have deserved the very contrary. But what I claim, I claim by right of a testament, and of the goodness of another; if it was not an unworthy act to leave such a legacy to me who am so unworthy, why should my unworthiness make me hesitate to accept it? Nay, the more unworthy I am, the more readily do I embrace this free favour from another." With such reasonings we must arm our own consciences against all their scruples and anxieties, that we may hold this promise of Christ with unhesitating faith. We must give the utmost heed not to approach in any confidence in our own confessions, prayers, and preparations; we must despair of all these and come in a lofty confidence in the promise of Christ—since it is the word of promise which alone must reign here—and in pure faith, which is the one and sole sufficient preparation.

We see from all this, how great the wrath of God has been which has permitted our impious teachers to conceal from us the words of this testament, and thus, as far as in them lay, to extinguish faith itself. It is self-evident what must necessarily follow this extinction of faith, namely, the most impious superstitions about works. For when faith perishes and the word of faith is silent, then straightway works, and traditions of works, rise up in its place. By these we have been removed from our own land, as into bondage at Babylon, and all that was dear to us has been taken from us. Even thus it has befallen us with the mass, which, through the teaching of wicked men, has been changed into a good work, which they call *opus operatum*, and by which they imagine that they are all powerful with God. Hence they have gone to the extreme of madness; and, having first falsely affirmed that the mass is of avail through the force of the *opus operatum*, they have gone on to say, that even if it be hurtful to him who offers it impiously, yet it is none the less useful to others. On this basis they have established their applications, participations, fraternities, anniversaries, and an infinity of lucrative and gainful business of that kind.

You will scarcely be able to stand against these errors, many and strong as they are, and deeply as they have penetrated, unless you fix what has been said firmly in your memory, and give the most steadfast heed to the true nature of the mass. You have heard that the mass is nothing else than the divine promise or testament of Christ, commended to us by the sacrament of His body and blood. If this is true, you will see that it cannot in any way be *a work*, nor can any work be performed in it, nor can it be handled in any way but by faith alone. Now faith is not a work, but the mistress and life of all works. Is there any man so senseless as to call a promise he has received, or a legacy that has been bestowed on him, a good work done on his part towards the testator? What heir is there, who thinks that he is doing a service to his father when he receives the testamentary documents along with the inheritance bequeathed to him? Whence then this impious rashness of ours, that we come to receive the testament of God as if we were doing a good work towards Him? Is not such ignorance of that testament, and such a state of bondage of that great sacrament, a grief beyond all tears? Where we ought to be grateful for blessings bestowed on us, we come in our pride to give what we ought to receive, and make a mockery, with unheard-of perversity, of the mercy of the Giver. We give to Him as a work of ours what we receive as a gift from Him; and we thus make the testator no longer the bestower of His good gifts on us, but the receiver of ours. Alas for such impiety!

Who has ever been so senseless as to consider baptism a good work? What candidate for baptism has ever believed he was doing a work which he might offer to God on behalf of himself and others? If then in one sacrament and testament there is no good work communicable to others, neither can there be any in the mass, which is itself nothing but a testament and a sacrament. Hence it is a manifest and impious error, to offer or apply the mass for sins, for satisfactions, for the dead, or for any necessities of our own or of others. The evident truth of this statement you will easily understand, if you keep closely to the fact, that the mass is a divine promise, which can profit no one, be applied to no one, be communicated to no one, except to the believer himself; and that solely by his own faith. Who can possibly receive or apply for another a promise of God, which requires faith on the part of each individual? Can I give another man the promise of God, if he does not believe it? or can I believe for another man? or can I make another believe? Yet all this I must be able to do if I can apply and communicate the mass to others; for there are in the mass only these two things, God's promise, and man's faith which receives that promise. If I can do all this, I can also hear and believe the gospel on behalf of other men, I can be baptized for another man, I can be absolved from sin for another man, I can partake of the Sacrament of the Altar for another man; nay, to go through the whole list of their sacraments, I can also marry for another man, be ordained priest for another man, be confirmed for another man, receive extreme unction for another man.

Why did not Abraham believe on behalf of all the Jews? Why was every individual Jew required to exercise faith in the same promise which Abraham believed? Let us keep to this impregnable truth;—where there is a divine promise, there every man stands for himself; individual faith is required; every man shall give account for himself, and shall bear his own burdens; as Christ says: "He that believeth and is baptized shall be saved; but he that believeth not shall be damned." (Mark 16:16.) Thus every man can make the mass useful only to himself, by his own faith, and can by no means communicate it to others; just as a priest cannot administer a sacrament to any man on behalf of another, but administers the same sacrament to each individual separately. The priests in their work of consecration and administration act as ministers for us; not that we offer up any good work through them, or communicate actively; but by their means we receive the promise and its sign, and communicate passively. This idea continues among the laity; for they are not said to do a good work, but to receive a gift. But the priests have gone after their own impieties and have made it a good work that they communicate and make an offering out of the sacrament and testament of God, whereas they ought to have received it as a good gift . . . .

This I readily admit, that the prayers which we pour forth in the presence of God, when we meet to partake of the mass, are good works or benefits, which we mutually impart, apply, and communicate, and offer up for one another; as the Apostle James teaches us to pray for one another and that we may be saved. Paul also exhorts that supplications, prayers, intercessions, and giving of thanks, be made for all men; for kings, and for all that are in authority. (1 Timothy 2:1, 2.) These things are not the mass, but works of the mass;—if, indeed, we can call the prayers of our hearts and our lips works—because they spring from the existence and growth of faith in the sacrament. The mass or promise of God is not completed by our prayers, but only by our faith; and in faith we pray and do other good works. But what priest sacrifices with the intention and idea of only offering up prayers? They all imagine that they are offering Christ himself to God the Father as an all-sufficient victim; and that they are doing a good work on behalf of all men, who, as they allege, will profit by it. They trust in the *opus operatum*, and do not attribute the effect to prayer. Thus, by a gradual growth of error, they attribute to the sacrament the benefit which springs from prayer; and they offer to God what they ought to receive as a gift from Him . . . .

To all these difficulties, which beset us so pertinaciously, we must oppose with the utmost constancy the words and example of Christ. Unless we hold the mass to be the promise or testament of Christ, according to the plain meaning of the words, we lose all the gospel and our whole comfort. Let us allow nothing to prevail against those words, even if an angel from heaven taught us otherwise. Now in these words there is nothing about a work or sacrifice. Again, we have the example of Christ on our side. When Christ instituted this sacrament and established this testament in the Last Supper, he did not offer himself to God the Father, or accomplish any work on behalf of others, but, as he sat at the table, he declared the same testament to each individual present and bestowed on each the sign of it. Now the more any mass resembles and is akin to that first mass of all which Christ celebrated at the Last Supper, the more Christian it is. But that mass of Christ was most simple; without any display of vestments, gestures, hymns, and other ceremonies; so that if it had been necessary that it should be offered as a sacrifice, His institution of it would not have been complete.

Not that any one ought rashly to blame the universal Church, which has adorned and extended the mass with many other rites and ceremonies; but we desire that no one should be so deceived by showy ceremonies, or so perplexed by the amount of external display, as to lose the simplicity of the mass, and in fact pay honour to some kind of transubstantiation; as will happen if we pass by the simple substance of the mass, and fix our minds on the manifold accidents of its outward show. For whatever has been added to the mass beyond the word and example of Christ, is one of its accidents; and none of these ought we to consider in any other light than we now consider monstrances—as they are called—and altar cloths, within which the host is contained. It is a contradiction in terms that the mass should be a sacrifice; since we receive the mass, but give a sacrifice. Now the same thing cannot be received and offered at the same time, nor can it be at once given and accepted by the same person. This is as certain as that prayer and the thing prayed for cannot be the same; nor can it be the same thing to pray and to receive what we pray for. . . .

Hence any one may easily understand that often-quoted passage from Gregory, in which he says that a mass celebrated by a bad priest is not to be considered of less value than one by a good priest, and that one celebrated by St. Peter would not have been better than one celebrated by the traitor Judas. Under cover of this saying some try to shelter their own impiety, and have drawn a distinction between the *opus operatum* and the *opus operans*; that they might continue secure in their evil living, and yet pretend to be benefactors to others. Gregory indeed speaks the truth, but these men pervert his meaning. It is most true that the testament and sacrament are not less effectively given and received at the hands of wicked priests than at those of the most holy. Who doubts that the gospel may be preached by wicked men? Now the mass is a part of the gospel; nay, the very sum and compendium of the gospel. For what is the whole gospel but the good news of the remission of sins? Now all that can be said in the most ample and copious words concerning the remission of sins and the mercy of God, is all briefly comprehended in the word of the testament. Hence also sermons to the people ought to be nothing else but expositions of the mass, that is, the setting forth of the divine promise of this testament. This would be to teach faith, and truly to edify the Church. But those who now expound the mass make a sport and mockery of the subject by figures of speech derived from human ceremonies.

As therefore a wicked man can baptize, that is, can apply the word of promise and the sign of water to the person baptized, so can he also apply and minister the promise of this sacrament to those who partake of it, and partake himself with them, as the traitor Judas did in the supper of the Lord. Still the sacrament and testament remains always the same; it performs in the believer its own proper work, in the unbeliever it performs a work foreign to itself. But in the matter of oblations the case is quite different; for since it is not the mass but prayers which are offered to God, it is evident that the oblations of a wicked priest are of no value. As Gregory himself says, when we employ an unworthy person as an advocate, the mind of the judge is prejudiced against us. We must not therefore confound these two things, the mass and prayer, sacrament and work, testament and sacrifice. The one comes from God to us through the ministry of the priest, and requires faith on our part; the other goes forth from our faith to God through the priest, and requires that He should hear us; the one comes down, the other goes upwards. The one therefore does not necessarily require that the minister should be worthy and pious, but the other does require it, because God does not hear sinners. He knows how to do us good by means of wicked men, but He does not accept the works of any wicked man, as He showed in the case of Cain. It is written: "The sacrifice of the wicked is an abomination to the Lord." (Proverbs. 15:8); and again: "Whatsoever is not of faith is sin." (Romans 14:23.)

We shall now make an end of this first part of the subject, but I am ready to produce further arguments when any one comes forward to attack these. From all that has been said we see for whom the mass was intended, and who are worthy partakers of it; namely, those alone who have sad, afflicted, disturbed, confused, and erring consciences. For since the word of the divine promise in this sacrament holds forth to us remission of sins, any man may safely draw near to it who is harassed either by remorse for sin, or by temptation to sin. This testament of Christ is the one medicine for past, present, and future sins; provided thou cleavest to it with unhesitating faith, and believest that that which is signified by the words of the testament is freely given to thee. If thou dost not so believe, then nowhere, never, by no works, by no efforts, wilt thou be able to appease thy conscience. For faith is the sole peace of conscience, and unbelief the sole disturber of conscience. . . .

On Holy Orders

Which of the ancient Fathers has asserted that by these words priests were ordained? Whence then this new interpretation? It is because it has been sought by this device to set up a source of implacable discord, by which clergy and laity might be placed farther asunder than heaven and earth, to the incredible injury of baptismal grace and confusion of evangelical communion. Hence has originated that detestable tyranny of the clergy over the laity, in which, trusting to the corporal unction by which their hands are consecrated, to their tonsure, and to their vestments, they not only set themselves above the body of lay Christians, who have been anointed with the Holy Spirit, but almost look upon them as dogs, unworthy to be numbered in the Church along with themselves. Hence it is that they dare to command, exact, threaten, drive, and oppress, at their will. In fine, the sacrament of orders has been and is a most admirable engine for the establishment of all those monstrous evils which have hitherto been wrought, and are yet being wrought, in the Church. In this way Christian brotherhood has perished; in this way shepherds have been turned into wolves, servants into tyrants, and ecclesiastics into more than earthly beings.

How if they were compelled to admit that we all, so many as have been baptized, are equally priests? We are so in fact, and it is only a ministry which has been entrusted to them, and that with our consent. They would then know that they have no right to exercise command over us, except so far as we voluntarily allow of it. Thus it is said: "Ye are a chosen generation, a royal priesthood, a holy nation." (1 Peter 2:9.) Thus all we who are Christians are priests; those whom we call priests are ministers chosen from among us to do all things in our name; and the priesthood is nothing else than a ministry. Thus Paul says: "Let a man so account of us as of the ministers of Christ, and stewards of the mysteries of God." (1 Corinthians 4:1.)

From this it follows that he who does not preach the word, being called to this very office by the Church, is in no way a priest, and that the sacrament of orders can be nothing else than a ceremony for choosing preachers in the Church. This is the description given of a priest: "The priest's lips should keep knowledge, and they should seek the law at his mouth; for he is the messenger of the Lord of hosts." (Malachi 2:7.) Be sure then that he who is not a messenger of the Lord of hosts, or who is called to anything else than a messengership—if I may so speak—is certainly not a priest; as it is written: "Because thou hast rejected knowledge, I will also reject thee, that thou shalt be no priest to me." (Hosea 4:6.) They are called pastors because it is their duty to give the people pasture, that is, to teach them. Therefore those who are ordained only for the purpose of reading the canonical Hours and offering up masses are popish priests indeed, but not Christian priests, since they not only do not preach but are not even called to be preachers; nay, it is the very thing intended, that a priesthood of this kind shall stand on a different footing from the office of preacher. Thus they are priests of Hours and missals, that is, a kind of living images, having the name of priests, but very far from being really so; such priests as those whom Jeroboam ordained in Beth-aven, taken from the lowest dregs of the people, and not from the family of Levi. . . .

Conclusion

It has seemed best, however, to consider as sacraments, properly so called, those promises which have signs annexed to them. The rest, as they are not attached to signs, are simple promises. It follows that, if we speak with perfect accuracy, there are only two sacraments in the Church of God, Baptism and the Bread; since it is in these alone that we see both a sign divinely instituted and a promise of remission of sins. The sacrament of penance, which I have reckoned along with these two, is without any visible and divinely appointed sign; and is nothing else, as I have said, than a way and means of return to baptism. Not even the schoolmen can say that penitence agrees with their definition; since they themselves ascribe to every sacrament a visible sign, which enables the senses to apprehend the form of that effect which the sacrament works invisibly. Now penitence or absolution has no such sign; and therefore they will be compelled by their own definition either to say that penitence is not one of the sacraments, and thus to diminish their number, or else to bring forward another definition of a sacrament.

Baptism, however, which we have assigned to the whole of life, will properly suffice for all the sacraments which we are to use in life; while the bread is truly the sacrament of the dying and departing, since in it we commemorate the departure of Christ from this world, that we may imitate Him. Let us then so distribute these two sacraments that baptism may be allotted to the beginning and to the whole course of life, and the bread to its end and to death; and let the Christian, while in this vile body, exercise himself in both, until, being fully baptized and strengthened, he shall pass out of this world, as one born into a new and eternal life, and destined to eat with Christ in the kingdom of his Father, as he promised at the Last Supper, saying: "I say unto you, I will not drink of the fruit of the vine until the kingdom of God shall come" (Luke 22:18). Thus it is evident that Christ instituted the sacrament of the bread that we might receive the life which is to come; and then, when the purpose of each sacrament shall have been fulfilled, both baptism and the bread will cease.

MARTIN LUTHER, *CONCERNING CHRISTIAN LIBERTY* (1520)

[from *Harvard Classics*, ed., Charles Eliot (New York: P. F. Collier and Son, 1910)]

Christian faith has appeared to many an easy thing; nay, not a few even reckon it among the social virtues, as it were; and this they do because they have not made proof of it experimentally, and have never tasted of what efficacy it is. For it is not possible for any man to write well about it, or to understand well what is rightly written, who has not at some time tasted of its spirit, under the pressure of tribulation; while he who has tasted of it, even to a very small extent, can never write, speak, think, or hear about it sufficiently. For it is a living fountain, springing up into eternal life, as Christ calls it in John 4.

Now, though I cannot boast of my abundance, and though I know how poorly I am furnished, yet I hope that, after having been vexed by various temptations, I have attained some little drop of faith, and that I can speak of this matter, if not with more elegance, certainly with more solidity, than those literal and too subtle disputants who have hitherto discoursed upon it without understanding their own words. That I may open then an easier way for the ignorant—for these alone I am trying to serve—I first lay down these two propositions, concerning spiritual liberty and servitude:—

> A Christian man is the most free lord of all, and subject to none; a Christian man is the most dutiful servant of all, and subject to every one.

Although these statements appear contradictory, yet, when they are found to agree together, they will make excellently for my purpose. They are both the statements of Paul himself, who says, "Though I be free from all men, yet have I made myself servant unto all" (I Corinthians 9:19), and "Owe no man anything but to love one another" (Romans 13:8). Now love is by its own nature dutiful and obedient to the beloved object. Thus even Christ, though Lord of all things, was yet made of a woman; made under the law; at once free and a servant; at once in the form of God and in the form of a servant.

Let us examine the subject on a deeper and less simple principle. Man is composed of a twofold nature, a spiritual and a bodily. As regards the spiritual nature, which they name the soul, he is called the spiritual, inward, new man; as regards the bodily nature, which they name the flesh, he is called the fleshy, outward, old man. The Apostle speaks of this: "Though our outward man perish, yet the inward man is renewed day by day" (II Corinthians 4:16). The result of this diversity is that in the Scriptures opposing statements are made concerning the same man, the fact being that in the same man these two men are opposed to one another; the flesh lusting against the spirit, and the spirit against the flesh (Galatians 5:17).

We first approach the subject of the inward man, that we may see by what means a man becomes justified, free, and a true Christian; that is, a spiritual, new, and inward man. It is certain that absolutely none among outward things, under whatever name they may be reckoned, has any influence in producing Christian righteousness or liberty, nor, on the other hand, unrighteousness or slavery. This can be shown by an easy argument.

What can it profit the soul that the body should be in good condition, free, and full of life; that it should eat, drink, and act according to its pleasure; when even the most impious slaves of every kind of vice are prosperous in these matters? Again, what harm can ill-health, bondage, hunger, thirst, or any other outward evil, do to the soul, when even the most pious of men and the freest in the purity of their conscience, are harassed by these things? Neither of these states of things has to do with the liberty or the slavery of the soul.

And so it will profit nothing that the body should be adorned with sacred vestments, or dwell in holy places, or be occupied in sacred offices, or pray, fast, and abstain from certain meats, or do whatever works can be done through the body and in the body. Something widely different will be necessary for the justification and liberty of the soul, since the things I have spoken of can be done by any impious person, and only hypocrites are produced by devotion to these things. On the other hand, it will not at all injure the soul that the body should be clothed in profane raiment, should dwell in profane places, should eat and drink in the ordinary fashion, should not pray aloud, and should leave undone all the things above mentioned, which may be done by hypocrites.

And, to cast everything aside, even speculation, meditations, and whatever else can be performed by the exertions of the soul itself, are of no profit. One thing, and one alone, it is necessary for life, justification, and Christian liberty; and that is the most holy word of God, the Gospel of Christ, as He says, "I am the resurrection and the life; he that believeth in Me shall not die eternally" (John 11:25), and also, "If the Son shall make you free, ye shall be free indeed" (John 8:36), and, "Man shall not live by bread alone, but by every word that proceedeth out of the mouth of God" (Matthew 4:4).

Let us therefore hold it for certain and firmly established that the soul can do without everything except the word of God, without which none at all of its wants are provided for. But, having the word, it is rich and wants for nothing, since that is the word of life, of truth, of light, of peace, of justification, of salvation, of joy, of liberty, of wisdom, of virtue, of grace, of glory, and of every good thing. It is on this account that the prophet in a whole Psalm (Psalm 119), and in many other places, sighs for and calls upon the word of God with so many groanings and words.

Again, there is no more cruel stroke of the wrath of God than when He sends a famine of hearing His words (Amos 8:11), just as there is no greater favour from Him than the sending forth of His word, as it is said, "He sent His word and healed them and delivered them from their destructions" (Psalm 107:20). Christ was sent for no other office than that of the word; and the order of the Apostles, that of bishops, and that of the whole body of the clergy, have been called and instituted for no object but the ministry of the word.

But you will ask, What is this word, and by what means is it to be used, since there are so many words of God? I answer, the Apostle Paul (Romans 1) explains what it is, namely the Gospel of God, concerning His Son, incarnate, suffering, risen, and glorified, through the Spirit, the Sanctifier. To preach Christ is to feed the soul, to justify it, to set it free, and to save it, if it believes the preaching. For faith alone and the efficacious use of the word of God, bring salvation. "If thou shalt confess with thy mouth the Lord Jesus, and shalt believe in thine heart that God hath raised Him from the dead, thou shalt be saved" (Romans 10:9); and again, "Christ is the end of the law for righteousness to every one that believeth" (Romans 10:4), and "The just shall live by faith" (Romans 1:17). For the word of God cannot be received and honoured by any works, but by faith alone. Hence it is clear that as the soul needs the word alone for life and justification, so it is justified by faith alone, and not by any works. For if it could be justified by any other means, it would have no need of the word, nor consequently of faith.

But this faith cannot consist at all with works; that is, if you imagine that you can be justified by those works, whatever they are, along with it. For this would be to halt between two opinions, to worship Baal, and to kiss the hand to him, which is a very great iniquity, as Job says. Therefore, when you begin to believe, you learn at the same time that all that is in you is utterly guilty, sinful, and damnable, according to that saying, "All have sinned, and come short of the glory of God" (Romans 3:23), and also: "There is none righteous, no, not one; they are all gone out of the way; they are together become unprofitable: there is none that doeth good, no, not one" (Romans 3:10–12). When you have learnt this, you will know that Christ is necessary for you, since He has suffered and risen again for you, that, believing on Him, you might by this faith become another man, all your sins being remitted, and you being justified by the merits of another, namely of Christ alone.

Since then this faith can reign only in the inward man, as it is said, "With the heart man believeth unto righteousness" (Roman 10:10); and since it alone justifies, it is evident that by no outward work or labour can the inward man be at all justified, made free, and saved; and that no works whatever have any relation to him. And so, on the other hand, it is solely by impiety and incredulity of heart that he becomes guilty and a slave of sin, deserving condemnation, not by any outward sin or work. Therefore the first care of every Christian ought to be to lay aside all reliance on works, and strengthen his faith alone more and more, and by it grow in the knowledge, not of works, but of Christ Jesus, who has suffered and risen again for him, as Peter teaches (I Peter 5) when he makes no other work to be a Christian one. Thus Christ, when the Jews asked Him what they should do that they might work the works of God, rejected the multitude of works, with which He saw that they were puffed up, and commanded them one thing only, saying, "This is the work of God: that ye believe on Him whom He hath sent, for him hath God the Father sealed" (John 6:27, 29).

Hence a right faith in Christ is an incomparable treasure, carrying with it universal salvation and preserving from all evil, as it is said, "He that believeth and is baptized shall be saved; but he that believeth shall not be damned" (Mark 16:16). Isaiah, looking to this treasure, predicted, "The consumption decreed shall overflow with righteousness. For the Lord God of hosts shall make a consumption, even determined (*verbum abbreviatum et consummans*), in the midst of the land" (Isaiah 10:22, 23). As if he said, "Faith which is the brief and complete fulfilling of the law, will fill those who believe with such righteousness that they will need nothing else for justification." Thus, too, Paul says, "For with the heart man believeth unto righteousness" (Romans 10:10).

But you ask how it can be the fact that faith alone justifies, and affords without works so great a treasure of good things, when so many works, ceremonies, and laws are prescribed to us in the Scriptures? I answer, Before all things bear in mind what I have said: that faith alone without works justifies, sets free, and saves, as I show more clearly below.

Meanwhile it is to be noted that the whole Scripture of God is divided into two parts: precepts and promises. The precepts certainly teach us what is good, but what they teach us is not forthwith done. For they show us what we ought to do, but do not give us the power to do it. They were ordained, however, for the purpose of showing man to himself, that through them he may learn his own importance for good and may despair of his own strength. For this reason they are called the Old Testament, and are so.

For example, "Thou shalt not covet," is a precept by which we are all convicted of sin, since no man can help coveting, whatever efforts to the contrary he may make. In order therefore that he may fulfill the precept, and not covet, he is constrained to despair of himself and to seek elsewhere and through another the help which he cannot find in himself; as it is said, "O Israel, thou hast destroyed thyself; but in Me is thine help" (Hosea 13:9). Now what is done by this one precept is done by all; for all are equally impossible of fulfillment by us.

Now when a man has through the precepts been taught his own impotence, and become anxious by what means he may satisfy the law—for the law must be satisfied, so that no jot or tittle of it may pass away, otherwise he must be hopelessly condemned—then, being truly humbled and brought to nothing in his own eyes, he finds in himself no resource for justification and salvation.

Then comes in that other part of Scripture, the promises of God, which declare the glory of God, and say, "If you wish to fulfill the law, and, as the law requires, not to covet, lo! Believe in Christ, in whom are promised to you grace, justification, peace, and liberty." All these things you shall have, if you believe, and shall be without them if you do not believe. For what is impossible for you by all the works of the law, which are many and yet useless, you shall fulfill in an easy and summary way through faith, because God the Father has made everything to depend on faith, so that whosoever has it has all things, and he who has it not has nothing. "For God hath concluded them all in unbelief, that He might have mercy upon all" (Roman 11:32). Thus the promises of God give that which the precepts exact, and fulfill what the law commands; so that all is of God alone, both the precepts and their fulfillment. He alone commands; He alone also fulfills. Hence the promises of God belong to the New Testament; nay, are the New Testament.

Now, since these promises of God are words of holiness, truth, righteousness, liberty, and peace, and are full of universal goodness, the soul, which cleaves to them with a firm faith, is so united to them, nay, thoroughly absorbed by them, that it not only partakes in, but is penetrated and saturated by, all their virtues. For if the touch of Christ was healing, how much more does that most tender spiritual touch, nay, absorption of the word, communicate to the soul all that belongs to the word! In this way therefore the soul, through faith alone, without works, is from the word of God justified, sanctified, endued with truth, peace, and liberty, and filled full with every good thing, and is truly made the child of God, as it is said, "To them gave He power to become the sons of God, even them that believe on His name." (John 1:12).

From all this it is easy to understand why faith has such great power, and why no good works, nor even all good works put together, can compare with it, since no work can cleave to the word of God or be in the soul. Faith alone and the word reign in it; and such as is the word, such is the soul made by it, just as iron exposed to fire glows like fire, on account of its union with the fire. It is clear then that to a Christian man his faith suffices for everything, and that he has no need of works for justification. But if he has no need of works, neither has he need of the law; and if he has no need of the law, he is certainly free from the law, and the saying is true, "The law is not made for a righteous man" (I Timothy 1:9). This is that Christian liberty, our faith, the effect of which is, not that we should be careless or lead a bad life, but that no one should need the law or works for justification and salvation.

Let us consider this as the first virtue of faith; and let us look also to the second. This also is an office of faith: that it honours with the utmost veneration and the highest reputation Him in whom it believes, inasmuch as it holds Him to be truthful and worthy of belief. For there is no honour like the reputation of truth and righteousness with which we honour Him in whom we believe. What higher credit can we attribute to any one than truth and righteousness, and absolute goodness? On the other hand, it is the greatest insult to brand any one with the reputation of falsehood and unrighteousness, or to suspect him of these, as we do when we disbelieve him.

Thus the soul, in firmly believing the promises of God, holds Him to be true and righteous; and it can attribute to God no higher glory than the credit of being so. The highest worship of God is to ascribe to Him truth, righteousness, and whatever qualities we must ascribe to one in whom we believe. In doing this the soul shows itself prepared to do His whole will; in doing this it hallows His name, and gives itself up to be dealt with as it may please God. For it cleaves to His promise, and never doubts that He is true, just, and wise, and will do, dispose, and provide for all things in the best way. Is not such a soul, in this its faith, most obedient to God in all things? What commandment does there remain which has not been amply fulfilled by such an obedience? What fulfillment can be more full than universal obedience? Now this is not accomplished by works, but by faith alone.

On the other hand, what greater rebellion, impiety, or insult to God can there be, than not to believe His promises? What else is this, than either to make God a liar, or to doubt His truth—that is, to attribute truth to ourselves, but to God falsehood and levity? In doing this, is not a man denying God and setting himself up as an idol in his own heart? What then can works, done in such a state of impiety, profit us, were they even angelic or apostolic works? Rightly hath God shut up all, not in wrath nor in lust, but in unbelief, in order that those who pretend that they are fulfilling the laws by works of purity and benevolence (which are social and human virtues) may not presume that they will therefore be saved, but, being included in the sin of unbelief, may either seek mercy, or be justly condemned.

But when God sees that truth is ascribed to Him, and that in the faith of our hearts He is honoured with all the honour of which He is worthy, then in return He honours us on account of that faith, attributing to us truth and righteousness. For faith does truth and righteousness in rendering to God what is His; and therefore in return God gives glory to our righteousness. It is true and righteous that God is true and righteous; and to confess this and ascribe these attributes to Him, this it is to be true and righteous. Thus He says, "Them that honour Me I will honour, and they that despise Me shall be lightly esteemed" (I Sam 2:30). And so Paul says that Abraham's faith was imputed to him for righteousness, because by it he gave glory to God; and that to us also, for the same reason, it shall be imputed for righteousness, if we believe (Romans 4) . . . .

And now let us turn to the other part: to the outward man. Here we shall give an answer to all those who, taking offence at the word of faith and at what I have asserted, say, "If faith does everything, and by itself suffices for justification, why then are good works commanded? Are we then to take our ease and do no works, content with faith?" Not so, impious men, I reply; not so. That would indeed really be the case, if we were thoroughly and completely inner and spiritual persons; but that will not happen until the last day, when the dead shall be raised. As long as we live in the flesh, we are but beginning and making advances in that which shall be completed in a future life. On this account the Apostle calls that which we have in this life the firstfruits of the Spirit (Romans 8:23). In future we shall have the tenths, and the fullness of the Spirit. To this part belongs the fact I have stated before: that the Christian is the servant of all and subject to all. For in that part in which he is free he does no works, but in that in which he is a servant he does all works. Let us see on what principle this is so.

Although, as I have said, inwardly, and according to the spirit, a man is amply enough justified by faith, having all that he requires to have, except that this very faith and abundance ought to increase from day to day, even till the future life, still he remains in this mortal life upon the earth, in which it is necessary that he should rule his own body and have intercourse with men. Here then works begin; here he must not take his ease; here he must give heed to exercise his body by fastings, watchings, labour, and other regular discipline, so that it may be subdued to the spirit, and obey and conform itself to the inner man and faith, and not rebel against them nor hinder them, as is its nature to do if it is not kept under. For the inner man, being conformed to God and created after the image of God through faith, rejoices and delights itself in Christ, in whom such blessings have been conferred on it, and hence has only this task before it: to serve God with joy and for nought in free love.

But in doing this he comes into collision with that contrary will in his own flesh, which is striving to serve the world and to seek its own gratification. This the spirit of faith cannot and will not bear, but applies itself with cheerfulness and zeal to keep it down and restrain it, as Paul says, "I delight in the law of God after the inward man; but I see another law in my members, warring against the law of my mind and bringing me into captivity to the law of sin" (Romans 7:22, 23), and again, "I keep under my body and bring it unto subjection, lest that by any means, when I have preached to others, I myself should be a castaway" (I Corinthians 9:27), and "They that are Christ's have crucified the flesh, with the affections and lusts" (Galatians 5:24).

These works, however, must not be done with any notion that by them a man can be justified before God—for faith, which alone is righteousness before God, will not bear with this false notion—but solely with this purpose: that the body may be brought into subjection, and be purified from its evil lusts, so that our eyes may be turned only to purging away those lusts. For when the soul has been cleansed by faith and made to love God, it would have all things to be cleansed in like manner, and especially its own body, so that all things might unite with it in the love and praise of God. Thus it comes that, from the requirements of his own body, a man cannot take his ease, but is compelled on its account to do many good works, that he may bring it into subjection. Yet these works are not the means of his justification before God; he does them out of disinterested love to the service of God; looking to no other end than to do what is well-pleasing to Him who he desires to obey most dutifully in all things.

On this principle every man may easily instruct himself in what measure, and with what distinctions, he ought to chasten his own body. He will fast, watch, and labour, just as much as he sees to suffice for keeping down the wantonness and concupiscence of the body. But those who pretend to be justified by works are looking, not to the mortification of their lusts, but only to the works themselves; thinking that, if they can accomplish as many works and as great as possible, all is well with them, and they are justified. Sometimes they even injure their brain, and extinguish nature, or at least make it useless. This is enormous folly, and ignorance of Christian life and faith, when a man seeks, without faith, to be justified and saved by works. . . .

True, then, are these two sayings: "Good works do not make a good man, but a good man does good works"; "Bad works do not make a bad man, but a bad man does bad works." Thus it is always necessary that the substance or person should be good before any good works can be done, and that good works should follow and proceed from a good person. As Christ says, "A good tree cannot bring forth evil fruit, neither can a corrupt tree bring forth good fruit" (Matthew 7:18). Now it is clear that the fruit does not bear the tree, nor does the tree grow on the fruit; but, on the contrary, the trees bear the fruit, and the fruit grows on the trees.

As then trees must exist before their fruit, and as the fruit does not make the tree either good or bad, but on the contrary, a tree of either kind produces fruit of the same kind, so must first the person of the man be good or bad before he can do either a good or bad work; and his works do not make him bad or good, but he himself makes his works either bad or good.

We may see the same thing in all handicrafts. A bad or good house does not make a bad or good builder, but a good or bad builder makes a good or bad house. And in general no work makes workman such as it is itself; but the workman makes the work such as he is himself. Such is the case, too, with the works of men. Such as the man himself is, whether in faith or in unbelief, such is his work: good if it be done in faith; bad if in unbelief. But the converse is not true that, such as the work is, such the man becomes in faith or in unbelief. For as works do not make a believing man, so neither do they make a justified man; but faith, as it makes a man a believer and justified, so also it makes his works good.

Since then works justify no man, but a man must be justified before he can do any good work, it is most evident that it is faith alone which, by the mere mercy of God through Christ, and by means of His word, can worthily and sufficiently justify and save the person; and that a Christian man needs no work, no law, for his salvation; for by faith he is free from all law, and in perfect freedom does gratuitously all that he does, seeking nothing either of profit or of salvation—since by the grace of God he is already saved and rich in all things through his faith—but solely that which is well-pleasing to God. . . .

From all this it is easy to perceive on what principle good works are to be cast aside or embraced, and by what rule all teachings put forth concerning works are to be understood. For if works are brought forward as grounds of justification, and are done under the false persuasion that we can pretend to be justified by them, they lay on us the yoke of necessity, and extinguish liberty along with faith and by this very addition to their use they become no longer good, but really worthy of condemnation. For such works are not free, but blaspheme the grace of God, to which alone it belongs to justify and save through faith. Works cannot accomplish this, and yet, with impious presumption, through our folly, they take it on themselves to do so; and thus break in with violence upon the office and glory of grace.

We do not then reject good works; nay, we embrace them and teach them in the highest degree. It is not on their own account that we condemn them, but on account of this impious addition to them. These things cause them to be only good in outward show, but in reality not good, since by them men are deceived and deceive others, like ravening wolves in sheep's clothing.

Now this leviathan, this perverted notion about works, is invincible when sincere faith is wanting. For those sanctified doers of works cannot but hold it till faith, which destroys it, comes and reigns in the heart. Nature cannot expel it by her own power; nay, cannot even see it for what it is, but considers it as a most holy will. And when custom steps in besides, and strengthens this pravity of nature, as has happened by means of impious teachers, then the evil is incurable, and leads astray multitudes to irreparable ruin. Therefore, though it is good to preach and write about penitence, confession, and satisfaction, yet if we stop there, and do not go on to teach faith, such teaching is without doubt deceitful and devilish. For Christ, speaking by His servant John, not only said, "Repent ye," but added, "for the kingdom of heaven is at hand" (Matthew 3:2).

For not one word of God only, but both, should be preached; new and old things should be brought out of the treasury, as well the voice of the law as the word of grace. The voice of the law should be brought forward, that men may be terrified and brought to a knowledge of their sins, and thence be converted to penitence and to a better manner of life. But we must not stop here; that would be to wound only and not to bind up, to strike and not to heal, to kill and not to make alive, to bring down to hell and not to bring back, to humble and to exalt. Therefore the word of grace and of the promised remission of sin must also be preached, in order to teach and set up faith, since without that word contrition, penitence, and all other duties, are performed and taught in vain.

There still remain, it is true, preachers of repentance and grace, but they do not explain the law and the promises of God to such an end, and in such a spirit, that men may learn whence repentance and grace are to come. For repentance comes from the law of God, but faith or grace from the promises of God, as it is said, "Faith cometh by hearing, and hearing by the word of God" (Romans 10:17), whence it comes that a man, when humbled and brought to the knowledge of himself by the threatenings and terrors of the law, is consoled and raised up by faith in the Divine promise. Thus "weeping may endure for a night, but joy cometh in the morning" (Psalm 30:5). Thus much we say concerning works in general, and also concerning those which the Christian practices with regard to his won body.

Lastly, we will speak also of those works which he performs towards his neighbour. For man does not live for himself alone in this mortal body, in order to work on its account, but also for all men on earth; nay, he lives only for others, and not for himself. For it is to this end that he brings his own body into subjection, that he may be able to serve others more sincerely and more freely, as Paul says, "None of us liveth to himself, and no man dieth to himself. For whether we live, we live unto the Lord; and whether we die, we die unto the Lord" (Romans 14:7, 8). Thus it is impossible that he should take his ease in this life, and not work for the good of his neighbours, since he must needs speak, act, and converse among men, just as Christ was made in the likeness of men and found in fashion as a man, and had His conversation among men.

Yet a Christian has need of none of these things for justification and salvation, but in all his works he ought to entertain this view and look only to this object—that he may serve and be useful to others in all that he does; having nothing before his eyes but the necessities and the advantage of his neighbour. Thus the Apostle commands us to work with our own hands, that we may have to give to those that need. He might have said, that we may support ourselves; but he tells us to give to those that need. It is the part of a Christian to take care of his own body for the very purpose that, by its soundness and well-being, he may be enabled to labour, and to acquire and preserve property, for the aid of those who are in want, that thus the stronger member may serve the weaker member, and we may be children of God, thoughtful and busy one for another, bearing one another's business and so fulfilling the law of Christ.

Here is the truly Christian life, here is faith really working by love, when a man applies himself with joy and love to the works of that freest servitude in which he serves others voluntarily and for nought, himself abundantly satisfied in the fullness and riches of his own faith. . . .

[A Christian] should reason thus: Lo! My God, without merit on my part, of His pure and free mercy, has given to me, an unworthy, condemned, and contemptible creature all the riches of justification and salvation in Christ, so that I no longer am in want of anything, except of faith to believe that this is so. For such a Father, then, who has overwhelmed me with these inestimable riches of His, why should I not freely, cheerfully, and with my whole heart, and from voluntary zeal, do all that I know will be pleasing to Him and acceptable in His sight? I will therefore give myself as a sort of Christ, to my neighbour, as Christ has given Himself to me; and will do nothing in this life except what I see will be needful, advantageous, and wholesome for my neighbour, since by faith I abound in all good things in Christ.

Thus from faith flow forth love and joy in the Lord, and from love a cheerful, willing, free spirit, disposed to serve our neighbour voluntarily, without taking any account of gratitude or ingratitude, praise or blame, gain or loss. Its object is not to lay men under obligations, nor does it distinguish between friends and enemies, or look to gratitude or ingratitude, but most freely and willingly spends itself and its goods, whether it lose them through ingratitude, or gains goodwill. For thus did its Father, distributing all things to all men abundantly and freely, making His sun to rise upon the just and the unjust. Thus, too, the child does and endures nothing except from the free joy with which it delights through Christ in God, the Giver of such great gifts.

You see, then, that, if we recognize those great and precious gifts, as Peter says, which have been given to us, love is quickly diffused in our hearts through the Spirit, and by love we are made free, joyful, all-powerful, active workers, victors over all our tribulations, servants to our neighbour, and nevertheless lords of all things. But, for those who do not recognize the good things given to them through Christ, Christ has been born in vain; such persons walk by works, and will never attain the taste and feeling of these great things. Therefore just as our neighbour is in want, and has need of our abundance, so we too in the sight of God were in want, and had need of His mercy. And as our heavenly Father has freely helped us in Christ, so ought we freely to help our neighbour by our body and works, and each should become to other a sort of Christ, so that we may be mutually Christs, and that the same Christ may be in all of us; that is, that we may be truly Christians.

Who then can comprehend the riches and glory of the Christian life? It can do all things, has all things, and is in want of nothing; is lord over sin, death, and hell, and at the same time is the obedient and useful servant of all. But alas! it is at this day unknown throughout the world; it is neither preached nor sought after, so that we are quite ignorant about our own name, why we are and are called Christians. We are certainly called so from Christ, who is not absent, but dwells among us—provided, that is, that we believe in Him and are reciprocally and mutually one the Christ of the other, doing to our neighbour as Christ does to us. But now, in the doctrine of men, we are taught only to seek after merits, rewards, and things which are already ours, and we have made of Christ a taskmaster far more severe than Moses.

The Blessed Virgin beyond all others, affords us an example of the same faith, in that she was purified according to the law of Moses, and like all other women, though she was bound by no such law and had no need of purification. Still she submitted to the law voluntarily and of free love, making herself like the rest of women, that she might not offend or throw contempt on them. She was not justified by doing this; but, being already justified, she did it freely and gratuitously. Thus ought our works too to be done, and not in order to be justified by them; for, being first justified by faith, we ought to do all our works freely and cheerfully for the sake of others.

Christ also, when His disciples were asked for the tribute money, asked of Peter whether the children of a king were not free from taxes. Peter agreed to this; yet Jesus commanded him to go to the sea, saying, "Lest we should offend them, go thou to the sea, and cast a hook, and take up the fish that first cometh up; and when thou hast opened his mouth thou shalt find a piece of money; that take, and give unto them for Me and thee" (Matthew 17:27).

This example is very much to our purpose; for here Christ calls Himself and His disciples free men and children of a King, in want of nothing; and yet he voluntarily submits and pays the tax. Just as far, then, as this work was necessary or useful to Christ for justification or salvation, so far do all His other works or those of His disciples avail for justification. They are really free and subsequent to justification, and only done to serve others and set them an example.

Such are the works which Paul inculcated, that Christians should be subject to principalities and powers and ready to every good work (Titus 3:1), not that they may be justified by these things—for they are already justified by faith—but that in liberty of spirit they may thus be the servants of others and subject to powers, obeying their will out of gratuitous love. . . .

From all this every man will be able to attain a sure judgment and faithful discrimination between all works and laws, and to know who are blind and foolish pastors, and who are true and good ones. For whatsoever work is not directed to the sole end either of keeping under the body, or of doing service to our neighbour—provided he require nothing contrary to the will of God—is no good or Christian work. Hence I greatly fear that at this day few or no colleges, monasteries, altars, or ecclesiastical functions are Christian ones; and the same may be said of fasts and special prayers to certain saints. I fear that in all these nothing is being sought but what is already ours; while we fancy that by these things our sins are purged away and salvation is attained and thus utterly do away with Christian liberty. This comes from ignorance of Christian faith and liberty.

This ignorance and this crushing of liberty are diligently promoted by the teaching of very many blind pastors, who stir up and urge the people to a zeal for these things, praising them and puffing them up with their indulgences, but never teaching faith. Now I would advise you, if you have any wish to pray, to fast, or to make foundations in churches, as they call it, to take care not to do so with the object of gaining any advantage, either temporal or eternal. You will thus wrong your faith, which alone bestows all things on you, and the increase of which, either by working or by suffering, is alone to be care for. What you give, give freely and without price, that others may prosper and have increase from you and your goodness. Thus you will be a truly good man and a Christian. For what to you are your goods and your works, which are done over and above for the subjection of the body, since you have abundance for yourself through your faith, in which God has given you all things. . . .

We conclude therefore that a Christian man does not live in himself, but in Christ and in his neighbour, or else is no Christian: in Christ by faith; in his neighbour by love. By faith he is carried upwards above himself to his neighbour, still always abiding in God and His love, as Christ says, "Verily I say unto you, Hereafter ye shall see heaven open, and the angels of God ascending and descending upon the Son of man" (John 1:51).

Thus much concerning liberty, which, as you see, is a true and spiritual liberty, making our hearts free from all sins, laws, and commandments, as Paul says, "The law is not made for a righteous man" (I Timothy 1:9), and one which surpasses all other external liberties, as far as heaven is above earth. May Christ make us understand and preserve this liberty. Amen.

[from J. J. Scarisbrick, *Henry VIII* (Berkeley: University of California Press, 1968); reprinted with permission of the publisher]

It is customary to label the growing opposition to the Church as anticlericalism. This is unexceptionable, provided it is recognized that the anticlericalism concerned was a many-headed hydra, an amalgam of what were often opposites or, at any rate, incompatibles. We may distinguish several strands. The first was a negative, destructive anticlericalism which could range from hostility to the local parson and resentment of tithes, of the workings of the ecclesiastical courts and of frivolous excommunications, etc., to a programme of wholesale dispossession of 'abbey-lubbers' and lordly bishops—a policy often innocent of much philosophical or theological implication. Though this may have been the most widespread and, in a sense, the most successful, it was not the only force pressing for action. Alongside this appetitive and basically selfish creed stood two of a higher order. For there indisputably was a positive and idealistic, though secular, anticlericalism (personified perhaps by a Thomas Cromwell) which argued that the Church needed radical purging, that society could no longer carry this uneconomic burden, this vast institution which absorbed so much manpower, sterilized so much wealth, took so much and gave back so little; that its energy and wealth should be turned to more positive ends, social and educational; that the English Church's dependence on a foreign power, the privileges and franchises of this great estate, and especially the autonomy of the Courts Christian, were an obstacle to political progress, a threat to jurisdictional wholeness; and that the flow of English money to Rome, so offensive to prevailing bullionist theory, damaged her economy. By such reckoning, therefore, the clerical estate must be both clipped and re-ordered—for the sake of the "Commonwealth". But there was also a positive, idealistic, and religious anti-clericalism, itself a thing of many shades, which would argue that, for the sake of Christian life in England, radical change must come. For some this may not have gone much further than a desire for traditional reforms; for others (like, say, a More, or even Fisher) it may have sought drastic attention to monasticism and the secular clergy, and some rehabilitation of the layman; for yet others it may have meant the full Erasmian programme—a simple, Biblical, strongly lay pietism.

Of course this picture is too easy. There may have been many who would not fit into any of these categories and some who moved from one to another or chose elements from all of them. It was certainly accompanied by a fourth which shaded imperceptibly into, and yet could easily be at cross-purposes with, all of them—namely the anticlericalism of heresy. It is beyond doubt that Lollardy, itself a very varied phenomenon, had survived intermittent repression, indeed had recently gained ground, and would now come to the surface to lend the voice of its strongly anti-sacerdotal, anti-sacramental creed to the clamour. And to this indigenous heresy, which was to provide a seedbed for it, was soon to be added the potent new life of the continental Reformation. Lutheranism had won converts in the English universities very quickly; Lutheran literature was in London and elsewhere in sufficient quantities to worry the authorities by the early 1520s and, when added to the writings of Zwingli, Oecolampadius and other Protestants, would give to the layman and the anticlerical cleric a lasting weapon against a clericalism which had so long oppressed and drained them.

Such, in heavy-schematized simplicity, were the basic forces of change building up against the established Church. How strong they were is impossible to gauge. But it is clear that, if the activists were a small minority, hostility to churchmen was widespread and often bitter, and the conviction intense that something must be done. There had been talk of reform for generations and nothing had come of it; but each time it was discussed and promised it was brought nearer because made more familiar. It had come to a crescendo with the humanists and, when uttered by an Erasmus or More, finally made respectable, indeed authoritative, for they spoke from the inside and the top. Nor was there merely talk. Not only were there germs of great things within the Catholic Church but, of course, the rebellion was well under way in Germany. There the *ancien régime* was crumbling like rotten wood and the massive success of the rebels could only serve as a stimulus, object lesson and warning elsewhere.

In the autumn of 1529 a momentous thing happened. Henry VIII threw in his lot with this anticlericalism, which could never have made full progress without him. He signaled his alliance with three actions: first, he dismissed Wolsey, the supreme clericalist, though less insensitive to the world of Erasmus than has been often supposed; secondly, Henry replaced him in a post hitherto regularly occupied by a cleric, but which he had determined should not be so occupied now, by a layman—and no ordinary layman either, but a semi-Erasmian radical and author of the most shocking book yet written in the English language, namely, *Utopia*; thirdly, he summoned Parliament, the organ through which, as nowhere else, anticlericalism could find expression, a parliament which, with his blessing, would immediately set about the chastisement of the clerical estate and end by ripping a large section of it to pieces..

Anticlericalism needed Henry if it were to succeed and Henry now needed it. The two have come together in a powerful partnership which was to produce what was both an act of state and (to fabricate an antithesis) an act of the community. But if Henry had made his new liaison clear he had left an important question unanswered: with which form of anticlericalism had he allied? It could not be with all of them, at least not permanently, because they were in reality pulling in several different directions. His upbringing, his papal title and so on might suggest that he would choose More's way, especially now that More was his chancellor. But his recent bullying of Clement had suggested other tendencies. The Boleyns had Lutheran connexions and Cranmer was not far away from the Court. Nor, for that matter, was Thomas Cromwell. Perhaps Henry had not made up his mind. Perhaps he did not want to, preferring to enjoy maximum support for as long as possible. Perhaps he had not yet perceived the necessity of choice—for, after all, he was a newcomer to the scene and its complexity may not yet have been evident. Perhaps he was not aware of what he had done. Wolsey had not been dismissed because he was the arch-priest of clericalism, but because he had failed the king; More did not replace him because he was radical, but because Henry wanted him. There is no sign that Henry had a prepared plan of campaign when Parliament assembled. Presumably he intended it to mark the end of a regime and perhaps deal with its author; to provide money; to be a stick with which to beat Clement for the sake of the divorce. But was that all?

SIMON FISH, *A SUPPLICATION FOR THE BEGGARS* (1529)

[Modernized from J. Meadows Cowper, ed., *Four Supplications: 1529–1553 A.D.* (London: Kegan Paul, Trench, Trubner, 1871); reprinted by Kraus Reprint, Millwood, N.Y, 1975. Words added to the text are in angled brackets (<>); words in square brackets ([]) explain the original, preceding term.]

TO THE KING OUR

SOVEREIGN LORD

Most <men> lamentably complain of their woeful misery unto your highness—these your poor daily beadsmen, the wretched hideous monsters (on whom scarcely for horror any of you dare look), the foul, unhappy sort of lepers, and other sore people; needy, impotent, blind, lame, and sick that live only by alms; how that their number is daily so sorely increased that all the alms of all the well-disposed people of this your realm are not half enough to sustain them, but for that very constraint they die for hunger. And this most pestilent mischief is common upon your said poor beadsmen, for in the times of your noble predecessors past, there craftily crept into this your realm another sort of beggars and vagabonds (not impotent, but strong, puissant, counterfeit holy, and idle), who since the time of their first entry, by all the craft and wiliness of Satan, are now increased under your sight, not only into a great number, but also into a kingdom. These are (not herds, but the ravenous wolves going in herds' clothing, devouring the flock) the bishops, abbots, priors, deacons, archdeacons, suffragans [assistant or auxiliary bishops], priests, monks, chanons, friars, pardoners, and summoners. And who is able to number this idle, ravenous sort, which (setting all labors aside) have begged so importunately that they have gotten into their hands more than the third part of all your realm. The goodliest lordships, manors, lands, and territories are theirs. Besides this, they have the tenth part of all the corn, meadow, pasture, grass, wool, colts, calves, lambs, pigeons, geese, and chickens. Over and besides, the tenth part of every servant's wage; the tenth part of the wool, milk, honey, wax, cheese, and butter. Ye, and they look so narrowly upon their profits that the poor wives must be accountable to them of every tenth egg or else she gets not her rights at Easter and shall be taken as a heretic. Hereto have they their four offering days. What money pull they in by probates of testaments, privy tithes, and by men's offerings to their pilgrimages, and at their first masses! Every man and child that is buried must pay somewhat for masses and dirges to be sung for him, or else they will accuse the dead man's friends and executioners <of his testament> of heresy. What money get they by mortuaries, by hearing of confessions (which they divulge) by hallowing of churches, altars, superaltars, chapels, and bells; by cursing of men and absolving them again for money? What a multitude of money do the pardoners gather in a year! How much money do the summoners get by extortion in a year, by taking people to the commissary's court, and afterwards dropping the charges for money! Finally, the infinite number of begging friars—what get they in a year? Here, if it please your grace to mark, you shall see a thing far out of joint. There are within your realm of England 52,000 parish churches; and with only ten households in every parish, there are 520,000 households. From each of these households each of the five orders of friars is due a penny a quarter; that is, for all the five orders, five pence a quarter from each house, or for all the five orders 20 pence a year from each house, for a sum total of £43,333 sterling. And yet, not 400 years ago they received not one penny.

Oh grievous and painful exactions thus yearly to be paid, from which the people of your noble predecessors, the kings of the ancient Britons, ever stood free. And this will the friars have, or else they will procure him that will not give it them to be taken as a heretic. What tyrant ever oppressed the people like this cruel and vengeful generation? What subjects shall be able to help their prince, who by this faction are yearly sheared? What good Christian people can be able to succor us poor lepers, blind, sore, and lame who are thus yearly oppressed? Is it any marvel that your people so complain of poverty? Is it any marvel that the taxes, fifteens [parliamentary grants to the king], and subsidies that your grace most tenderly of great compassion have taken among your people to defend them from the threatened ruin of their commonwealth have been so slothfully, ye, painfully levied—seeing that almost the utmost penny that might have been levied has been gathered before by this ravenous, cruel, and insatiable generation? Neither the Danes nor the Saxons, in the time of the ancient Britons, would ever have been able to have brought their armies from so far hither into your land to have conquered it if they had had at that time such a sort of idle gluttons to find at home. The noble king Arthur would never have been able to have carried his army to the foot of the mountains to resist the coming down of Lucius the emperor <6ᵗʰ century> if such yearly exactions had been taken of his people. The Greeks would never have been able to have so long continued the siege of Troy if they had had at home such an idle sort of cormorants to find. The ancient Romans would never have been able to have put all the whole world under their obeisance if their people had been thus yearly oppressed. The Turk now, in your time, would never have been able to get so much ground of Christendom if he had in his empire such a sort of locusts to devour his substance. Lay then these sums to the foresaid third part of the possessions of the realm, that you may see whether or not they draw unto themselves nearly half of the entire substance of the realm; so shall you find that they draw far above. Now let us then compare the number of this unkind, idle sort with the number of the lay people, and we shall see whether it be indifferently shifted or not that they should have half. Compare them to the number of men, so are they not but one in 100 persons. Compare them to men, women, and children; then are they not but one in 400 persons. One part therefore in 400 parts divided would still be too much for them unless they did labor. What an unequal burden is it that they have half with the multitude and are not of their number a 400ᵗʰ of the whole. What tongue will be able to tell that ever there was any commonwealth so sore oppressed since the world first began?

And what do all these greedy sort of sturdy, idle, holy thieves, with these yearly exactions that they take from the people? Truly nothing but exempt themselves from the obedience due your grace. Nothing but translate all rule, power, lordship, authority, obedience, and dignity from your grace unto themselves. Nothing but contrive to have all your subjects fall into disobedience and rebellion against your grace and be under them. As they did unto your noble predecessor king John, which, because he would have punished certain traitors who had conspired with the French king to have deposed him from his crown and dignity (among the which was a clerk called Stephen, whom afterward against the king's will the pope made bishop of Canterbury), they interdicted his land. For the which matter your most noble realm has wrongfully (alas, shamefully) stood tributary (not unto any kind of temporal prince, but unto a cruel, devilish bloodsucker, drunken in the blood of the saints and martyrs of Christ) ever since. Here were a holy sort of prelates, who thus cruelly could punish such a righteous king, all his realm and succession for doing right!

Here were a charitable sort of holy men that could thus interdict a holy realm and pluck away the obedience of the people from their natural liege lord and king, for none other cause but for his righteousness! Here were a blessed sort, not of meek herds, but of bloodsuckers that could set the French king upon such a righteous prince to cause him to lose his crown and dignity, to make effusion of the blood of his people unless this good and blessed king of great compassion, more fearing and lamenting the shedding of the blood of his people than the loss of his crown and dignity against all right and conscience, had submitted himself unto them! O case most horrible that ever so noble a king, realm, and succession should thus be made to stoop to such a sort of bloodsuckers! What has become of his sword, power, crown, and dignity whereby he might have done justice in this manner? What has become of their obedience that should have been subject under his high power in this matter? Ye, what has become of the obedience of all his subjects that for maintenance of the commonwealth should have helped him manfully to have resisted these bloodsuckers to the shedding of their blood? Was not all together by their [the clergy's] policy translated from this good king unto them? Ye, and what do they more? Truly nothing but apply themselves, by all the sleights they may, to have to do with every man's wife, every man's daughter, and every man's maid, that cuckoldry and baudry should reign over all among your subjects, that no man should know his own child, that their [the clergy's] bastards might inherit the possessions of every man to put the right begotten children clear besides their inheritance, in subversion of all estates and godly order. These be they that by their abstaining from marriage do let the generation of the people, whereby all the realm at length, if it should be continued, should be made desert and uninhabitable.

These be they that have made a hundred-thousand idle whores in your realm, which would have gotten their living, in the sweat of their faces, had not their superfluous riches elected them to unclean lust and idleness. These be they that corrupt the whole generation of mankind in your realm, that catch the pokes [bags] of one woman and bear them to another, that be brent with [take the goose of] one woman and bear it to another, that catch the leprosy of one woman and bear it to another. Ye, some one of them shall boast among his fellows that he has meddled with a hundred women. These be they that when they have once drawn men's wives to such incontinency, spend away their husbands' goods, make the women to run away from their husbands; ye, run away themselves both with wife and goods, bringing both man, wife, and children to idleness, theft, and beggary.

Ye, who is able to number the great and broad, bottomless ocean sea, full of eels, that this mischievous and sinful generation may lawfully bring upon us unpunished? What has become of your sword, power, crown, and dignity that should punish (by punishment of death, even as other men are punished) the felonies, rapes, murders, and treasons committed by this sinful generation? What has become of their obedience that should be under your high power in this matter? Have these not been taken from you and translated to them? Yes, truly. What an infinite number of people might have been increased to have peopled the realm if these sort of folk had been married like other men? What breach of matrimony is there brought in by them? Such truly as was never since the world began among the whole multitude of heathen.

Who is she that will set her hands to work to get 3d. [denarius—old silver penny] a day, when she may get at least 20d. a day to sleep an hour with a friar, a monk, or a priest? Who is he that would labor for a grote a day [1/8 of an ounce of silver], when he may have at least 12d. a day to be baud to a priest, a monk, or a friar? Who are they that marry priests' sovereign ladies in order to cloak the priests' incontinency and to get a living from the priests themselves for their labor? How many thousands does such lubricite [shiftiness] bring to beggary, theft, idleness who would have kept their good name and have set themselves to work had there not been this excessive treasure of the spirituals? What honest man dares take any man or woman in his service that has been at such a school with a spiritual man? Oh the grievous shipwreck of the commonwealth, which in ancient time, before the coming in of these ravenous wolves was so prosperous that then there were but few thieves! Ye, theft was at that time so rare that Caesar was not compelled to make penalty of death upon felony, as your grace may well perceive in his institutes. There was also at that time but few poor people, and yet they did not beg, but there was given them enough unasked; for there was at that time none of these ravenous wolves to ask it from them, as it appears in the acts of the apostles. Is it any marvel though that there be now so many beggars, thieves, and idle people? Nay truly.

What remedy: make laws against them? I am in doubt whether you would be able. Are they not stronger in your own parliament house than yourself? What a number of bishops, abbots, and priors are lords of your parliament! Are not all the learned men of your realm in fee with [employed by] them to speak in your parliament house for them against your crown, dignity, and commonwealth of your realm, a few of your own learned counsel only excepted? What law can be made against them that may be available? Who is he—though he be ever so grieved for the murder of his ancestor, ravishment of his wife, of his daughter, robbery, trespass, mayhem, debt, or any other offense—who would dare lay charges against them? And if he does, then is he by and by, by their wiliness, accused of heresy. Ye, they will so handle him that unless he bear a faggot [a bundle of sticks carried by recanting heretics] for their pleasure, he shall be excommunicated, and then all of his actions will be dashed. So captive are your laws unto them that no man that they list to excommunicate may be admitted to sue any action in any of your courts. If any man in your sessions dare be so hardy to indict a priest of any such crime, he will have, before the year is out, such a yoke of heresy laid on his neck that it will make him wish that he had not done it. Your grace may see what a work there is in London, how the bishops raged against the indictment of certain curates for extortion and incontinency during the last year of the Warmoll Quest [annual inquiry into abuses]. Had Richard Hunne not commenced action of praemunire against a priest <1514>, he would have been yet alive—and no heretic—at all, but honest man.

Did not divers of your noble progenitors—seeing their crown and dignity run into ruin and to be thus craftly translated into the hands of this mischievous generation—make divers statutes for the reformation thereof, among which was the statute of mortmain [lands held inalienably by the church]—the intent of which statute being that after that time they should have no more given unto them?

But what availed it? Have they not since gotten into their hands more lands than any duke in England has, the statute notwithstanding? Ye, have they not for all that translated into their hands, from your grace, thoroughly half of your kingdom? Has not your ancient kingdom (which was before theirs, and out of which theirs is grown) been cut in twain: the spiritual kingdom (as they call it, and which they name first), and your temporal kingdom? And which of these two kingdoms (suppose you) is likely to overgrow the other—ye, to put the other clear out of memory? Truly the kingdom of the bloodsuckers; for to them is given daily out of your kingdom, and what once is given to them never comes back again from them; for such laws have they that none of them may either give or sell anything.

What law can be made so strong against them that they, either with money or else with other policy, will not break and set at naught? What kingdom can endure that always gives thus from him and receives nothing again? O, how all the substance of your realm, your sword, power, crown, dignity, and obedience of your people, runs headlong into the insatiable whirlpool of these greedy goulafers [gulfs] to be swallowed and devoured!

Neither have they any other color [reason] to gather these yearly exactions into their hands but that they say they pray for us to God to deliver our souls out of the pains of purgatory, without whose prayer, they say, or at least without the pope's pardon, we could never be delivered thence; which, if it be true, then is it good reason that we give them all these things, even were it hundred times as much. But there are many men of great literature and judgment that, for the love they have unto the truth and unto the commonwealth, have not feared to put themselves into the greatest infamy that may be, in abjection [degradation] of all the world, ye, in peril of death, to declare their opinion in this matter, which is that there is no purgatory, but that it is a thing invented by the covetousness of the spirituality, only to translate all kingdoms from other princes unto them, and that there is not one word spoken of it in all holy scripture. They say also, that if there were a purgatory, and also if the pope with his pardons for money may deliver one soul thence; he may deliver him as well without money; if he may deliver one, he may deliver a thousand; if he may deliver a thousand, he may deliver them all, and so destroy purgatory. And then is he a cruel tyrant without all charity if he keep them there in prison and in pain till men will give him money.

Likewise say they of all the whole sort of the spirituality that if they will not pray for any man except for them that give them money, they are tyrants and lack charity and suffer those souls to be punished and pained uncharitably for lack of their prayers. These sort of folks they call heretics; these they burn; these they rage against, put to open shame and make them bear faggots. But whether they are heretics or not, well I know that this purgatory, and the pope's pardon, are all the cause of translation of your kingdom so fast into their hands; wherefore it is manifest that it cannot be of Christ, for he gave more to the temporal kingdom; he himself paid tribute to Caesar, he took nothing from him, but taught that the high powers should be always obeyed; ye, he himself (even though he was the most free lord of all, and innocent) was obedient unto the high powers unto death. This is the great scab why they will not let the New Testament go abroad in your mother tongue, lest men should espy that they [the clergy], by their cloaked hypocrisy, do translate thus fast your kingdom into their hands; that they are not obedient unto your high power; that they are cruel, unclean, unmerciful, and hypocrites; that they seek not the honor of Christ, but their own; that remission of sins are not given by the pope's pardon, but by Christ, for the sure faith and trust that we have in him. Here may your grace well perceive that, unless you allow their hypocrisy to be disclosed, all is like to run into their hands; and as long as it is covered, so long shall it seem to every man to be a great impiety not to give to them. For this I am sure your grace thinks, (as is the truth), that I [your grace] am as good a man as my father; why then may I not as well give them [the people] as much as my father did? And of this mind I am sure are all the lords, knights, squires, gentlemen, and yeomen in England. Ye, and until it is disclosed, all your people will think that your statute of mortmain was never made with any good conscience, seeing that it takes away the liberty of your people, in that they may not buy their souls out of purgatory by giving to the spirituals as lawfully as their predecessors did in times passed.

Wherefore, if you will eschew the ruin of your crown and dignity, let their hypocrisy be uttered; and that shall be more speedful in this matter than all the laws that may be made, be they ever so strong. For to make a law for the punishment of any offender, unless to give other men an example to beware committing such like offense, what should it avail? Did not doctor Allen [judge in Cardinal Wolsey's legantine court], in your own time, most presumptuously and against all his allegiance, do all that he could to keep from you the knowledge of such pleas as belong in your high courts, so as to put them in another court in derogation of your crown and dignity? Did not also doctor Horsey [chancellor of London] and his accomplices most heinously, as all the world knows, murder in prison that honest merchant, Richard Hunne, for bringing a writ of praemunire against a priest who had wrongfully taken him [Hunne] to spiritual court for a matter that belonged in your high courts? And what punishment was there done that any man may take example of to beware of like offense? Truly none, other than that the one [Allen] paid £500 (as it is said) to the building of your Star Chamber; and when that payment was once passed, the captains of his kingdom [high clergy] (because he fought so manfully against your crown and dignity) have helped him to benefice upon benefice, so that he is rewarded ten times as much [e.g., archbishop of Dublin]. The other [Horsey] (as it is said) paid £600 for himself and his accomplices, which, because he had likewise fought so manfully against your crown and dignity, was immediately (as he had obtained your most gracious pardon) promoted by the captains of his kingdom with benefice upon benefice, to the value of 400 times as much. Who can take example of this punishment to beware of such like offense? Who is he of their kingdom that will not rather take courage to commit like offense, seeing the promotions that flow to the men for their so offending? So weak and blunt is your sward to strike at one of the offenders of this crooked and perverse generation!

And this is the reason that the chief instrument of your law, ye, the chief of your counsel, and he who has your sword in his hand, and to whom also all the other instruments are obedient, is always a spiritual man; who has ever such an inordinate love unto his own kingdom, that he will maintain that, though all the temporal kingdoms and commonwealth of the world should therefore utterly be undone. Here we leave out the greatest matter of all, lest we, by declaring such a horrible carrion of evil against the ministers of iniquity should seem to reveal the ignorance of our <king>, our best beloved minister of righteousness, which is to be hid till he, by these small enormities that we have spoken of, comes to know it plainly himself. But what remedy is there to relieve us your poor, sick, lame, and sore beadsmen? To make many hospitals for the relief of the poor people? Nay truly. The more the worse, for ever the best parts are taken by the priests. Divers of you noble predecessors, kings of this realm, have given lands to monasteries to give a certain sum of money yearly to the poor people; but not in all that time have they given one penny. Your predecessors likewise have given money to priests to have certain masses said for them; but the priests never say one. If the abbot of Westminster should sing every day as many masses for his founders as he is bound to do by his foundation, 1000 monks would be too few. Wherefore, if your grace will build a sure hospital that never shall fail to relieve us, all your poor beadsmen, take from them all these things. Set these sturdy louts abroad in the world to get themselves wives of their own, to get their living with their labors in the sweat of their faces, according to the commandment of God, Genesis 3:19, to give other idle people, by their example, occasion to go to labor. Tie these holy, idle thieves to the carts to be whipped naked about every market town till they will fall to labor, that they, by their importunate begging, take not away the alms that the good Christian people would give unto us sore, impotent, miserable people, your beadsmen. Then shall decrease the number of our foresaid monstrous sort—bauds, whores, thieves, and idle people. Then shall these great yearly exactions cease. Then shall not your sword, power, crown, dignity, and obedience of your people be translated from you. Then shall you have full obedience of your people. Then shall the idle people be set to work. Then shall matrimony be much better kept. Than shall the generation of your people be increased. Then shall your commons increase in riches. Then shall the gospel be preached. Then shall no one beg our alms from us. Then shall we have enough, and more than shall suffice us; which shall be the best hospital that every was founded for us. Then shall we daily pray to God for your most noble estate long to endure.

SIR THOMAS MORE, *A SUPPLICATION OF SOULS* (1529)

[Thomas More's *A Supplication of Souls* was written in response to Simon Fish's *Supplication of Beggars* and printed in the autumn of 1529. This defense of the clergy and of the doctrine of purgatory is put into the mouths of souls suffering in purgatory, who will benefit from the reader's prayers here on earth and whose prayers will in turn benefit living Christians. It is divided into two books. The first book takes up the "secular" arguments that Fish makes, arguing that the clergy does not own as much property or exact anything like the amount of money that Fish alleges; that they don't accuse those who attack them of heresy; that the king is not weakened by the clergy but, on the contrary, that the presence of the clergy ensures good order in the commonwealth; that their celibacy does not result in underpopulation or the corruption of women; that they are indeed subject to the law of praemunire. He argues at the end of Book I that these various accusations are really a cover for the Protestant attempt to undermine Catholic faith. The second book, from which the following passages are taken, is a full scale defense of the existence of purgatory. The page numbers refer to Volume 7 of *The Yale Edition of the Works of Thomas More.*

The English language of the early sixteenth century differs greatly from modern English, and in nothing so much as sentence structure. Sentences were often long and leisurely, and they could be modeled on Latin prose, in which it is easier to identify subject, object, and verb in a given sentence. In working with long sentences students are advised to look for the main verb, which often comes toward the end of the sentence. Here punctuation and spelling have been modernized. Difficult words are glossed in square brackets [] and words that are added or substituted are enclosed in angle brackets <>. Passages in **boldface** are summaries or introductions.]

[174-5 To take away purgatory would encourage people to sin.]

For albeit that [although] God of his great mercy may forthwith forgive some folk freely their sin and pain . . . and also that the better passion of our Savior beside the remission of the perpetuity of our pain do also lessen our purgatory and stand us here in marvelous high stead, yet if He should use this point for a general rule—that at every conversion from sin with purpose of amendment and recourse to confession, He shall forthwith fully forgive without the party's pain or any other recompense [i.e. punishment] for the sins committed save only Christ's passion paid for them all—then should He give great occasion of [opportunity for] lightness [wantonness] and bold courage to sin.

For when [if] men were once persuaded that—be their sins never so sore, never so many, never so mischievous [evil], never so long continued—yet they shall never bear pain [punishment] therefore, but <merely> by their . . . faith and their baptism with a short return again to God shall have all their sin and pain also clear forgiven and forgotten (nothing else but only to cry him mercy as one woman would that treadeth on another's train [gown]) this way would as we said give the world great occasion [cause] and courage not only to fall boldly to sin and wretchedness, but also careless to continue therein, presuming upon that thing that such heretics have persuaded unto some men already—that three or four words ere they die shall sufficiently serve them to bring them straight to heaven.

But] . . . if they believe . . . that . . . great and long pain abideth [keeps] them here among us [souls in purgatory] . . . this thing we say (as it is true indeed, so if the world well and firmly for a sure truth believe<s> it) can not fail to be to many folk a good bridle and a sharp bit to refrain them from sin. And on the other side, the contrary belief [in the absence of purgatory] would send many folk forward to sin and thereby in stead of purgatory into everlasting pain.

[The existence of purgatory is proven by passages out of Scripture, including 2 Mac. 12:43–45 and 1 Cor.3:12–15]

[189–90 The pains of hell can be compared to seasickness, in that some people get sicker than others.]

And for as much as ye never can conceive a very right imagination of these things which ye never felt, for it is not possible to find you any example in the world very like unto the pains that sely [helpless] souls feel when they be departed thence, we shall therefore put you in remembrance of one kind of pain which . . . may . . . somewhat be resembled [compared] by reason of the fashion and manner. If there were embarked many people at once . . . by ship conveyed a long journey by sea of such as never came [on ship] before and should hap [happen] all the way to have the seas rise high and sore wrought, and sometime soon upon a storm to lie long after wallowing at an anchor: there should ye find diverse fashions of folk, some peradventure (of them very few) <shall be> so clean from all evil humors and so well attempred [healthy] of themselves, that they shall be all on that long voyage by sea as lusty and as jocund as if they were on land. But for the most part shall ye see sore sick, and yet in many sundry [differing] manner, some more, so less, some longer time diseased, and some much sooner amended. And divers that a while had went [believed] they should have died for pain, yet after one vomit or twain, <are> so clean rid of their grief [discomfort] that they never feel displeasure of it after. And this happeth after [takes place according] as the body is more or less disposed in itself thereto. But then shall ye sometime see there [on ship] some other whose body is so incurably corrupted that they shall walter and tolter [stumble and flounder], and wring their hands, and gnash their teeth, and stomach wamble [be nauseous] and all the body shiver for pain and yet shall never vomit at all, or if they vomit, yet shall they vomit still [continually], and never find ease thereof. Lo, thus fareth it as a small thing may be resembled to a great by the souls deceased and departed the world—that such as be clean and unspotted can in the fire feel no disease at all, and on the other side such as come in thence so deadly poisoned with sin that their spots be indelible and their filthiness unpurgeable, lie fretting and frying in the fire for ever. And only such as neither be fully cleansed nor yet sore defiled but that the fire may fret out [get rid of] the spots of their sin: of this sort only [solely] be we that here lie in purgatory, which [whom] these cruel heretics would make you believe that we feel none harm at all . . . .

[The souls end this section by stating that the words of the Bible are not necessary for belief; the authority of the Church over the ages is enough.]

[196–97   Protestants blasphemously say that they have never seen a spirit from purgatory, but if they have not, then they haven't seen a blessed spirit or a damned spirit either, and there are many people, including Protestants, who have. It is better to believe in hell than to end up seeing it.]

[Against the charge that the pope's charity should extend to all those in purgatory, whether they give alms or not, More says that the pope is doing the will of God. If the pope were simply to allow all out of purgatory, it would be an encouragement to evil.]

For else if either the pope or God should always forthwith deliver [free] every man here [in purgatory] or rather keep every man hence as these heretics [Protestants] would make men believe that God doth indeed, and wills that the world should so take it—then should God or the pope as we somewhat have said before give a great occasion to men boldly to fall in sin and little to care . . . how slowly they rise again. Which thing neither were meet [right] for the pope's office nor for his mercy. For by that mean should he give innumerable folk great occasion of [opportunity for] damnation, which [who] presuming upon such easy short remission would lustily draw to lewdness with little care of amendment.

[Protestants make two objections to purgatory: 1) that you can't profit from the good works of others—but you profit from Christ's good works. 2) You won't try to save yourself if you expect others to help you—but of course you need to help yourself also.]

[202–3 If you are not in a state of grace [i.e. ultimately destined to be saved] you can't profit from other's prayers. But purgatorial souls are in a state of grace, halfway between angels and men—and hence do need your prayers.]

But sith that [since] we be not in that case [of damnation], but have with the help of God's grace deserved to be partners of such good deeds as ye that are our friends will of goodness do for us, ye may by your merits highly relieve us here and help to get us hence. And surely great wonder were it if we should not be able to take profit of your prayers. For there will no wise man doubt but that the prayer of any member of Christendom may profit any other that it is made for, which [who] hath need and is a member [part] of the same [of the mystical body of the church]. But none is there yet living that is more very [truly] member of Christ's mystical body that is his church than we be, nor no man living that hath more need of help than we. For in surety [certainty] of salvation we be fellows with angels: in need of relief [from present pain] we be yet fellows with you.

[There's no need of any other proof of this need of prayer for those in purgatory than the fact that Christians have prayed for them in times past.]

And finally for this point that the suffrages of the church and the prayers of good Christian people stand us here in relief and comfort there needeth in this world . . . none other manner proof than that all Christendom has ever used to do so [been accustomed to], and have thought themselves<s> always bounden to do, damning always for heretics all <those> that would affirm the contrary.

And in this point may they [i.e the Protestants] have a marvelous great thing against them in the judgment of every good man, the great antiquity of Christ's church by which the church hath so long ago customably [by custom] recommended in their prayers all Christian souls to God . . . Go then to the old time and to the good men that then were [Christians who lived in earlier times] and hear what they said and see what they did and believe and follow them.

[205 Giving of alms enables mutual charity.]

But now though the priests pray for us of their own charity, yet when good people desire them thereto and give them their alms therefore—then are they [the priests] double bounden and then rises there much more good and profit upon all sides. For then take we fruit both of the prayer[s] of the one [priests] and the alms of the other [laymen]. And then taketh the priest benefit of his own prayer made both for the giver and for us—the giver also getting fruit both of his own merciful alms and of double prayer also, that is to wit both the prayer of the priest that prayeth for us, which commonly pray for him too, and also the prayer of us, which [who] with great fervor of heart pray for our benefactors incessantly, and are so far forth in God's undoubted favor that very few men living upon earth are so well heard as we. Besides that of all kind of alms that any man can give, the most meritorious is that which is bestowed upon us . . . .

[207 Better to err on the side of belief even if you're wrong.]

. . . he that believes that there were purgatory and that his prayer and good works wrought for his friend's soul might relieve them therein [those in purgatory]. And because thereof [of his belief] used much prayer and alms for them, he could not lose the reward of his good will although his opinion were untrue and that there were no purgatory at all, no more than he loses his labor not that prayeth for one whom he feareth to lie in purgatory when he is already in heaven. But on the other side, he that believeth there is none [no purgatory], and therefore prayeth for none, if his opinion be false and that there be purgatory indeed as indeed there is, he loseth much good and geteth him also much harm, for he both feareth much the less to sin and to lie long in purgatory, saving that [except that] his heresy shall save him thence and send him down deep into hell.

[A story to make the point]

And it fareth [it happens] between these two kind of folk as it fared between a lewd gallant and a poor friar. Whom when the gallant saw going barefoot in a great frost and snow, he asked him why he did take such pain. And he [the friar] answered that it was very little pain if a man would remember hell. Ye, friar, quoth the gallant, but what [if] there be none hell? then art though a great fool. Ye, master, quoth the friar, but what [if] there be hell? then is your mastership a much more fool.

[218 A final plea to remember the souls in purgatory]

But letting pass over such heretics as are our malicious mortal enemies, praying God of his grace to give them better mind, we shall turn us to you that are faithful folk and our dear loving friends, beseeching your goodness of your tender pity that we be remembered with your charitable alms and prayer . . . If ye are < of those who have forgotten us> behold in what heavy plight we lie. Your sloth would soon be quickened and your oblivion turn to fresh remembrance.

[The wrongness of forgetting souls of those you have loved while they burn in purgatory and the shame of coming among them and realizing your own cold-heartedness.]

For your father, your mother, your child, your brother, your sister, your husband, your wife or a very stranger to lie in your sight somewhere in fire, <if> that your means might help him—what heart were so hard, what stomach [disposition] so stony that could sit [at] rest at supper or sleep in rest abed, and let a man lie and burn? We find therefore full true that old saw "out of sight is out of mind." And yet surely to say the truth we cannot therein with reason much complain upon you. For while we were with you there, for wantonness of that wretched world we forgot in likewise our good friends here. And therefore can we not marvel much though the justice of God suffer us to be forgotten of you as others have been before forgotten of us.

But we beseech our Lord for both our sakes to give you the grace to mend for your part that common fault of us both, lest when ye come hither hereafter, God of like justice suffer you to be forgotten of them that ye leave there behind you, as you forgot us that are come hither before you. But albeit we cannot well as we say for the like [same] fault in our self greatly rebuke or blame this negligence and forgetfulness in you; yet would we for the better wish you that ye might without your pain [i.e. without actually suffering punishment] once at the leastwise behold, perceive and see what heaviness of heart and what a sorrowful shame the sely [miserable] soul hath at his first coming hither, to look his old friends in the face here, whom he remembreth himself to have so foul forgotten while he lived there. When albeit [while although] in this place no man can be angry, yet their piteous look and lamentable countenance casteth his unkind forgetfulness into his mind. Wit [know] ye well dear friends that among the manifold great and grievous pains which he suffereth here . . . the grudge and grief of his conscience in the consideration of his unkind forgetfulness is not of them all the least. Therefore dear friends let our folly learn you wisdom. Send hither your prayer; send hither your alms before you; so shall we find ease thereof and yet shall ye find it still. For as he that lighteth another the candle hath never the less light himself, and he that bloweth the fire for another to warm doth warm himself also therewith . . . .

[221–2. Those suffering in purgatory cannot feel less pain if they are temporarily out of purgatory and in the world again.]

". . . And like as the body that hath a hot fever as fervently burneth if he ride a horseback as if he [lay] in his bed, so carry we still about us no less heat with us than if we lay bounden here. And yet the despiteful sights that our evil angels [devils] bring us to behold abroad so far augmenteth our torment, that we would wish to be drowned in the darkness that is here rather than to see the sights that they show us there.

[Devils torment those in purgatory by showing them their friends and relatives making merry with their goods.]

For among us they [the devils] convey us into our own houses, and there double is our pain with sight sometime of the self same things which while we lived was half our heaven to behold. There show they us our substance [possessions] and our bags stuffed with gold, which when we now see we set much less by them [value them less] than would an old man that found a bag of cherry stones which he laid up when he was a child. What a sorrow hath it been to some of us when the devils <have> in despiteful mocking cast in our teeth our old love born to our money and then showed us our executors as busily riffling and ransacking our houses as though they were men of war, that [who] had taken a town by force.

How heavily hath it (think you) gone unto our heart when our evil angels have grinned and laughed and showed us our late wives soon waxen wanton and forgetting us their old husbands (that have loved them so tenderly and left them so rich), sit and laugh and make merry—and more too sometime<s>—with their new whores [gigolos] while our keepers [the devils] in despite keep us there in pain to stand still and look on. Many times would we then speak if we could be suffered [allowed] and sore we long to say to her: "Ah, wife, wife, I wisse [know] this was not covenant [our agreement], wife, when ye wept and told me that if I left you <riches> to live by you would never wed again. We see there our children, whom we loved so well, pipe, sing, and dance and no more think on their fathers' souls than on their old shoes—save that sometimes cometh out "God have mercy on all Christian souls." But that cometh out so coldly and with such dull affection [feeling] that it lyeth but in the lips and never came near the heart. . . .

But when we find in this wise our wives or children and friends so soon and so clearly forget us and see our executors rap and rend unto themselves, catch every man what he can and hold fast [to] that he catcheth and care nothing for us—Lord God what it greveth us that we left so much behind us and had not sent hither more of our substance before us by our own hands. For happy find we him among us that sendeth before all that may be forborne [done without].

[224 The dead wives also appeal to their living husbands.]

[225 A plea for pity from the souls whose pain exceeds all that living men can know.]

Finally, all our other friends and every good Christian man and woman, open your hearts and have some pity upon us. If ye believe not that we need your help, alas the lack of faith. If ye believe our need and care not for us, alack the lack of pity. For who so [whoever] pityeth not us, whom can he pity? If ye pity the poor, there is none so poor as we that have not a brat [rag] to put on our backs. If you pity the blind, there is none so blind as we which are here in the dark saving for sights unpleasant and loathsome till some comfort come. If ye pity the lame, there is none so lame as we, that neither can creep one foot out of the fire nor have one hand at liberty to define our face from the flame. Finally, if ye pity any man in pain, never knew ye pain comparable to ours, whose fire as far passeth in heat all the fires that ever burned upon earth, as the hottest of all those passeth a feigned [imagined] fire painted on a wall. If ever ye lay sick and thought the night long, and longed sore for day while every hour seemed longer than five—bethink you then what a long night we sely [miserable] souls endure, that lie sleepless, restless, burning and broiling in the dark fire one long night of many days, of many weeks, and some of many years together. We walter peradventure and tolter in sickness from side to side and find little rest in any part of the bed: we lie bounden to the brands [sticks of burning wood] and cannot lift up our heads. Ye have your physicians with you that sometime cure and heal you; <but> no physic will help our pain nor no plaster [medical dressing] cool our heat. Your keepers do you great ease and put you in good comfort; our keepers are such as God keep you from, cruel damned spirits, odious, envious, and hateful, dispitious enemies and despiteful tormentors, and their company more horrible and grievous to us than is the pain itself and the intolerable torment that they do us wherewith from top to toe they cease not continually to tear us.

[226 Defends talking about the pains of hell by likenesses, since one can't communicate the reality of the afterlife in mortal speech.]

[A final urging]

Think how soon ye shall come hither to us; think what great grief and rebuke will then your unkindness be to you; what comfort on the contrary part when all we shall thank you; what help ye shall have here of your good [goods] sent hither. Remember what kin ye and we be together; what familiar friendship hath ere this been between us; what sweet words ye have spoken and what promise ye have made us. Let now your words appear and your fair promise be kept. Now, dear friends, remember how nature and Christendom bindeth you to remember us. If any point of your old favor, any piece of your old love, any kindness of kindred, any care of acquaintance, any favor of old friendship, any spark of charity, any tender point of pity, any regard of nature, any respect of Christendom be left in your breasts; let never the malice of a few fond fellows, a few pestilent persons borne toward priesthood, religion and your Christian faith, raze out of your hearts the care of your kindred, all force of your old friends and all remembrance of all Christian souls. Remember our thirst while ye sit and drink; our hunger while ye be feasting; our restless watch [sleeplessness] while ye be sleeping; our sore and grievous pain while ye be playing; our hot burning fire while ye be in pleasure and sporting: so may God make your offspring after remember you, so God keep you hence or not long here; but bring you shortly to bliss, to which for our Lord's love help you to bring us, and we shall set hand to help you thither to us.

"REFORM LEGISLATION"

[from David H. Pill, *The English Reformation, 1529–58* (London: University of London Press; 1973)]

The Acts of 1529

In the Parliament's first session the Commons introduced legislation to deal with a number of clerical abuses and to reduce the fees the clergy received. One of the new Acts reduced probate fees to fixed and moderate proportions. Another fixed the mortuary fees on a graduated scale from 17p [pence] up to 50p, according to the value of the deceased person's property. When the goods of the deceased were worth less than ten marks and in the case of married women, children, persons who were not householders, and wayfarers, no mortuary was to be taken.

Pluralism and non-residence were attacked in a bill which forbade clergy to take to farm land beyond what was necessary for the support of their household, to keep a brewery or a tannery, or otherwise directly or indirectly trade for gain. Pluralities were forbidden with respect to benefices above an annual value of £8. On the face of it this move to keep the clergy at their pastoral work in the parishes was a worthy one. However, the rich pluralist was to be a feature of the ecclesiastical scene for many years to come; for, although clerics were forbidden to accept papal licenses for pluralities, members of the King's Council were to be allowed to hold 3 benefices with cure of souls, and chaplains of the King or nobility two. And, although residence was made obligatory, dispensations could be obtained from the King by his and the nobles' chaplains, clerics of noble origin, and doctors and bachelors in divinity or law. Since a large number of existing pluralists fell into these categories, the situation was but little improved; only the poor priest who wished to augment his income by part-time work suffered.

Nor did these Acts have a mollifying effect on the Pope. If they had any effect at all it was the reverse. Clement summoned Henry to appear before the *Rota*, the supreme court in Rome. And then, as if to scotch rumours that he was privately expressing a wish that the King would marry Anne and settle the matter once and for all without involving the Holy See, he issued a series of bulls threatening excommunication if he should do any such thing. He also prohibited anyone from speaking or writing against the validity of Catherine's marriage, and any court or other body from attempting to pass judgment on it.

The Pardoning of the Clergy

Henry's reaction was to inform the papal nuncio of the existence of the law of *Praemunire*, which declared that those who brought or received papal bulls into England which touched "our Lord the King, against him, his crown, and royalty or his realm" should be "put out of the King's protection, and their lands, tenements, goods and chattels forfeited to our Lord the King, and that they be attached by their bodies . . . and brought before the King and his Council."

In the summer of 1530 he decided to show the world that these were not empty words. Writs of *Praemunire facias* were issued against eight bishops and seven other leading clergy. The charge was that they had aided Wolsey in his offences by handing over part of their income to him. This had indeed happened, but the reason had not been to help Wolsey exercise his papal powers but rather to restrict them. The bishops had bribed him in order to prevent him from overriding their episcopal authority.

Before a decision had been reached in this case, the whole clerical estate were accused of *praemunire*. Although from the existing evidence the charge is not clear, it was probably either one of accepting Wolsey's legatine authority or of exercising their jurisdiction in the Church courts. When Convocation met in January 1531, those who had bribed Wolsey bought off the wrath of the Crown. In return for a pardon, the Convocation of Canterbury agreed to pay £100,000 and that of the much poorer province of York, £18,840. His Majesty's allies, the laity, on the other hand were freely forgiven their *praemunire*. In addition to paying him money, the clergy agreed to acknowledge Henry as their "singular protector, only and supreme lord . . . even Supreme Head," but with the important proviso "so far as the law of Christ allows." If this submission was a result of a deliberate campaign to deprive the Pope of all his rights over the English Church (and some would deny that it was) then victory was not yet complete . . . .

The Supplication Against the Ordinaries

In 1532 the legislative independence of the English Church was destroyed. Ironically, it happened at a time when Convocation was embarking on an impressive programme of reform, issuing canons which put a tighter control on the qualifications of ordinands, attempted to compel clergy to reside, increased the penalties for fornication and imposed a weekly minimum of six hours' scriptural study on incumbents. Such measures, of course, did not please those who wished to see the Church discredited.

The destructive process began with the presentation to Henry by the Commons of their Supplication against the Ordinaries, a document which some scholars believe Cromwell first drafted as an ordinary member of the House in 1529. Its demands for a single sovereignty and undivided allegiance in the realm certainly savour of what are known to have been his views. The draft of 1532 linked together the power of the Church courts, which the Commons disliked, and the legislative power of Convocation, which the Crown wished to control. To some this suggests that the presentation of the document was government inspired. It attacked the power of Convocation to make laws without the consent of the laity. It protested against prosecution over trivial matters in the Church courts, and against high legal fees. It also contained a number of accusations against the church not connected with the ecclesiastical jurisdiction, including the sale of sacraments and the presentation of minors to benefices, and it criticized the neglect of work through an excessive number of holy days. The clergy made an appeal for the King's protection but Henry's response was to encourage the Commons to continue their attack, and to demand that Convocation should pass no new legislation unless he licensed them to do so. He also insisted that existing canons should be referred for approval or disapproval to a royal commission of thirty-two members, half of them laymen. The following day, he explained to the Speaker and a delegation from Commons what he had done. He informed them that he had discovered that "all the prelates at their consecration make an oath to the Pope clean contrary to the oath they make to us, so that they seem his subjects not ours." Both King and Commons had long been aware of this, but the latter were dutifully horror-stricken, and Henry asked them to consider what might be done. Perhaps fearing the Commons might decide that appropriate action would be the complete destruction of their courts and law-making powers by Act of Parliament, Convocation submitted to the King's demands, and the next day the perceptive Sir Thomas More resigned the chancellorship. Having used the Commons to persuade Convocation to surrender its legislative powers, Henry ignored their other demands.

The Conditional Restraint of Annates

While the Supplication was still being debated by Commons and Convocation, Henry was encouraging the Lords to legislate against annates. The preamble to their bill described them as "great and inestimable sums of money" which were "daily conveyed out of this realm to the impoverishment of the same," something we know to have been an exaggeration. It was stated that payments were to cease but that the bill was not to become law until confirmed by letters patent from the King. Henry was trying to bully the Pope into doing what he wished by applying economic blackmail. He had some difficulty getting both Houses to agree to it. Even the people who had suffered directly from annates, the bishops and abbots, voted against it. Perhaps they still felt some loyalty to Rome; the Commons may have feared reprisals, such as the stopping of the valuable wool trade with Charles V's Flanders. At any rate Henry felt it necessary to be present in the House at the time of the division on the bill. Yet he tried to win the Pope's favour by pretending that he was standing in the way of an all but overwhelming demand by Parliament for the abolition of the payments to the Holy See. He instructed his agents in Rome to "instil into their ears how incessant have been our efforts to resist importunity of our people from passing the statute." The Act anticipated retaliation from Rome by declaring that should the Pope delay or deny bulls of consecration, bishops might be consecrated by English authority alone. Should he decide on excommunication or interdict (banning the English people from all ecclesiastical rites), the King and his lay subjects might "without any scruple of conscience" continue to receive the sacraments and attend the services of the Church.

The Act in Restraint of Appeals

. . . A bill was introduced into Parliament to prevent any attempt by Catherine to appeal against the Archbishop's verdict on her marital status to the Holy See; its phraseology had convinced many that the mind behind it was Cromwell's not Henry's.

. . . this realm of England is an empire, and so hath been accepted in the world, governed by one Supreme Head and King . . . unto whom a body politic, compact of all sorts and degrees of people, divided in terms, and by names of spirituality and temporality, be bounden and owe to bear, next to God, a natural and humble obedience.

These words and those which followed could indeed be said to echo the words of Marsiglio but the theory that England was an empire or sovereign state was an old tradition based on the legendary descent of the monarch from Constantine the Great. There was a further appeal to the past in a reference to the laws of previous reigns (Provisors and *Praemunire*) which had been designed to keep England "free from the annoyance as well of the see of Rome as from the authority of other foreign potentates." These laws had proved insufficient, for they did not cover "causes testamentary, *causes of matrimony and divorces*, rights of tithes, oblations [donations for pious uses] and obventions [fees occasionally received]." The "part of the body politic, called the spirituality, now being usually called the English Church" was, however, capable of dealing with such matters itself and would in the future do so, thus saving the King and his subjects "great inquietation, vexation, trouble, cost and charges" and preventing "great delay and let to the true and speedy determination of the said causes."

The Annulment

The Act having been passed (not without resistance from a Commons still worried about the wool trade), further steps were taken to clear the way for the annulment of the King's first marriage. A depleted Convocation passed resolutions that the Pope had had no right to permit the marriage of Henry and Catherine after the consummation of Catherine's marriage to Arthur, and that consummation had been adequately proved. Then on 23 May 1533, at a special court meeting at Dunstable, Cranmer [Warham's successor as Archbishop] declared the King's first marriage null and void from the beginning. He followed this up with a decree proclaiming Henry's marriage with Anne valid; and the new Queen was crowned. If Henry thought that the Pope would accept the Archbishop's verdict because, as he had stated when giving it, he was "Legate of the Apostolic See," he was mistaken. Clement's idea of legality was different from Henry's. In July he declared that Anne was not the King's wife, and Henry was excommunicated. However the sentence was suspended till September to give him time to repent and put away his mistress. In that month his daughter Elizabeth was born. Though she was not the boy he had hoped for, she was duly recognized as his heir.

The Act for the Submission of the Clergy

The Pope's attitude resulted in a spate of legislation which, during the early months of 1534, brought the English Church more and more under the royal thumb. One of the new laws put the clergy's submission following the Commons' Supplication of 1532 into statutory form, and the penalty of fine or imprisonment at the King's pleasure was imposed on all who should act contrary to its provisions. Appeals to Rome, which the Act of the previous year had prohibited only in certain cases, were now, under penalty of *praemunire*, forbidden in any case whatsoever. In lieu of the right thus abolished, it was decreed that appeals from the archbishop's court should be made to commissioners appointed under the Great Seal, that is to the King in Chancery.

The Act in Absolute Restraint of Annates

In the previous July the King had put the provisions of the Act of Annates into operation. Now Parliament confirmed his action by passing a new statute which referred to the failure of the "Bishop of Rome," as the Pope was now called in English official documents, to make use of the opportunity given to him to redress grievances relating to the payments. Not only did the new Act stop the Pope from receiving them once and for all, it also forbade Englishmen to procure papal bulls for the consecration of bishops and abbots. And it confirmed the existing practice whereby the King chose his own bishops, making statutory the attendant formalities. Chapter was obliged to elect the person named in letters missive sent within the *congé d'éliore*. Failure to do so within twelve days would cause the chapter to lay themselves open to a charge of *Praemunire*, and the King would then appoint by letter patent.

The Act Forbidding Papal Dispensations and Payment of Peter's Pence

Another Act, usually called the Dispensations Act, stopped *all* payments to Rome, including Peter's Pence, and said that dispensations allowing departures from canon law should in the future be issued by the Archbishop of Canterbury. *Praemunire* featured here too, for its penalties were to be incurred by anyone suing to Rome for any bulls, licenses or instruments forbidden by the Act. Strange as it may seem, however, it is possible that even at this late stage Henry was hoping to make his peace with Rome, for the Act was not to take effect until the feast of St John the Baptist, three months later, unless the King should decide to the contrary. In addition the King was empowered to annul the whole or any part of the Act at any time before the feast day. However, that he did not do, for on 23 March 1534 Clement closed the royal case, which had all this time been "'under consideration" in Rome, by solemnly pronouncing Henry's first marriage valid. The immediate answer was a proclamation ordering the Pope's name to be struck out of all prayer books, that it be "never more (except in contumely and reproach) remembered, but perpetually suppressed and obscured."

Act of Supremacy

By the time the first parliamentary session of 1534 ended in that same month of March, the King had an annulment which he found satisfactory, a new wife and a new heir; the Pope had lost all his rights in England except those which he shared with all other bishops, namely his sacramental ones; and the English Church had more than ever been subjected to the royal will. The King's claim to appoint bishops had statutory power behind it; the legislation of the church was subject to lay approval; its judicial powers were limited by appeal to the Chancery. When Parliament met for a second session in

November, what this state of affairs really amounted to was recognized in a statute which declared:

Albeit the King's Majesty justly and rightfully is and oweth to be Supreme Head of the Church of England, and so is recognized by the clergy of this realm in their Convocations, yet nevertheless for corroboration and confirmation thereof, and for the increase of virtue in Christ's religion within this realm of England, and to repress and extirp all errors, heresies and other enormities and abuses heretofore used in the same; be it enacted by the authority of this present Parliament, that the King our Sovereign Lord, his heirs and successors, kings of this realm, shall be taken, accepted, and reputed the only Supreme Head on earth of the Church of England.

The first great act of nationalization was over. The King's new title was clearly stated; no allowance was made for convenient consciences with the words "so far as the law of Christ allows." However, the Pope had claimed to exercise two kinds of power, entitled *potestas jurisdictionis* and *potestas ordinis*. In this statute the monarch was given *potestas jurisdictionis*, the power to subject the clergy to all the laws of the realm, to define doctrine and ensure the teaching of the same, to hold visitations and reform abuses; he did not have *potestas ordinis*, the right to administer the sacraments, to excommunicate or to preach, for he was not a priest, so he had none of the spiritual powers of a Pope, only the administrative ones. The Church in England might have become the Church of England, but in its hierarchy, its sacraments and its doctrine it remained, for the time being at least, Catholic.

The Act Annexing First Fruits and Tenths to the Crown

With the Church firmly under its control, the Crown, impoverished by an active but futile foreign policy and extravagance at court, began to tap its wealth. Though the Act in Conditional Restraint of Annates had condemned those payments to Rome as an 'intolerable burden', they were now made payable to the Crown by all those entering any new living or church office, secular or monastic, high or low. Not only that, but all beneficed clergy were to pay a tenth of their net incomes to the King annually. And he was not going to be content with an assessment made in 1292 as the Pope had been. To make sure he got what he was entitled to, Cromwell, now Henry's Vicar-General in ecclesiastical matters, ordered the compilation of the *Valor Ecclesiasticus*, a detailed account of all clerical incomes. A wonder book of information for the historian, it is the Domesday Book of its time. The result of all this labour was the addition £40,000 a year to the royal income, though as time went on inflation increased the value of livings and the *Valor*'s assessments, though still applied, became as unrealistic as those of the *Taxation* of 1292.

STATUTES OF THE REFORMATION PARLIAMENT

[From *Statutes of the Realm*, volume 3 (London: Dawsons of Pall Mall, 1963); modernized and redacted, but without ellipses to indicate excisions or brackets to indicate additions, replacements, or explanations, because the changes made are too many.]

November 1529 _____

An Act concerning Fines and Sums of Money To Be Taken by the Ministers of Bishops and Other Ordinaries of Holy Church for the Probate of Testament

Probate reform—restrictions on clerical fees charged for processing of wills (pp.285–88)

Whereas in the parliament held at Westminster in the thirty-first year of the reign of the noble King of famous memory Edward III, upon the complaint of his people for the outrageous and grievous fines and sums of money taken by the ministries of bishops of the Holy Church for the probate of testaments; the said noble King in the same parliament openly charged and commanded the archbishop of Canterbury and the other bishops that for the time being amendment of said practices should be had; and that if no amendment were forthcoming, the King, by the authority of the same parliament, should make inquiry by his justices of such oppression and extortions. And whereas at the parliament held at Westminster in the third year of the reign of King Henry V, it was recited that the commons of the realm had often complained that divers ordinaries take for the probation of testaments sometimes 40 shillings, sometimes 60 shillings, and sometimes more against right and justice, whereas in the time of King Edward III, men were wont to pay for such causes but 2 shillings, 6 pence, or 5 shillings at the most; it was then enacted for the avoiding of such oppression that no ordinary from thenceforth should take for the probation of testament any more than was accustomed and used in the time of the said noble King Edward III, upon pain to yield to the party so grieved three times as much as the said ordinaries did so receive; <u>which act did endure but to the next parliament following by reason that the ordinaries did then promise to reform and amend their oppressions and extortions; notwithstanding said promise, these unlawful exactions were not reformed nor amended but greatly augmented and increased, against right and justice, and to the great impoverishment</u> of the King's subjects. Accordingly, the King our Sovereign Lord by the assent of the Lords Spiritual and Temporal and the Commons in this present parliament assembled and by authority of the same <u>has ordained, established, and enacted that from the first day of April 1530 nothing shall be demanded, received, nor taken by any bishop ordinary for probation of testament where the goods of the testator so dying do not amount above the value of 100 shillings sterling.</u> The bishop ordinary shall not refuse to approve any such testament being lawfully tended or offered to him to be approved. And when the goods of the testator do amount above the value of 100 shillings and do not exceed the sum of £40 sterling, that then no bishop ordinary shall take of any person more than 3 shillings, and 6 denarius.

V

And it is enacted that every bishop ordinary that shall do or attempt anything against this act shall forfeit and lose for every time so offending to the party grieved so much money as he shall take contrary to the act; and over that shall lose and forfeit £10 sterling, whereof the one half shall be given to the King our Sovereign Lord and the other half to the party grieved who will sue by action of debt bull in any of the King's courts for the recovery of the same.

An Act concerning the Taking, Demanding, Receiving, or Claiming of Mortuaries

Mortuary reform—restrictions on clerical fees charged for burials (pp. 288–89)

Forasmuch as there has been much ambiguity and doubt in the demanding, receiving, and claiming of mortuaries, as well as much complaint that the greatness and value of the same has been excessive to the poor people and other persons of this realm; and forasmuch as mortuaries have been demanded from those that have no goods at the time of their deaths and from wayfaring travelers in the places where they have chanced to die: To the intent that all doubt, contention, and uncertainty herein may be removed, as well as the generality of the King's people therein remedied, and the vicars, parish priests, and curates provided for; be it enacted, ordained, and established by the King our Sovereign Lord, the Lords Spiritual and Temporal, and the Commons of this parliament assembled that no person shall take, receive, or demand any mortuary, any sums of money, or any other thing worth more than what is hereafter mentioned. Nor shall any persons take legal action for the recovery of any such mortuary, upon pain of forfeiting as much in value as they shall take above the sum limited by this act.

II

First, it is ordained, established, and enacted that no manner of mortuary shall be taken from any person who at the time of his death has under 10 marks in movable goods. Also, that no mortuary shall be given, asked, or demanded but only in such place where heretofore mortuaries have been used to be paid; nor that any person pay mortuaries in more places than one, and in that place of his most frequent dwelling and habitation. And while mortuaries shall rise with the worth of the person dying or dead, in no case shall fees exceed 10 shillings.

III

No manner of mortuary is to be asked of married women, children, or persons keeping house; nor of any wayfaring man except in the place where he had the longest period of habitation.

IV

Always it shall be lawful for vicars, curates, parish priests, and other spiritual persons to take and receive any sum of money or other thing which by any person dying shall chance to be disposed, given, or bequeathed unto them, or to the high altar of the church. In places where mortuaries have been accustomed to be taken of less value than is aforesaid, no person shall be compelled to pay in any such place any other mortuary, or more for any mortuary than has been accustomed.

An Act . . . for Plurality of Benefices; and for Residence

Limitations on benefices and prohibitions on non-residency (pp. 292–96)

IX

Be it enacted that if any person having one benefice with cure of souls, being of the yearly value of £8 or above, accept and take any other benefice with cure of souls, and be instituted and inducted in possession of the same, then immediately after such possession had thereof, the first benefice shall be adjudged in the law to be void. And that it shall be lawful to every patron having the avowson thereof to present another, and the presentee to have the benefit of the same in such like manner and form as though the incumbent had died or resigned. And that if any person at any time after the first day of April in the year of our Lord God 1530 procure and obtain at the Court of Rome or elsewhere any license to receive and take any more benefices with cure than is above limited, such person shall incur the danger, pain, and penalty of £20 sterling and also lose the whole profit of every such benefice he receives, the one half of which forfeiture to go to the King our Sovereign Lord and the other half to him who will sue for the same in any of the King's courts.

X

Provided always that this act not extend nor be prejudicial to any person who at any time prior to the first day of April 1530 shall be really entitled and possessed of not more than four benefices with cure of souls.

XI

Provided also that all spiritual men now being or who hereafter shall be of the King's Council may purchase license for three benefices with cure of souls—etc.

XV

Be it also furthermore enacted that every spiritual person of the rank of archdeacon and above shall be personally resident and abiding in his said benefice, or at any one of them at the least.

XVI

And if any person procure at the Court of Rome or elsewhere any manner of license to be non-resident at their benefice contrary to this act, then every such person shall incur the penalty, damage, and pain of £20 sterling for every time so doing, to be forfeited and recovered as is above said, and such license to be void and of none effect.

XVII

Provided always that this act of non-residence shall not in any way extend nor be prejudicial to any such spiritual person as shall chance to be in the King's service beyond the sea, nor to any person going to any pilgrimage or holy place beyond the sea; nor to any scholar abiding for study at any university within this realm or without—etc.

XVIII

Provided also that it shall be lawful to every spiritual person being chaplains to the King our Sovereign Lord to accept any benefice which it shall please his Highness to give, of what number soever it be, without incurring the danger, penalty, and forfeiture in this statute comprised. And that also it shall be lawful to the King's Highness to give license to any of his own chaplains for non-residence upon their benefices.

An Act to Release the King His Highness from Such Sums of Money as May Be Required of Him by Any Subject for Any Reason

Repudiation of royal debts (pp. 315–16)

The King's humble, faithful, and loving subjects the Lords Spiritual and Temporal and the Commons in this present parliament assembled, considering and calling to their remembrance the inestimable costs, charges, and expenses which the King's Highness has necessarily been compelled to support and sustain since the assumption of his royal estate and dignity, as well as his exertions in defense of the church, rent by schism and the kingdom, threatened by war; and considering that when the entire Christian world was all death and destruction, the King's subjects in all this time, by the high providence and politic means of his Grace, were nevertheless preserved, defended, and maintained from all these inconveniences and dangers and were free to exercise their traffics of merchandise and order their crafts and occupations for their livings, which could not possibly have been brought about except by the continual studies, travails, and pains of the King's Highness, and the charges and expenses he has incurred, for the reducing of enemies unto peace. Considering furthermore that in all these duties, the King has employed both the contributions of his loving subjects, whether procured by loan or by tax, as well as his own treasure and yearly revenue, which his Grace might have kept and reserved for his own use: We, the present parliament and representatives of the whole realm, do freely, liberally, and absolutely give and grant unto the King's Highness all and every sum and sums of money which to his subjects is due by reason of any money or any other thing to his Grace at any time heretofore was advanced or paid; and we remit, release, and quite claim unto his Highness, his heirs and successors forever, all and every of the same sums of money and every parcel thereof; and all suits, petitions, and demands which his subjects or their heirs might hereafter file or submit, we declare void and of none effect.

An Act concerning Punishment of Beggars and Vagabonds

Begging rights for certain of the poor, and punishments for others (pp. 328–32)

Whereas in all places throughout this realm, vagabonds and beggars have of long time increased and daily do increase in great and excessive numbers by the occasion of idleness, the mother of all vices, causing continual thefts, murders, and other heinous offenses and great enormities to the high displeasure of God and the inquiet and damage of the King's people and to the marvelous disturbance of the commonweal of this realm;

and whereas many and sundry good laws have before this time been devised and made as well by the King our Sovereign Lord and by his predecessors, yet notwithstanding which the vagabonds and beggars have not diminished, but rather daily augmented and increased into great companies: <u>Be it therefore enacted</u> by the King our Sovereign Lord, and by the Lords Spiritual and Temporal and the Commons in this parliament assembled, <u>that justices of the peace in every county shall have power to make diligent search and inquiry of all aged, poor, and impotent persons which live, or of necessity be compelled to live, by alms of the charity of the people; and that after such search, said justice shall have power to grant licenses to impotent persons, by which they may go begging within the limits of city, town, or parish, but not without.</u> The names of said impotent persons shall be registered and written in a bill or role, and a letter containing the names of the same and specifying the limits within which they be authorized to beg shall be issued by the above said justices. Impotent persons begging outside their limits shall be set in the stocks with only bread and water; thereafter they shall be sworn to return again to the city, town, or parish wherein they be authorized to beg.

II
Beggars without letters shall be stripped naked from the middle upwards and whipped within the towns where they be taken, or set in the stocks, at the discretion of the justice.

III
And be it further enacted by the authority aforesaid that if any person or persons, being whole and mighty in body and capable of labor, who be taken in begging, or be vagrant and able to give no reckoning of how he does lawfully get his living, shall be tied to the end of a cart naked and be beaten with whips throughout the town until his body be bloody; and after such punishment and whipping had, the person so punished, by the discretion of the justice, shall be enjoined upon his oath to return forthwith to the place where he was born or where he last dwelled for the space of three years and there put himself to labor. Cities, towns, or parishes that be negligent and not punish every such impotent and strong beggar according to the form of this statute, shall suffer and pay a fine, the half of which to be given to the King our Sovereign Lord and the other half to him that will sue for the same by any bull of information.

IV
And be it enacted that scholars of the Universities of Oxford and Cambridge that go about begging without sufficient authority; and shipmen pretending losses of their ships and goods; and all other idle persons using divers and subtle crafty and unlawful games and plays, and some of them feigning to have knowledge of physics, physiognomy, palmistry, or other crafty sciences whereby they pretend to tell the destinies, deceases, fortunes, and such other like fantastical imaginations to the great deception of the King's subjects: that these offenders shall be punished by whipping after the manner before rehearsed. And if any offend in a like offense a second time, he shall be scourged, put upon the pillory, and suffer the loss of one ear; and if he offend a third time, the same and the loss of the other ear.

VI
And furthermore be it enacted that any person giving harbor, money, or lodging to any strong beggars able in their bodies to work, shall make payment of a fine to the King.

An Act concerning the Pardon Granted to the King's Spiritual Subjects of the Provinces of Canterbury for the Praemunire

King's pardon for clergy accused of praemunire (pp. 334–38)

The King our Sovereign Lord calling to his blessed and most gracious remembrance that his good and loving spiritual subjects of the archbishopric of Canterbury have fallen into divers dangers by things done, perpetrated, and committed contrary to the order of his laws, and especially contrary to the form of the statute of provisors, provisions, and praemunire; and having a tender eye with mercy and pity and compassion toward his said spiritual subjects, gives and grants them his free pardon to be taken and enjoyed by them and every of them by virtue of this present act. The King's Highness, in consideration that the archbishop, bishops, and clergy of the said province of Canterbury in their said Convocation now sitting, have given and granted to him a subsidy of £100,000 of lawful money current in this realm, is fully and resolutely contented and pleased that it be ordained, established, and enacted by authority of this his said parliament that all spiritual subjects of the province of Canterbury, by authority of this present pardon, be acquitted, pardoned, released, and discharged against his Highness, his heirs, successors, and executors, and every of them, of all and all manner offenses, contempts, and trespasses committed or done against all and each statute and statutes provisors, provisions, and praemunire.

An Act concerning the Pardon Granted to the King's Temporal Subjects for Praemunire

King's pardon for laity accused of praemunire (p. 338)

The King our Sovereign Lord does remember the manifold great offenses committed by divers and many of his temporal and lay subjects against his Highness contrary to the statutes of provisions, provisors, and praemunire, by reason whereof they so offending have incurred the dangers and penalties of law and so now are liable to forfeiture of lands, goods, and chattels and to loss of his gracious protection. Nevertheless, his royal Majesty, having always most tender zeal, favor, and affection for his loving subjects, and not wishing to enforce his penal laws upon them, does remit and mitigate the full rigor of the same; and of his mere motion, high benignity, special grace, pity, and liberality has given and granted, and by authority of this present parliament does give and grant a general and free pardon to all and each of his temporal and lay subjects and temporal bodies politic and corporations for all offenses committed against the said statutes of provisions, provisors, and praemunire.

An Act concerning Restraint of Payment of Annates to the See of Rome

Conditional cessation of Annates payments to Rome (pp. 385–88)

The Noblemen of this realm, and the wise, sage, politic Commons of the same, assembled in this present parliament, considering that the Court of Rome ceases not to tax, take, and exact the great sums of money under the title of Annates or First Fruits, to the great disadvantage of the prelates and this realm, which Annates or First Fruits were first suffered to be taken within the same realm only for the defense of Christian people against the infidels, and now they be claimed and demanded as mere duty, only for lucre, against all right and conscience, insomuch that it is evidently known that there has passed out of this realm unto the Court of Rome since the second year of the reign of the most noble prince of famous memory, King Henry VIII, unto this present time, the sum of 800,000 ducats, amounting to in sterling money at the least eight score £1000; and albeit that our said Sovereign Lord the King and all his natural subjects, both spiritual and temporal, be as obedient, devout, Catholic, and humble children of God and Holy Church as any people be within any realm christened, yet the said exactions of Annates or First Fruits be so intolerable and importable to this realm that it is considered and declared that the King's Highness before almighty God is bound as by the duty of a good Christian prince, for the conservation and preservation of the good estate and commonwealth of this his realm, to do all that is in him to obviate, repress, and redress the said exactions of Annates or First Fruits; and because divers prelates of this realm be now in extreme age and in other debilities of their bodies, so that of likelihood bodily death in short time shall or may succeed unto them, by reason whereof great sums of money shall shortly after their deaths be conveyed unto the Court of Rome for the unreasonable and uncharitable causes abovesaid, to the universal damage, prejudice, and impoverishment of this realm, if speedy remedy be not in due time provided: It is therefore ordained, established, and enacted by the authority of this present parliament that the unlawful payments of Annates or First Fruits for any archbishopric or bishopric shall from henceforth utterly cease, and that no manner person or persons hereafter to be named, elected, presented, or postulated to any archbishopric or bishopric within this realm shall pay the said Annates or First Fruits upon pain of forfeiture to our said Sovereign Lord the King, his heirs and successors, all manner of his goods and chattels forever, and all the temporal lands and possessions belongs to the archbishoprics or bishoprics during the time that he or they which shall offend do have, possess, or enjoy the same.

II
And furthermore, should any person hereafter named by the King or any of his heirs or successors to serve as bishop of any see or diocese within this realm be deferred or delayed at the Court of Rome by means of restraint of bulls apostolic: Be it enacted that every such person so presented shall be consecrated here in England by the archbishop in whose province the bishopric shall be; and should any person named by the King to serve as archbishop be delayed at the Court of Rome, said same person shall be consecrated and invested by any other two bishops within this realm whom the King's Highness will assign and appoint for the same, according and in like manner as divers other archbishops

and bishops have heretofore in ancient times been consecrated and invested by the King's most noble progenitors.

IV

And it is also further ordained and enacted by the authority of this present parliament that any time prior to the feast of Easter of 1533, the King, by letters patent, may and shall have full power and liberty to declare whether any part of this act and statute of parliament shall be observed, obeyed, executed, or performed.

V

If our Holy Father the Pope should at any time hereafter vex and molest the realm with excommunication or interdiction: Be it enacted that our Sovereign Lord, his heirs or successor kings of England, and his spiritual and lay subjects, shall, without any scruple of conscience, minister or cause to be ministered all sacraments, ceremonies, or other divine services as they heretofore have been virtuously used within this realm; nor shall any papal censures be published by any prelates or spiritual fathers of this region.

Commons' Supplication against the Ordinaries

Petition to revoke or curtail legislative power of Convocation (in State Papers of Henry VIII, volume 1, number 22)

First, the clergy of this your realm, being your subjects, make in their Convocation divers laws and ordinances concerning temporal things, some of which be repugnant to the laws and statutes of your realm. Not requiring your assent to these laws, they yet declare that the infringers of these same laws incur not only the terrible censures of excommunication but also the detestable crime and sin of heresy. Your humble lay subjects are then brought into ambiguity as to whether they may execute your laws according to your royal jurisdiction for dread of the same pains and censures comprised in the said ecclesiastical laws. Also, many of your subjects, especially the poorest sort, are daily summoned before the bishops, called spiritual ordinaries, for displeasure without any probable cause and sometimes committed to prison without bail, and there sometime lie half a year. There they are constrained to answer many subtle interrogations only invented at the pleasure of said ordinaries, by which the simple and unlearned may be trapped and induced by an ignorant answer to accept open penance to their shame or else redeem the same penance for money. Additionally, if witnesses are called, they are but two in number and never of great credence, and are used also to induce the subject to pay redemption money. Also, many of your subjects, who are cited to appear out of the diocese they dwell in, may be excommunicated for small causes made under a pretended seal of an archdeacon with no warning. And yet, when absolved, they will be forced to pay their proctor, as well as the proctor who is against them, and the scribe, to the great impoverishing of your said subjects. Also, your subjects are grieved with excessive fees in the spiritual courts, and the probate of testaments. And there is exacted and demanded of your subjects in divers parishes of this your realm other manner of tithes than have been customary this past 100 years. Likewise, since the statute of mortuaries was made, where any mortuary is due after the rate of the statute, sometimes curates, before they will demand it, will bring citations for it and then will not receive the mortuary till they may have such costs as they say they have laid out for suit for the same. Also, oftentimes, when many spiritual persons are presented by your Highness or by other patrons to divers benefices and other spiritual promotions, said ordinaries not only do take of them many great sums of money and rewards, but also do long delay them without reasonable cause before they will admit, institute, and induct them; because said ordinaries will have the profits of the benefice during vacancy, unless the presentees do agree that after their institution they will share some part of the profits of their benefice with the ordinaries. Furthermore, spiritual ordinaries do daily confer and give sundry benefices to certain young folks, calling them nephews or kinsfolk, which being in their minority are unable to serve the cure of any such benefice; whereby the said ordinaries do keep the fruits of the same benefices in their own hands, while the poor silly souls of your people, for lack of good curates, do perish without good example, doctrine, or any good teaching.

February–April 1533_____

An Act in Restraint of Appeals

Rome no longer recognized as court of appeals for cases arising in England (pp. 427–29)

Whereby in divers sundry old authentic histories and chronicles it is manifestly declared and expressed that this realm of England is an empire, and so has been accepted in the world, governed by one supreme head and king having the dignity and royal estate of the imperial crown of the same, unto whom a body politic composed of all degrees of people is bound to bear a natural obedience, next only to God; the King, being furnished by Almighty God with plenary power, preeminence, authority, prerogative, and jurisdiction, may render justice and final determination to all manner of folks resident or subjects within this realm in all causes, matters, debates, and contentions happening to occur within the limits thereof, without restraint by any foreign princes of the world. Likewise, the spiritual body, now being usually called the English Church, has the power, knowledge, integrity, and sufficiency of number, when any cause of law divine comes into question, to determine all such doubts without the intermeddling of any exterior persons, and to administer all such duties as do appertain to their offices. For the due administration whereof, and to keep them from corruption and sinister affection, the King's most noble progenitors, and the ancestors of the Nobles of this realm, have sufficiently endowed the said Church both with honor and possession. And the temporal laws for trial of propriety of lands and goods, and for the conservation of the people of this realm in unity and peace, were and still are administered by sundry judges of the other part of the said body politic called temporality, and both their authorities and jurisdictions do conjoin together in the due administration of justice. The King and his predecessors have made laws and provisions for the prerogatives, liberties, and preeminences of the said imperial crown of this realm, and of the jurisdictions spiritual and temporal of the same, to keep them from the annoyance of the See of Rome or from the authority of other foreign potentates attempting the diminution or violation thereof.. But notwithstanding the said good statutes and ordinances past made, divers and sundry inconveniences and dangers not provided for plainly by the said former acts have risen and sprung by reason of appeals sued out of this realm to the See of Rome, in causes testamentary, causes of matrimony and divorces, and right of tithes, not only to the great vexation and cost of the King's Highness and many of his subjects, but also to the great delay in the true and speedy determination of these causes. Furthermore, as Rome is so far distant from this realm, neither the necessary proofs nor the true knowledge of the cause can be there so well known, nor the witnesses there so well examined as within this realm, so that the parties grieved by means of the said appeals be most times without remedy. <u>In this consideration whereof, the King's Highness, his Nobles and Commons, considering the great enormities, dangers, long delays, and hurts that do daily ensue, do therefore enact, establish, and ordain that all causes testamentary, causes of matrimony and divorce, and rights of tithes already commenced or hereafter coming in contention, debate, or question within this realm, whether they concern the King, his family, or any other subjects within the realm, shall be from henceforth heard, examined, discussed, and definitively adjudged and determined within the King's jurisdiction and authority and not elsewhere, in such courts spiritual and temporal as shall be required.</u> Any foreign appeals, summons, citations, suspensions, interdictions, excommunications, restraints, or judgments from the See of Rome or any other foreign courts or potentates of the world are henceforth no impediment. It shall be lawful to the King and his subjects within this realm, notwithstanding any possible punishments, to pursue, execute, have, and enjoy the effects, profits, and benefits of all such processes, sentences, judgments, and determinations in any court spiritual or temporal as the cases shall require within the limit of the King's realm. Also, all spiritual prelates may use, minister, execute, and do all sacraments, sacramentals, divine services, and all other things unto all subjects within the realm as Catholic and Christian men owe to do, any foreign citations, inhibitions, suspensions, interdictions, excommunications, or appeals touching any of the aforementioned causes to or from the See of Rome or any other foreign court to the contrary thereof notwithstanding. And if any of the spiritual persons by the occasion of the said fulminations or other foreign citations do refuse to minister the said sacraments, they shall, for every such time that they do refuse to do so, have one year's imprisonment and make fine and ransom at the King's pleasure.

II

And it is further enacted that if any persons do move to or purchase from the See of Rome or any foreign court any appeal or summons, or do execute any of the same process, or do any act to impede or derogate any process, sentence, or judgment made in any of the courts of this realm, then every person so doing shall incur the same pains, penalties, and forfeitures ordained by the statue of provision and praemunire made in the 16th year of the reign of King Richard II.

III

And furthermore in eschewing the great delays and expenses sustained in pursuing such appeals, let it therefore be ordained and enacted that in such cases where until now any of the King's subjects have procured an appeal to the see of Rome, they may and shall use their appeals within this realm and not elsewhere, in the manner and form as hereafter ensues and not otherwise; that is to say, first from the archdeacon, if the matter be there begun, to the diocesan bishop within 15 days following judgment; or if it be commenced before the diocesan bishop, to the archbishop of the province, and there to be definitively and finally determined without any other or further process or appeal thereupon to be had or sued.

IV

And in every cause which may touch the King or his heirs, the party grieved may appeal to the spiritual prelates and other abbots and priors of the Upper House assembled by the King's writ in Convocation within the province where the same matter of contention was begun; so that every such appeal be taken by the party grieved within 15 days following judgment or sentence given. And whatsoever be affirmed or determined by the aforesaid prelates of the Upper House of Convocation shall stand and be taken for a final decree and the same matter never to come into question again. And if it shall happen that any person pursues an appeal contrary to the effect of this act, then every person so doing shall incur the penalties provided in the statue of provision and praemunire.

January–March 1534_____

An Act for the Submission of the Clergy to the King's Majesty

Parliamentary codification of Convocation's declaration of submission (pp. 460–61)

Where the King's humble and obedient clergy of this realm of England have not only acknowledged that Convocation is always and ought to be assembled only by the King's writ, but also have promised that they will never from henceforth attempt, allege, claim, promulgate, or execute any new canons, constitutions, or provincial ordinances in Convocation unless the King's assent may to them be had. And where divers constitutions, ordinances, and canons, provincial or synodal, which heretofore have been enacted and be thought not only to be prejudicial to the King's prerogative and repugnant to the laws of this realm, but also onerous to his Highness and his subjects, the said clergy have most humbly besought the King's Highness that the <u>said constitutions and canons may be subjected to the judgment of his Highness and of 32 persons of the King's subjects whereof 16 are to be of the Upper and Nether House of the parliament of the temporality, and the other 16 to be of the clergy of the realm, and all the said 32 persons to be chosen and appointed by the King's Majesty. Be it therefore now enacted by the authority of this present parliament that no clergy shall presume to attempt, allege, or claim any constitutions or ordinances, provincial or synodal, or execute any of the same without the King's most royal assent and license, upon pain of imprisonment and fine at the King's will.</u>

II

And forasmuch as such <u>canons formerly made</u> by the clergy cannot now be reviewed at this present session of parliament, by reason of shortness of time, let it therefore be enacted that the King's Highness shall have power and authority to nominate and assign at his pleasure the said 32 persons, and that <u>the same 32 shall have power and authority to review, search, and examine</u> the said canons; and such of them as the King's Highness and the commission of 32 shall deem and adjudge worthy to be continued and obeyed, they shall from thenceforth be kept within the realm.

III

Provided always that no canons, constitutions, or ordinances shall be made or put in execution by authority of Convocation which shall be contrary or repugnant to the King's royal prerogative, or the customs, laws, or statutes of this realm.

IV

And be it further enacted that no manner of appeals shall be had to the Bishop of Rome in any cause or contention that has its commencement in any court of this realm; but that all appeals shall be made within this realm in the causes of matrimony and tithes, by a statute made and established since the beginning of this present parliament. And for lack of justice at or in any of the courts of the archbishops of this realm, it shall be lawful for grieved parties to appeal to the King's Majesty and that upon every such appeal a commission chosen by the King shall hear and definitively determine the matter.

V

And if any person sue any manner of appeal to the Bishop of Rome, then every such person so doing shall incur the penalties contained in the act of provision and praemunire.

An Act Restraining the Payment of Annates

Absolute cessation of Annates payments to Rome (pp. 462–64)

At the beginning of this present parliament, it was ordained and established by act that the payment of the Annates or First Fruits for any archbishopric or bishopric or for any bulls to be obtained from the See of Rome for the said purpose should utterly cease.

And albeit the Bishop of Rome, otherwise called the Pope, has been informed and certified of the effectual contents of the said act, to the intent that by some genteel ways the said exactions might have been redressed and reformed; yet nevertheless the said Bishop of Rome hitherto has made no answer of his mind therein to the King's Highness, nor devised any reasonable ways to rectify the problem. Wherefore his most Royal Majesty has not only put his most gracious and royal assent to the foresaid act, but also ratified and confirmed the same and every clause and article therein contained.

II

And forasmuch as in the said act it is not plainly and certainly expressed in what manner and fashion archbishops and bishops shall be elected, presented, invested, and consecrated within this realm and in all other of the King's dominions: Be it now therefore enacted, by the King our Sovereign Lord, by the assent of the Lords Spiritual and Temporal, and the Commons in this present parliament assembled and by the authority of the same, that the said act and every thing therein contained shall be and stand in strength, virtue, and effect; except only that no person nor persons hereafter shall be presented, nominated, or commended to the said Bishop of Rome to or for the dignity or office of any archbishop or bishop within this realm or in any other of the King's dominions, nor shall send nor procure there for any manner of bulls, briefs, palls, or other things requisite for an archbishop or bishop, nor shall pay any sums of money for Annates, First Fruits, or otherwise for expedition of any such bulls, briefs, or palls; but that by the authority of this act all such payments and actions shall utterly cease and no longer be used within this realm or within the King's dominions.

III

And furthermore be it ordained and established by the authority aforesaid that at every vacancy of every archbishopric or bishopric within this realm or in any of the King's dominions, the King our Sovereign Lord, his heirs and successors may grant unto the prior and convent, or the dean and chapter of the cathedral churches or monasteries where the see of such archbishopric or bishopric shall happen to be void, a license under the great seal, as of old time has been the custom, to proceed to election of an archbishop or bishop of the see so being void, with a letter missive containing the name of the person which they shall elect and choose. By virtue of which license, the said dean and chapter or prior and convent shall with all speed and celerity in due form elect and choose the said person named in the said letters missive to the dignity and office of the archbishopric or bishopric so being void, and none other. And if they do defer or delay their election above 12 days next after such license and letters missive to them delivered, then for every such default the King Highness, his heirs and successors at their liberty and pleasure shall nominate and present, by their letters patent under their great seal, such a person to the said office and dignity so being void as they shall think able and convenient for the same.

VI

And be it further enacted by the authority aforesaid that if the prior and convent of any monastery, or dean and chapter of any cathedral church where the see of an archbishop or bishop is within any of the King's dominions shall proceed not to election and signify the same according to the tenor of this act within the space of 20 days next after such license shall come to their hands, or shall refuse and do not confirm, invest, and consecrate with all due circumstance as is aforesaid, or shall execute any censures, excommunications, interdictions, or inhibitions to the contrary of this act, then every person so offending and doing contrary to this act shall run into the dangers, pains, and penalties of the statute of provision and praemunire made in the 25th year of the reign of King Edward III and in the 16th year of King Richard II.

An Act for the Exoneration from Exactions Paid to the See of Rome

Cessation of dispensations sought from Rome and of household taxes paid thereto (pp. 464–71)

We your obedient and faithful subjects of Commons of this present parliament assembled do most humbly beseech your Royal Majesty that where your subjects of this your realm by many years past have been greatly decayed and impoverished by such intolerable exactions of great sums of money as have been claimed and taken out of this your realm by the Bishop of Rome called the Pope, as well as in pensions, Peter's pence, fruits, bulls for archbishoprics and bishoprics, appeals, and jurisdictions legantine; and also for dispensations, licenses, and other infinite sorts of instruments of sundry natures, heretofore practiced and obtained otherwise than by the laws of this realm; wherein the Bishop of Rome has not only to be blamed for his usurpation in the premises but also for his abusing and beguiling your subjects, pretending and persuading them that he has full power to dispense with all human laws, uses, and customs of all realms in all causes which be called spiritual, which matter has been usurped and practiced by him and his predecessors for many years in great derogation of your imperial crown and authority royal, contrary to right and conscience. For where this your Grace's realm, recognizing no superior under God but only your Grace, has been and is free from subjection to any man's laws but only to such as have been devised, made, and ordained within this realm for the wealth of the same, or to such other as by sufferance of your Grace and your progenitors the people of this your realm have taken at their free liberty by their own consent to be used among them, and not as to the observance of the laws of any foreign prince, potentate, or prelate: It stands therefore with natural equity and good reason that in all and every such laws human, made within this realm, your Royal Majesty and your Lords Spiritual and Temporal and Commons, representing the whole state of your realm, have full power and authority not only to dispense but also to authorize some elect person or persons to dispense with those and all other human laws of this your realm and with every one of them, as the quality of the persons and matter shall require; and also the said laws and every of them to abrogate, annul, amplify, or diminish as it shall be seen unto your Majesty and the Nobles and Commons of your realm meet and convenient for the wealth of your realm. And because it is now in these days present seen that the dignity of the imperial crown is much and sore decayed and diminished, and the people of this realm thereby impoverished and be like to continue if remedy be not therefore shortly provided: It may therefore please your most noble Majesty that no person or persons of this your realm shall henceforth pay any pensions, Peter's pence, or any other impositions to the use of the said Bishop or of the See of Rome, and that all such payments shall from henceforth clearly surcease and never more be levied nor paid to any person or persons in any manner whatsoever.

II

And be it further enacted that neither your Highness nor any of your subjects shall from henceforth sue to the said Bishop of Rome for licenses, dispensations, delegacies, or any other instruments or writings for any cause for the which any license, dispensation, etc. heretofore has customarily been obtained from the See of Rome. But that from henceforth every such license, dispensation, etc., necessary for your Highness and your subjects shall be granted and obtained within this your realm in the manner and form following, which is to say: the Archbishop of Canterbury shall have power and authority to give, grant, and dispose unto your Majesty such licenses, dispensations, etc., for causes not contrary or repugnant to the Holy Scriptures and laws of God as shall be convenient and necessary for the honor and surety of your Highness, your heirs and successors, and the wealth and profit of this your realm.

XIII

Be it understood that by this act your Grace, your Nobles and subjects, mean not to decline or vary from the congregation of Christ's Church in any things concerning the very articles of the Catholic faith or Christendom, or in any other things declared by Holy Scripture and the word of God necessary for your and their salvations.

An Act for the Establishing of the King's Succession

Recognition of Anne Boleyn as lawful queen, and placement of the royal succession in Henry and Anne's heirs (pp. 471–74)

Your most humble and obedient subjects, the Lords Spiritual and Temporal and the Commons of this present parliament assembled, do humbly show unto your Majesty that it is the natural inclination of every man gladly and willingly to provide for the surety of both his title and succession; and although we doubt not of your princely heart and wisdom, mixed with natural affection to the same, to foresee and provide for the perfect surety of both yourself and of your most lawful succession and heirs, upon which depends all our joy and wealth; we your said most humble and obedient subjects still call to remembrance the great divisions which in times past have afflicted this realm by reason of several titles pretended to the imperial crown, which sometimes and for the most part were occasioned by ambiguity and doubts in the designation of true heirs, and whereof ensued great effusion of blood and destruction of many Nobles and other subjects; by reason whereof the Bishop of Rome, contrary to the jurisdiction given by God to emperors, kings, and princes in succession to their heirs, has presumed in times past to invest whoever should please him to inherit in other men's kingdoms and dominions, which thing we your most humble subjects do abhor and detest. And sometimes other foreign princes, wanting dissension and discord to continue in the realm rather than charity, equity, or unity, have also supported wrong titles, whereby they might the more easily and facilely aspire to the superiority of the same. But the continuance of these practices is too dangerous to be suffered any longer and too much contrary to our unity, peace, and tranquillity.

In consideration whereof your said most humble and obedient subjects, realizing that the unity, peace, and wealth of this realm consists and rests in the certainty and surety of the procreation and posterity of your Highness, in whose most royal person at this present time is no manner of doubt nor question, <u>do therefore most humbly beseech your Highness, that it may please your Majesty, that with the assent of parliament, your marriage to Lady Catherine, being before lawful wife to Prince Arthur your elder brother, who by him was carnally known, as was duly proven by Thomas, the Archbishop of Canterbury, shall, by authority of this present parliament, be definitely, clearly, and absolutely declared to be against the laws of Almighty God and utterly void and annulled, and that Lady Catherine shall be from henceforth reputed only dowager to Prince Arthur and not queen of this realm. And the lawful matrimony solemnized between your Highness and your most dear and entirely beloved wife Queen Anne shall be established and taken for true and perfect ever hereafter, according to the judgment of the said Thomas, Archbishop of Canterbury, whose grounds for judgment have been confirmed</u>

by the clergy of this realm in Convocation, and by both universities thereof, as by the universities of Bologna, Padua, Paris, Orleans, Toulouse, Angers, and many others, and also by the private writings of many well learned men; which grounds so confirmed and the judgment of the said Archbishop concluding the same, we your said subjects do accept, approve, and ratify your marriage as consonant to the laws of Almighty God, and most humbly beseech your Majesty that it may be so established forever by your most gracious and royal assent.

IV

And also be it enacted that all the issue had and procreate between your Highness and your wife Queen Anne shall be your lawful children, and shall inherit, according to the laws of this realm, the imperial crown of the same, with all dignities, honors, preeminences, prerogatives, authorities and jurisdictions to the same belonging, the inheritance thereof to be and remain to your said children and right heirs in manner and form as hereafter shall be declared: That is to say, first, the said imperial crown shall be to the first son lawfully begotten between your Highness and Queen Anne; and for default of such heirs, then to the second son and his heirs, all lawfully begotten, and so to every son of your body of the body of said Queen Anne begotten. And if it shall happen that your beloved wife, Queen Anne, dies without male issue of the body, then the same imperial crown goes to the son and male heir of your body lawfully begotten. And for the default of such issue, then to your second son and his heirs all lawfully begotten. And if is shall happen that no male heir survives to inherit, then the imperial crown shall go to the first of the eldest issue female, which is the Lady Elizabeth, now princess, and to the heirs of her body lawfully begotten, and for default of such issue then to the second female issue, and so forth.

V

And be it further enacted that by the first of day of May next coming, proclamations shall be made in all shires of this realm of the tenor and contents of this act. And if any person, of what estate, dignity, or condition soever they be, by writing, or imprinting, or by any exterior act or deed maliciously procure or do anything to the prejudice, slander, disturbance, or derogation of the said lawful matrimony between your Majesty and the said Queen Anne, or to the peril, slander, or disinheriting of any of your royal heirs, whereby they might suffer disturbance or interruption in the title of inheritance to the crown of this realm; then every such offender, as well as their counselors, maintainers, and abettors, shall be adjudged high traitors, and being lawfully convicted according to the customs and laws of this realm, shall suffer pains of death as in cases of high treason; and they shall lose and forfeit to your Highness and to your heirs all such manors, lands, tenements, rents, or annuities which they had in possession as owners. Also, they shall forfeit any interests for years of lands, and their goods, and debts from the time of attainder, and their heirs shall also forfeit by reason of attainder any claim to said lands or goods.

VI

And be it further enacted that if any person, after the said first day of May, by any words without writing or any exterior deed or act, maliciously and obstinately publish, divulge, or utter anything to the peril of your Highness, or to the slander or prejudice of the said matrimony solemnized between your Highness and the said Queen Anne, or to the slander or disinheriting of their lawful heirs eligible to inherit the crown of this realm, then every such offense shall be taken and adjudged for <u>misprision of treason</u> [complicity]. And every person so doing and offending, and being thereof lawfully convicted, <u>shall suffer imprisonment</u> of their bodies at the King's will, and shall lose as well all their goods, chattels, and debts, and any interests they shall have in lands, rents, or hereditaments held at the time of conviction and attainder of such offense.

IX

And be it further enacted that all the Nobles of your realm Spiritual and Temporal, as well as all your other subjects, <u>shall make a corporal oath</u> in the presences of your Highness or your heirs, or those deputied for the same, that they shall truly, firmly, and constantly without fraud or guile observe, fulfill, maintain, defend, and keep to their cunning, wit, and uttermost of their powers the whole effects and contents of this present act. <u>And if any person obstinately refuse to swear this oath, then every person so doing shall be taken and accepted for offender in misprision of high treason.</u>

November 1534_____

An Act concerning the King's Highness To Be Supreme Head of the Church of England and To Have Authority To Reform and Redress All Errors, Heresies, and Abuses in the Same

Establishment of the king as the supreme head of the church with authority to supervise its spiritual business (p. 492)

Albeit the King's majesty is justly and rightfully the supreme head of the Church of England, and is so recognized by the clergy of this realm in their Convocation; yet nevertheless for corroboration and confirmation thereof, and for increase of virtue in Christ's religion within this realm of England, and to repress and extirpate all errors, heresies, and other enormities and abuses heretofore used in the same: <u>Be it enacted by authority of this present parliament that the King our Sovereign Lord, and his heirs and successors, shall be taken, accepted, and reputed as the only supreme head on earth of the Church of England, called *Anglicana Ecclesia*, and shall have united to the imperial crown of this realm the title and style thereof, as well as all honors, dignities, preeminences, jurisdictions, privileges, authorities, immunities, profits, and commodities belonging and appertaining to the said dignity of supreme head of the same Church. And our Sovereign Lord, and his heirs and successors, shall have full power and authority to visit, repress, redress, reform, order, correct, restrain, and amend all such heresies and abuses,</u> whatever they be, which by spiritual authority may lawfully be reformed or redressed to the pleasure of Almighty God, the increase of virtue in Christian religion, and for the conservation of the peace, unity, and tranquillity of this realm, any foreign authority notwithstanding.

An Act Ratifying the Oath that Every of the King's Subjects Have Taken and Shall Hereafter Be Bound To Take for Due Observation of the Act Made for the Surety of the Succession of the King's Highness in the Crown of the Realm

An accompaniment to the Act of Succession requiring individuals to affirm their fealty (pp. 492–93)

At the day of the last prorogation of this present parliament, the Nobles Spiritual and temporal as well as the Commons most lovingly accepted and took such an oath as then was devised in writing for the maintenance and defense of the act made earlier for the establishment of the succession, and meant and intended at that time that every other of the King's subjects should be bound to accept and take the same upon pains contained in the said act, the tenor of which oath is now given: <u>You shall swear to bare faith, truth, and obedience alone to the King's Majesty and to the heirs of his body and of his most dear, entirely beloved, and lawful wife, Queen Anne, begotten and to be begotten; and further to the heirs of our Sovereign Lord according to the limitations mentioned and contained in the statute made for the surety of his succession to the crown of this realm, and not to any other within this realm nor foreign authority or potentate. And in case any oath be made or has been made by you to any person contrary to this act, then you are to repute said oath as vain. And using your cunning wit and uttermost powers, without guile, fraud, or other undue means, you shall observe, keep, maintain, and defend the said *Act of Succession* and all the whole effects and contents thereof, and all other acts made in confirmation or for the execution of the same. And this you shall do against all manner of persons of what estate, dignity, degree, or condition soever they be; and in nowise do or attempt, nor to your power suffer to be done or attempted, directly or indirectly, anything privately or publicly to the hindrance, damage, or derogation thereof or of any part of the same. So help you God, all saints, and the holy evangelists.</u>

And forasmuch as it is convenient for the sure maintenance and defense of the same act that the said oath should not only be authorized by the authority of parliament, but also be interpreted and expounded by the whole assent of this present parliament, saying that it was meant and intended by the King's Majesty, the Lords and Commons of the parliament, at the said day of the said last prorogation, that every subject should be bound to take the same oath according to the tenor and effect thereof upon the pains and penalties contained in the said; <u>therefore be it enacted that the said oath above rehearsed shall be the oath taken by all subjects of the realm.</u>

And be it further enacted that the commissioners that hereafter shall be appointed to receive such oath of the King's subjects shall have power and authority to certify unto the King's Bench by writing under their seals every refusal that hereafter shall be made of the same oath by any person coming before them to take the oath. And every such certificate made by such commissioners shall be taken as strong and as available in the law as an indictment of 12 men lawfully finding the same. The person named in any such certificate shall be compelled to answer as if he were indicted; and any judgment executed against said offender shall have the same standing as if it had been a lawful indictment according to the due course and order of the common laws of this realm.

An Act whereby Divers Offenses Be Made High Treason, and Taking Way All Sanctuaries for All Manner of High Treasons

Sundry actions labeled treasonous and their consequent penalties (pp. 508–09)

Forasmuch as it is most necessary, both for common police and duty of subjects, to prohibit, provide, and restrain all manner of shameful slanders, perils, or imminent dangers which might happen to our Sovereign Lord the King, the Queen, or their heirs, which, when they be noticed and understood, cannot but be abhorred by all true and loving subjects, if at any point they may touch the King, his Queen, their heirs or successors, upon which depend the whole unity and universal weal of this realm, such behavior being considered the unreasonable liberty of cankered and traitorous hearts—for which of the King's loving subjects should not declare unto their Sovereign Lord their undoubted sincerity and truth? <u>Be it therefore enacted</u>, by the assent of our Sovereign Lord and the Lords Spiritual and Temporal and the Commons of this present parliament assembled, <u>that if any persons after the first day of February next do maliciously wish, will, or desire by words or writing, or invent by craft any bodily harm to be done to the King's most royal person, or the Queen's, or their heir's apparent, or to deprive them of the dignity, title, or name of their royal estates, or slanderously and maliciously publish and pronounce, by express writing or words, that the King should be a heretic, schismatic, tyrant, infidel, or usurper of the crown, or rebelliously do detain, keep, or withhold from our Sovereign Lord any his castles, fortresses, or holds within this realm; or any of his ships, ordinance, artillery, or other munitions or fortifications of war; and do not humbly render and give up to our said Sovereign Lord the same within six days after they be commanded to by our Sovereign Lord by open proclamation under the great seal, that then every such person so offending, their aiders, counselors, and abettors, shall be adjudged traitors and lawfully convicted according to the laws and customs of this realm.</u> Every such offense done after the first day of February shall be adjudged high treason and subject offenders to suffer such pains of death and other penalties as is limited and accustomed in cases of high treason.

II
And to the intent that all treasons should be the more dread, and also because ill-disposed persons are often tempted to adventure and embrace their malicious intents and enterprises: <u>Be it therefore enacted that no offender in any kind of high treasons, nor his aiders, counselors, and abettors, shall be allowed to have the benefit or privilege of sanctuary.</u>

III
And over that be it enacted further that if any of the King's subjects or denizens do commit or practice out of the limit of this realm any such offences which by this act are made treason, then such treasons, whatsoever they be or wheresoever they shall happen, shall be inquired into and presented, by the oaths of 12 good and lawful men upon good and probable evidence and witnesses in such places and before such persons as it shall please the King's Highness to appoint by commission, in like manner and form as is used for treasons committed within this realm. And upon every indictment and presentment found and made of such treasons, and certified unto the King's Bench, like process shall be made against the offenders as if the same treasons so presented had been done within

the limits of this realm. All processes of outlawry hereafter made against any offenders living outside of the limits of the realm at the time of the outlawry pronounced against them shall be as good and as effectual in the law to all intents and purposes as if such offenders had been resident and dwelling within the realm at the time.

IV

And be it further enacted that every offender convicted of high treason according to the due course and custom of the common laws of this realm shall forfeit to the King's Highness all such lands, tenements, and hereditaments which any such offender shall have in his possession at the time of any such treason.

An Act Containing a Grant of Subsidy unto the King for a XVth and Xth

King's tax imposed upon the orders for the defense of the realm (pp. 516–24)

The King's most loving subjects in this present parliament assembled, calling to their remembrance not only the manifold and great benefits which they have received by the wise and politic governance of this realm, which under the reign of our Sovereign Lord the King has been for the space of 25 years most prudently governed, protected, and defended, and his most loving subjects of the same maintained and kept in wealth, unity, rest, and quietness, to the high pleasure of Almighty God; but also considering the great sums of money and other charges sustained by his Highness in his past and present wars, in the repair and improvement of the fortresses and harbor made at Calais, and in the construction of a new port and harbor made at Dover, and in the fortification and strengthening of the frontiers, coasts, and borders of this realm, for the surety and commodity of his subjects and friends passing the seas and for the common annoyance of his enemies—do grant to the King's Highness one whole fifteenth and tenth to be levied of goods movable, cattle, and other things.

III

And because the said fifteenth and tenth granted as is aforesaid extends but to a small sum of money towards the recompense of the charges of our said Sovereign Lord, his loving commons have granted unto the King one subsidy of 12 pence to be levied of all manors, lands, and tenements.

IV

Likewise every spiritual person shall be rated and made to pay according to the clear value of lands, tenements, and other hereditaments.

VI

Further, every person of the estate of a baron and above shall be examined of their freehold and value and charged according to their said examination.

An Act concerning Decay of Houses and Enclosures

Penalties for neglect of farm buildings and enclosure of farmland (pp. 553–54)

Inasmuch as many divers and sundry persons which hold not their lands and tenements immediate from the King's Highness have and do let decay and fall down no small number of houses of husbandry, and also do convert the lands of the same from tillage and husbandry into pasture, to the most perilous example of all others being in like case and to the greatest abuse and disorder of the natural soil that by any manner of invention could be practiced or imagined: Be it therefore enacted that the King our Sovereign Lord, his heirs and successors shall take and have one half of all revenues, rents, and profits coming and growing of all lands and tenements now and remaining enclosed, decayed, or converted from tillage into pasture, being so found by office and verdict of 12 men, until such time as the said owners shall have built and refurbished in convenient places, for every 50, 40, or 30 acres of land, one sufficient tenement suitable for an honest man to dwell in, and also until such time as the same owners shall have converted the said lands so misused from pasture into tillage again, according to the nature of the soil and course of husbandry used in the country where such lands do lie.

An Act for Punishment of Sturdy Vagabonds and Beggars

Public assistance to the poor, in addition to punishments for the able-bodied (pp. 558-62)

IV

It is ordained and enacted that every mayor, governor, and head officer of every city, borough, and town corporate, and the Church wardens shall in goodness and charity take such discrete and convenient order by gathering and procuring of such charitable and voluntary alms of the good Christian people within the same, with boxes every Sunday, holy day, and other festival day, or otherwise among themselves, so that the poor, impotent, lame, feeble, and diseased people, being not able to work, may be provided help and relief, and so that none of them be suffered to go openly in begging; and that such as be lusty or having their limbs strong enough to labor may be daily kept in continual labor, whereby everyone of them may get their own substance and living with their own hands.

V

It is enacted that all <u>lepers</u> and poor bedridden creatures whatsoever they be may at their own liberty remain and continue in such place where they be, and shall not be compelled to repair into the country.

IX

It is enacted that every preacher and vicar curate of this realm, in all their sermons, biddings, confessions, and at the making of wills or testaments, shall exhort, move, and provoke people to be liable and bountifully to extend their good and charitable alms and contributions toward the comfort and relief of the said poor, decrepit, indigent, and needy people.

XIII

And for the avoiding of all such inconveniences as oftentimes do chance among the people by common and open doles: Be it is therefore enacted that no man shall make any such common or open dole, or shall give any ready money in alms, otherwise than to the common boxes and common gatherings in every city, town, parish, and hamlet for the putting in plain and due execution the good and virtuous intents contained in this present act, upon pain of loss and forfeiture ten times the value of all such ready money as shall be given in alms contrary to the tenor and purport of the same.

XV

And it is ordered that within the cities and towns corporate, the mayor, aldermen, governor, bailiff, or constable shall name and appoint certain of the said poor people found of the common alms to collect and gather broken meats and fragments and the refuse drink of every householder within every such parish, which shall be by the discretion of these same town officials distributed evenly among the poor.

XXIV

Be it understood that neither the mayor, aldermen, sheriffs, bailiffs, constables, or other head officers of said cities and towns, nor also the whole of them in general, shall be constrained to any such certain contribution but as their free wills and charities shall extend.

XXVII

Inasmuch as friars mendicant have little or nothing to live upon but only by the charity and alms of Christian people, be it also understood that in this act nothing prejudicial or hurtful be intended unto any person giving to them in general or particular any manner of alms in money, victuals, or other thing.

XXVIII

Be it further understood that in this act nothing hurtful or prejudicial be intended unto any abbot, prior, or other person of the clergy who be bound to give yearly, weakly, or daily alms in money, victuals, lodging, clothing, or other things, to any monastery, alms house, hospital, or other foundations or brotherhoods established for the maintenance of the poor.

An Act whereby All Religious Houses of Monks, Chanons, and Nuns which May Not Dispend Manors, Lands, Tenements, and Hereditaments above the Clear Yearly Value of £200 Are Given to the King's Highness, His Heirs and Successors Forever

The dissolution and transferral to the king of all religious houses under a certain value (pp. 575–78)

Forasmuch as manifest sin, vicious, carnal, and abominable living, is daily used and committed among the little and small abbeys, priories, and other religious houses of monks, chanons, and nuns, where the congregation is under 12 persons; whereby the governors of such religious houses and their convent spoil, destroy, consume, and utterly waste as well their churches, monasteries, priories, principal houses, farms, granges, lands, tenements, and hereditaments, as the ornaments of their churches and their goods and chattels to the high displeasure of Almighty God, slander of good religion, and to the great infamy of the King's Highness and the realm, if redress should not be had thereof; and albeit that many continual visitations have been heretofore conducted over the last 200 years and more for an honest and charitable reformation of such unthrifty, carnal, and abominable living, yet nevertheless little or no amendment is hitherto had, but their vicious living shamelessly increases and augments, and by a cursed custom so rooted and infested that a great multitude of the religious persons in such small houses do rather choose to rove abroad in apostasy than to conform themselves to the observation of good religion; so that unless such small houses be utterly suppressed and the religious persons therein committed to great and honorable monasteries of religion in this realm, where they may be compelled to live religiously for reformation of their lives, there can else be no reformation in this behalf. In consideration whereof the King's most Royal Majesty, being supreme head on earth under God of the Church of England, daily finding and devising the increase, advancement, and exaltation of true doctrine and virtue in the said Church, to the only glory and honor of God and the total extirpating and destruction of vice and sin, having knowledge that the premises be true, as well by the accounts of his late visitations as by sundry credible informations, considering also that divers and great solemn monasteries of this realm wherein, thanks be to God, religion is right well kept and observed, be destitute of such full numbers of religious persons as they ought and may keep, has thought good that a plain declaration should be made of the premises to the Lords Spiritual and Temporal as well to his other loving subjects the Commons in this present parliament assembled; whereupon the said Lords and Commons by a great deliberation finally be resolved that it is and shall be much more to the pleasure of Almighty God and for the honor of this his realm that the possessions of such spiritual religious house, now being spent, spoiled, and wasted for increase and maintenance of sin, should be used and converted to better uses, and the unthrifty religious persons so spending the same to be compelled to reform their lives; and thereupon most humbly desire the King's Highness that it may be enacted by authority of this present parliament, that his Majesty shall have and enjoy to him and to his heirs forever all and singular monasteries, priories, and other religious houses of monks, chanons, and nuns, of what kinds or diversities of habits, rules, or orders so ever they be called or named, which have not in lands and tenements, rents, tithes, portions, and other hereditaments above the clear yearly value of £200; and in like manner shall have and enjoy the sites and circuits of all such religious houses, and all their properties, in as large a manner as their current governors now have; and that also his Highness shall have to him and to his heirs all and singular such monasteries, abbeys, and priories which, at any time within one year next afore the making of this act, have been given and granted to his Majesty by any abbot, prior, abbess, or prioress under their convent seals, or that otherwise have been suppressed or dissolved.

VIII

Furthermore, his Majesty is pleased and contented of his most excellent charity to provide to every chief head and governor of every such religious house during their lives such yearly pensions or benefices as for their degrees and qualities shall be reasonable and convenient; wherein his Highness will have most tender respect to such of the said chief governors as well and truly conserve and keep the goods and ornaments of their houses to the use of his Majesty, without spoil, waste, or embezzling the same. And also his Majesty will ordain and provide that the convents of every such religious house shall have the capacity, if they will, to live honestly and virtuously abroad, and some convenient charity disposed to them toward their living, or else shall be committed to such honorable great monasteries of this realm wherein good religion is observed as shall be limited by his Highness, there to live religiously during their lives.

IX

And it is ordained that the chief governors and convents of such honorable great monasteries shall take and accept into their houses from time to time such number of the persons of the said convents as shall be assigned and appointed by the King's Highness, and keep them religiously during their lives within their said monasteries in like manner and form as the convents of such great monasteries be ordered and kept.

An Act Establishing the Court of Augmentations

Creation of court meant to receive confiscated properties of dissolved religious houses (pp. 569–74)

Be it enacted by the assent of the King's Majesty, his Lords Spiritual and Temporal, and the Commons in this present parliament assembled that the King our Sovereign Lord ordains and establishes a certain court commonly to be called the Court of Augmentations of the Revenues of the King's Crown, which court continually shall be a court of record and shall have one great seal and one privy seal.

II

Also be it enacted that there shall be one certain person to be named and assigned by the King's Highness which shall be chancellor of the said court and shall be the chief and principal officer of the same court and shall have the keeping of the said great seal and privy seal. Also that there shall be one person to be named by the King's Highness which shall be called the King's treasurer of the Court of Augmentations of the Revenues of the King's Crown and shall be the second officer of the same court.

III

Also it is ordained that there shall be one person learned in the laws of the land to be named the King's attorney of the said court; one person named the King's solicitor; ten persons named auditors; 16 named receivers; one named clerk; one named usher; and one named messenger.

V

Also be it enacted that all the monasteries, priories, and other religious houses which be dissolved and come or shall come to the King's Highness by the act aforesaid shall be in the order, survey, and governance of the said court and of the officers and ministers thereof, except those which the King's Majesty shall decide to preserve in their essential state as they were before the making of the said act.

Appendix B: Bibliography

RESERVE BOOKS

Roland Bainton, *The Reformation of the Sixteenth Century* (Boston: Beacon Press,1952), Introduction, chs. 1–3
Excellent introduction to medieval Catholicism and Lutheranism.

Joseph S. Block, *Factional Politics and the English Reformation, 1520–1540* (Woodbridge, Suffolk: Boydell Press, 1993)
The personnel and policies of court and parliamentary factions during the reform years.

A. G. Dickens, *The English Reformation*, second edition (University Park: Pennsylvania State University Press, 1989).
History, beliefs, practices of medieval Catholicism and of reform denominations.

_____, *Thomas Cromwell and the English Reformation* (London: English Universities Press, 1959)
The life and thoughts of the man most responsible for the English Reformation.

G. R. Elton, *Reform and Reformation: England, 1509–1558* (Cambridge: Harvard University Press, 1977)
A penetrating study of domestic and foreign policy during Henry's reign (and beyond); strongly supportive of Cromwell.

J. A. Guy, *The Public Career of Sir Thomas More* (New Haven: Yale University Press, 1980)
More's career as lawyer, diplomat, and minister; good on the factions in court and parliament.

Stanford Lehmberg, *The Reformation Parliament, 1529-1536* (Cambridge: Cambridge University Press, 1970)
The best account of the composition of the Reformation Parliament and of its legislative agenda.

Conyers Read, ed., *Bibliography of British History, Tudor Period, 1485–1603* (Oxford: Clarendon Press, 1959)
A useful, if now dated, bibliography organized by subject, e.g., Tudor economics; reference book not on reserve (Z2018.R28).

Richard Rex, *Henry VIII and the English Reformation* (New York: St. Martin's Press, 1993)
> An analysis of issues rather than a narrative of events, with a qualified defense of the Catholic church in Chapter 2.

Jasper Ridley, *Statesman and Saint: Cardinal Wolsey, Sir Thomas More, and the Politics of Henry VIII* (New York: Viking Press, 1982)
> A dual biography, particularly critical of More.

J. J. Scarisbrick, *Henry VIII* (Berkeley: University of California Press, 1968)
> The best biography, in the opinion of some; a large book, but the relevant chapters are 8–10.

David Starkey, *The Reign of Henry VIII: Personalities and Politics* (New York: Franklin Watts, 1986)
> Faction in the royal court, with a particular focus on the Privy Chamber.

Statutes of the Realm, volume 3 (London: Dawsons of Pall Mall, 1963) (KD.132 1810A.3—oversize)
> Full texts of all of the legislation of the Reformation Parliament.

Alison Weir, *Henry VIII: The King and His Court* (New York: Ballantine Books, 2001)
> A delightful, detailed account of the daily doings of Henry and his court; a "lifestyles of the rich and famous" type of book.

FILMS

A Man for All Seasons (feature film starring Paul Scofield and Robert Shaw)

Anne of a Thousand Days (feature film starring Richard Burton and Genevieve Bujold)

Henry VIII (Masterpiece Theater film starring Ray Winstone)

Minions of the Race (play about More, Cromwell, and Wolsey)

The Six Wives of Henry VIII (documentary)

Henry VIII, Scandals of a King (documentary)

Luther (feature film starring Stacy Keach)

Luther (feature film starring Joseph Fiennes)

HISTORICAL NOVELS

Margaret George, *The Autobiography of Henry VIII*

Robin Maxwell, *The Secret Diary of Anne Boleyn*

Carolly Erickson, *Mistress Anne*

Philippa Gregory, *The Other Boleyn Girl: A Novel*

Charles Major, *When Knighthood Was in Flower*
    (Charles Brandon's courtship of Mary Tudor).

Lucy Beckett, *A Time before You Die: A Novel of the Reformation*
    (Story of a monk cast out of his monastery; told in counterpoint with story of
    Reginald Pole)

H.F.M. Prescott, *The Man on a Donkey*
    (Robert Aske and the Pilgrimage of Grace).

MUSIC

Songs, Ballads and Instrumental Pieces Composed by Henry the Eighth, ed., Lady Mary
    Trefusis (Oxford, 1912)
    (Contains all vocal music).

Music at the Court of Henry VIII, ed., J. Stevens, MB, xviii (London, 1962)
    (Contains all secular vocal and untexted ensemble music).

Google.com, The Music of Henry VIII

ARCHITECTURE

Simon Thurley, *The Royal Palaces of Tudor England*